The Many Voices of Lydia Davis

Edinburgh Critical Studies in Literary Translation
Series Editors: Stuart Gillespie and Emily Wilson

The series reflects the current vitality of the subject and will be a magnet for future work. Its remit is not only the phenomenon of translation in itself, but the impact of translation too. It also draws on the increasingly lively fields of reception studies and cultural history. Volumes will focus on Anglophone literary traditions in their foreign relations.

Published Titles

The English Aeneid: *Translations of Virgil, 1555–1646*
Sheldon Brammall

The Many Voices of Lydia Davis: Translation, Rewriting, Intertextuality
Jonathan Evans

The Many Voices of Lydia Davis
Translation, Rewriting, Intertextuality

Jonathan Evans

EDINBURGH
University Press

Edinburgh University Press is one of the leading
university presses in the UK. We publish
academic books and journals in our selected
subject areas across the humanities and social
sciences, combining cutting-edge scholarship
with high editorial and production values to
produce academic works of lasting importance.
For more information visit our website:
edinburghuniversitypress.com

Edinburgh University Press Ltd
The Tun – Holyrood Road
12(2f) Jackson's Entry
Edinburgh EH8 8PJ

First published in hardback by Edinburgh University Press 2016

Typeset in 10.5/13 Sabon by
Servis Filmsetting Ltd, Stockport, Cheshire,
and printed and bound by CPI Group (UK) Ltd
Croydon, CR0 4YY

A CIP record for this book is available from the
British Library

ISBN 978 1 4744 0017 6 (hardback)
ISBN 978 1 4744 3156 9 (paperback)
ISBN 978 1 4744 0018 3 (webready PDF)
ISBN 978 1 4744 1787 7 (epub)

Contents

Series Editors' Preface

Translators, Pushkin's 'post-horses of enlightenment', play a central role in every society's reception of other cultures. The study of translation – in theory, in practice and in relation to broader narratives in literary and cultural history – is now a vibrant scholarly field. It is key to current debates on literary canons in an increasingly global world, and on the possibility of World Literature. Edinburgh Critical Studies in Literary Translation addresses translation as a literary and historical phenomenon and is the first monograph series to do so.

Some of these studies engage with the approaches individual authors have taken to translation. Some deal with the impact of particular source texts or of particular translations on the societies in which they were produced. A central concern of the series is with interactions between translation and other forms of creative work and with the part translation can play in forging the identity of individual authors. We are no less interested in the way translation can set directions for literary cultures at large.

There are no constraints on historical period. The emphasis of the series is in the first instance on translations involving the English language, whether in the context of ancient or modern literature. Our scholarly territory straddles the disciplines of English Literature, Classical Studies, Comparative Literature and Modern Languages. Contributors necessarily work at their frontiers, using innovative tools on interdisciplinary topics.

Stuart Gillespie and Emily Wilson

Acknowledgements

A book of this length requires a large amount of support from various people, and this book is no exception. I am grateful for two sets of funding from the Centre for European and International Studies at the University of Portsmouth that made it possible. The first (2007–10) paid for the initial research, while teaching relief in 2015 allowed me to complete the manuscript.

My thanks go to Edinburgh University Press for all their help. I am especially grateful to the series editors, Stuart Gillespie and Emily Wilson, who have supported me throughout the writing of the book and offered thoughtful and helpful suggestions on the manuscript. Jackie Jones and Adela Rauchova at the press have also provided much needed aid. I also want to thank my two anonymous reviewers for their feedback on the proposal.

A great many people have helped me over the years and it's impossible to mention them all here. I want to thank Bran Nicol and Carol O'Sullivan, who supervised the PhD that this book is based on. Mona Baker and Charlotte Bosseaux gave helpful feedback at a Translation Research Summer School in 2009. Sue Wright helped sharpen up my initial book proposal. Justin Parks found me a copy of a very hard to find Blanchot translation in SUNY Buffalo library, while Stefan Tobler gave me a copy of a pamphlet by Davis and accompanied me to see her reading in London. I cannot list everyone who I've discussed this with: thanks to all of you.

Earlier versions of chapters have been presented at a number of conferences over the years, including ones at University College London, University of Portsmouth, Heriot-Watt University and University of Manchester. Thanks to organisers and audiences for providing the opportunity for early feedback.

Some parts of the book have been published in different versions in the following publications:

Part of Chapter 2 was published in an earlier form as 'Translation and Response between Maurice Blanchot and Lydia Davis' in *TranscUlturAl*, 4:2 (2011), 49–61 <https://ejournals.library.ualberta.ca/index.php/TC/article/view/19230>.

Part of Chapter 3 was published in an earlier form in *CLCWeb: Comparative Literature and Culture*. Copyright release by Purdue University 2015: Evans, Jonathan. "Davis's Poetic Dialogue with Leiris's Autobiography." *CLCWeb: Comparative Literature and Culture*, 14.1 (2012) <http://dx.doi.org/10.7771/1481-4374.1755>.

Chapter 4 was published in an earlier form as 'Lydia Davis' Rewritings of Proust' in *Translation and Literature*, 21 (2012), 175–95.

Chapter 6 was published in an earlier form as 'At the Borders Between Translation and Parody: Lydia Davis's Story about Marie Curie' in *TTR*, 25:2 (2012), 167–91.

My grateful thanks to the journals for permission to republish these items.

Finally, I owe my family, both young and old, a huge debt of gratitude. My parents, Ian and Maureen Evans, gave lots of initial encouragement as well as reading various drafts. My wife, Ting Guo, has supported my writing in all sorts of ways, for which I am truly grateful, not least for taking care of Rowan Guo Evans in order to let me finish the manuscript. The book is dedicated to Maureen Evans and Rowan Guo Evans.

Chapter 1

Introduction

Lydia Davis has long been regarded as a 'writer's writer'. Her working form is the short story and often these are very short, some only one sentence long. In a reading public used to novels, it's easy for Davis' work to slip between the cracks. The publication of her *Collected Stories*, in 2009, gave a much more substantial view of her career as a writer than had previously been available in one place. Davis won the 2013 Man Booker International prize, giving her much more international recognition.

Yet Davis had already received international recognition as a translator. She became a Chevalier de l'Ordre des Arts et Lettres in France in 1999. She has translated a substantial number of books from French, including, most famously, a new translation of Marcel Proust's *Du côté de chez Swann* (Proust 2002). She has also translated five of Maurice Blanchot's fictional texts, including *Death Sentence* (Blanchot 1978), and two volumes of the surrealist poet Michel Leiris' autobiography, *Scratches* (Leiris 1997a) and *Scraps* (Leiris 1997b). Most recently, in 2010, she published a new translation of Flaubert's *Madame Bovary*. These are only the most high profile translations; between 1978 and 2002 she translated over twenty book-length works, including four novels by Pierre-Jean Jouve, two novels by Conrad Detrez, a travelogue by Michel Butor, a biography of Alexis de Tocqueville, as well as a book on masculine identity by Elizabeth Badinter, and several more novels and non-fiction works.[1] Davis' career as a translator began at the same time as her career as a writer: she published her first book-length translation, with Paul Auster, in 1975. The pair went on to translate four more books together, including a book of Sartre's interviews and a novel, *Aboard the Aquitaine*, by Georges Simenon.

Davis' work, I argue in this book, challenges the separation between writing and translating. Through an exploration of the relationship between her translations and her own work, as well as an investigation into how Davis uses translation in her stories, *The Many Voices of Lydia Davis* questions the division between her roles as a writer and as a translator and the separation between the two modes of creativity. It therefore follows in the wake of work such as Stephen Yao's *Translation and the Languages of Modernism* (2002), Daniel Katz's *American Modernism's Expatriate Scene* (2007), Stuart Gillespie's *English Translation and Classical Reception* (2011) and Matthew Reynolds' *The Poetry of Translation* (2011) in arguing that translation is an integral part of English language literature. Davis' work demonstrates why it is impossible to ignore translation, both as a practice and as a form of reception, when conceptualising English language literature. *The Many Voices of Lydia Davis* shows, as have Yao, Katz and many others, that American literature is entwined with literatures from around the world.[2] There are numerous points of correspondence, both thematic and formal, between Davis' stories and her translations, suggesting a continuity of project that makes her translations into part of her *œuvre*. I argue in this book that some of Davis' translations enter into significant, often dialogic relationships with her other work, making them central to her authorship. Not all of Davis' translations do so, as she translated to earn a living for much of her career, and some of the texts she translated have no apparent connection to her other work.

Davis started publishing her stories with small presses in the 1970s. Her first collection, *The Thirteenth Woman and other stories*, was published in 1976 by Living Hand Press, which was an extension of *Living Hand*, the little magazine that Davis edited with her then husband Paul Auster. A second small press collection, *Story and other stories*, was published in 1983 by The Figures. The stories from both of these collections reappeared throughout her later books. In her next book, *Break It Down* (1986), which contains thirty-five stories, sixteen came from *Story and other stories* and a further six from *The Thirteenth Woman* (Perloff 1989: 206n5). *Break It Down* was the first of Davis' collections to be published by a major publisher, Knopf. She published a novel, *The End of the Story*, in 1995, which was quickly followed in 1997 by Davis' next collection, *Almost No Memory*. These and Davis' 2007 collection, *Varieties of Disturbance*, were published by Farrar Straus Giroux (FSG). Her 2001 collection *Samuel Johnson is Indignant* was, however, first published by the independent publisher McSweeney's as a hardback, but subsequent paperback editions have been published by Picador, which is owned by the same group as Farrar Straus Giroux. A *Collected Stories* was published by FSG in 2009, which brought together the four books previously published by mainstream publishers. Her most recent collection is 2014's *Can't and Won't*, which was also published by FSG in the USA and Hamish Hamilton in the UK.

In a reversal of the usual hierarchy of writing as primary and translation as secondary, Davis' translations are so substantial in number and importance that her reputation as a translator has, at times, overshadowed her reputation as a writer. As James Wood comments in his review of her *Collected Stories*, when he first heard of Davis in the mid-1990s, '[s]he was known as a translator of the French autobiographer Michel Leiris and the philosopher and critic Maurice Blanchot'. She was known as a translator first and foremost, while her stories were secondary. Wood adds that Davis' work is considered 'glamorous in literary circles', leading to the risk of reading her as a 'writer's writer' (Wood 2009: 88). She has since become better known as a writer, with the award of the Man Booker International Prize, as well as the effect of the *Collected Stories*. But her reputation – both as a writer and as a translator – was also bolstered by her translation of *Madame Bovary* in 2010, which received much critical attention (some of which I discuss in Chapter 5) and which was a bestseller. Her identity as a writer is inextricable from her identity as a translator.

Davis' stories are often experimental in form, avoiding or complicating standard ideas of narrative. Some of them are one line long, seemingly nothing more than an observation. For example, the story 'Hand' from Davis' 2007 collection *Varieties of Disturbance* is, in its entirety, the following sentence:

> Beyond the hand holding this book that I'm reading, I see another hand idle and slightly out of focus – my extra hand. (Davis 2007a: 30)

Davis' stories are often more developed than this short example suggests, but it shares a characteristic re-evaluation of the quotidian that appears in many of her stories. Even in a text as short as 'Hand' there is a questioning of the individual's perception of self. The speaker (it is too much to say narrator) exhibits a detached relationship to their own body, which is slightly alien to them. The story highlights the focus that one has when reading, a focus that can leave the body behind (the other hand) as well as alter the reader's perception of reality. Intellect and body are linked, though the link is sometimes confusing for the self.

Davis' characters often exhibit a similar sort of self-consciousness. In 'Break it Down' (Davis 1986: 20–30), for example, the central character is struggling to come to terms with a brief but emotionally powerful love affair. To do so, he analyses what its financial cost was. He concludes that the good times cost about three dollars an hour, if you include all the thinking about it beforehand and the memories afterwards. This figure does not include the pain, which comes afterwards, and which the character says cannot be measured (Davis 1986: 30). The story questions its own logic as it develops, posing intellectual questions about cost to cover the more emotional question about whether or not the pleasure outweighs the pain.[3]

Davis' self-reflexive characters led the critic Marjorie Perloff to state that 'the question of interpretation is Davis's real subject' (Perloff 1989: 208). Many of her stories fold back in on themselves, focusing not on the events of their narrative but on a character's interpretation of those events. Karen Alexander (2008) views this as a focus on analysis in the stories. The central characters of Davis' fiction tend to spend their time listening to themselves think, thinking about themselves thinking, trying to understand. Davis' fiction revolves around understanding and interpretation, suggesting that even when translation is not explicitly invoked, it is never far away. The metaphorical relationship with translation in her stories makes a reading of how her translations relate to those stories all the more necessary.

I am not the first person to notice the link between writing and translation in Davis' work. Other critics have not ignored Davis' translations, although what little critical work there is about her focuses on her other writing. The comments that are made are often speculations on what influence translating has had on Davis' short fiction, and no critic investigates the relationship beyond general speculations. Perloff, in her groundbreaking essay on Davis' work, wondered in a footnote what influence translating Leiris and Blanchot had had on Davis' own writing (Perloff 1989: 205n4). She does not develop this thought and her placement of it in a footnote is telling: it separates it from the body of her essay, reducing the question to something not properly part of her discussion of Davis.

Influence features heavily in other comments on the relationship between Davis' work and her translations of Blanchot. Beverly Haviland remarks that 'Davis's excellent work as a translator of Maurice Blanchôt [sic] seems to have made her as distrustful of language as he is' (Haviland 1989: 153). Haviland here reinforces the notion that the influence of translation on a writer moves only in one direction; I would argue that Davis' distrust of language could equally have led her to translate Blanchot. Josh Cohen (2005, 2010) uses ideas from Blanchot's critical writings to read stories by Davis, suggesting that these ideas offer a privileged insight into Davis' writing precisely because she translated Blanchot. Cohen (2010: 504) also suggests that Davis' translation activity mirrors her focus on form at the expense of content in her own writing, yet, as I will show throughout *The Many Voices of Lydia Davis*,

Davis is equally concerned with emotional states and how they are affected by language.

Other critics have remarked on the influence of translating in general on Davis' writing, which, as Christopher Knight puts it, 'has left an imprint on her fiction' (Knight 1999: 525). Larry McCaffery sees evidence of this imprint in 'the recurrence . . . of a set of concerns that all fundamentally have to do with the slipperiness of language' (McCaffery 1996: 59), as well as the presence of French and translated materials in her stories. Again, there is little here that could be considered substantial analysis, although McCaffery offers new ways of thinking about how translating has influenced Davis. Rather than just the influence of the writers she has translated, he suggests that translation may have influenced Davis' style and subject matter.

Influence feels, however, too simple an idea to describe the relationship between Davis' work and her translations. While I do not doubt that there is a possible relationship of influence between some of Davis' translations and her fiction, there is more to the relationship between her writing and translating than just influence from the translated texts. Some of Davis' translations bear traces of her own writing, such as a use of French words in her translations of Leiris, a technique which also appears in her stories 'The Letter' (Davis 1986: 49–56) and 'French Lesson 1: Le Meurtre' (Davis 1986: 128–36). Ben Marcus (2007) also suggests that Davis' own minimal aesthetic shines through her translation of Proust, which he says put 'Scott-Montcrieff's seminal translation on a diet'. Marcus reverses the common reading of translation as training for a writer, suggesting that Davis' own writing influences her translation activity. But again, he does not develop this thought. In other cases, themes and motifs from the texts that Davis has translated appear revised in her own stories, and her fiction can be read as responding to some of her translations. This is not so much a form of influence, as a form of textual dialogue between Davis and the other writer. Her translation offers another facet of that dialogue.

In this book, then, I go beyond previous commentary on Davis' work, breaking new ground by exploring in-depth how her translations relate to her own stories. To do so I use a methodology that has its roots in both comparative literature and translation studies. I use comparative readings of Davis' writing with texts that she has translated to look for connections, searching for echoes, parallels and responses to her translations in Davis' work. In addition, I analyse how she has translated a work, looking for clues to her relationship with that text and for echoes of her own writing techniques in her translation strategies. This combined methodology allows me to tease out the many subtle connections between the texts. My choice of what to analyse is influenced by Davis' own pronouncements on her translations, in interviews and significantly in her short book *Proust, Blanchot and a Woman in Red*, where she writes about her translations of Proust, Blanchot and Leiris. All three, she says, 'have been very important in [her] career as a translator' (Davis 2007b: 7). I will argue, in Chapters 2, 3 and 4, that they have also been important in her career as a writer. I also analyse her relation to Flaubert's work, which is complicated by her appropriation[4] of some of his letters in her own 'Stories from Flaubert', first published in 2010. But, as I have already said, Davis' interest in translation is not only confined to texts that can be defined clearly as translations: she also uses translation as a method and as a focal point in some of her stories. I analyse these stories in Chapters 6 and 7.

There are certain limits on what this book can do. It is impossible here to fully address the complex question of Davis' relationship with postmodernism and contemporary writing. That would, I fear, be another book-length study. However, some consideration of the relationship between postmodernism and Davis' work is unavoidable. Davis' stories could be considered experimental, or even 'post-experimental' as Ivan Callus (2014) argues, as some try to find new narrative techniques. The inclusion of a study of Davis in *Breaking the Sequence* (Friedman and Fuchs 1989), a collection of essays on women's experimental fiction, supports this position. Yet many of her stories have a more complex relationship with narrative, often doubting its possibility while at the same time producing it. Her novel *The End of the Story* offers a good example of telling a story and simultaneously questioning the possibility of telling it (see Chapter 4). This relationship is similar to the mix of subversion and belonging that Linda Hutcheon (1988: 3–15) characterises as specific to postmodern art. Davis' conscious use of intertextuality in her stories, which I analyse in Chapter 7, is also reminiscent of postmodernist writers such as Kathy Acker and William Burroughs. I argue in that chapter that Davis' work draws on a tradition of collage and montage that dates back at least as far as the early twentieth century and arguably much longer. Equally, Davis could be seen as participating in what Perloff calls a 'translational poetics', alongside contemporary writers such as Kenneth Goldsmith, Charles Bernstein and Susan Howe, studied in Perloff's *Unoriginal Genius* (2010). Davis' use of translation in her fiction could also place her among writers of what Klaus Kaindl and Karlheinz Spitzl (2014) have called 'transfiction', fiction that narrativises and dramatises translation. Yet, as I shall show in Chapter 7, Davis' use of translation differs from many of the more typical 'transfiction' authors.

Nor would it be possible here to explore in-depth Davis' complex relationship to American literature. Davis' choice of working mainly in the very short story and in translation shows an interest in what are marginal literary forms in a culture where the novel is dominant.[5] Davis' stories are often focused on small events, rather than the grand schemes of the energetic, large novels by writers such as Thomas Pynchon and David Foster Wallace, that Wood (2005: 167–83) calls 'hysterical realist'. Davis' work slips in-between the cracks in many ways and has often been overlooked because of her choice of literary forms; as I noted at the beginning, it was really only her *Collected Stories* from 2009 that brought her to many people's attention. By focusing on how she uses translation in this book, I hope to show how important translating is for her as a writer as well as demonstrating how translation contributes to literatures in English, not only as a way of importing texts and ideas but as a creative form.

Davis' own comments on her relationship to American literature often demonstrate a somewhat complex relationship to it. She cites European writers such as Samuel Beckett, Franz Kafka and Vladimir Nabokov among her influences (see, for example, McCaffery 1996: 66–7), and she has stated that she has 'very strong ties to Europe' (Knight 1999: 548). However, her stories often seem to have American settings. *The End of the Story*, for example, is set somewhere on the west coast of the USA. She has also mentioned the American writer Russell Edson (McCaffery 1996: 67). Edson writes short, surreal prose texts which do not fall neatly into any genre, like Davis' stories. While Edson's are published as poetry (for example, Edson 1994), Davis prefers to call her short texts 'stories', although they have also been published in *The Best American Poetry 2001* (Hass and Lehman 2001: 67) and *The Best American Prose Poetry* (Lehman 2003: 191–2). Davis is also connected through friendship to contemporary poets: Ron Silliman reports that she is part of a group of people to whom the poet Rae Armantrout sends drafts of her poems (Silliman 2001: xiii). Davis certainly has roots in European literature, but she is also an American writer, and her writing reflects both of these backgrounds.

My reading of Davis' translations is written against a tendency in translation studies to view translators as what Anthony Pym (1998: 161) calls 'mono-professionals', as I investigate the porous border between Davis as a translator and Davis as a writer. Pym explains that this tendency came about through the professionalisation of translation in the 1980s:

[t]he rapid expansion of translator training in the late 1980s has been bolstered by an institutional discourse that posits a social need for specialist translators and interpreters, implicitly people trained to work in this field and no other. The result is a widespread belief in what we might call the ideal 'mono-professionalism' of translators. (Pym 1998: 161)

The institutional discourse on translating (and interpreting) helped to create the perception that translators' sole professional activity is translating.[6] As Pym is careful to highlight, this is only a 'widespread belief': he goes on to show that relatively few translators have lived off translating (ibid.: 162). The institutional move towards a discourse of the translator-professional may have also been a response to what Lawrence Venuti (1986, 1995) has called 'the translator's invisibility': the way that translators' work tends to be obscured and hidden in the publication of translated fiction, through lack of acknowledgement or through the choice of a fluent translation style that hides the foreign origin of the text. By focusing on translation and translators, to the exclusion of their other activities, translation studies would make translation visible.

This does not mean that there is no work that analyses a writer's translations. George Steiner's *After Babel* (1998) is full of analyses of writers' translations, as is Venuti's *The Translator's Invisibility* (1995). These two well-known examples do not, however, link the writers' translations with their other writing, and are indicative of the general tendency of the discipline in this. By focusing on translations alone, the equally interesting connections between those translations and the other literary productions of a writer are eclipsed. There have been other studies that analyse the relationship between writers' translations and their other writing, ranging from Timothy Webb's 1976 study of Shelley's translations to Martine Hennard Dutheil de la Rochère's 2013 book on the role of translation in Angela Carter's work.[7] Recent work by Gillespie (2011) and Reynolds (2011) has highlighted the importance of translation in English literary history, though both these writers focus on poetry, whereas I am focusing on prose. While none of these earlier studies take Davis as an example, they form a background to how I've approached Davis.

In order to analyse the relationship between Davis' writing and translation, it is necessary to revisit the concept of authorship, especially the idea of an authorial *œuvre*, which allows us to link the two forms of creative output. An *œuvre*, following Michel Foucault (1994: 795), posits a unity across the different texts by an author. Foucault describes this unity as problematic, as it is an expectation of the reader rather than a demonstrable textual quality: readers expect a certain coherence and uniformity across the work of an author. However, as Foucault points out, that unity is an illusion: the concept of an author, he writes, 'c'est . . . ce qui permet de surmonter les contradictions qui peuvent se déployer dans une série de textes' ('is what makes it possible to overcome the contradictions that may be spread through a series of texts'; ibid.: 802). The author is not therefore identical to the writer, but a construct of the text. The author is not a living person who writes, eats, sleeps, drives to the shops, plays tennis, fills out tax forms, watches movies and so on, but rather the figure of the author that the reader imagines for themselves from the texts. Lydia Davis as author is not, therefore, Lydia Davis the flesh-and-blood person, but a textual construct.

The texts that can be associated with an author are more limited than those which the actual writer can produce. Readers will not accept just any text as part of an *œuvre*: there must be some sort of connection and uniformity with the other texts (Foucault 1994: 801–2). Following this theory, only those which demonstrate this uniformity 'really' belong to an author's *œuvre*; the rest can be ignored. This would mean ignoring notebooks, drafts, letters, shopping lists and other non-literary forms of writing, or anything by an author which was not of equal value to the rest of their literary works, such as juvenilia or pornography. The construction of an *œuvre* revolves around the exclusion of texts which are not considered to have relevant, significant connections with other works by an author.

Translations' dual status, as both original texts and derivative works, causes translations to take a problematic place in a writer-translator's *œuvre*. Translations are original as they are a new text, one that has not existed before in the language and which is the creative work of the translator. At the same time, they are derivative as they are based on and translate another text in another language. Because the translated texts may be written in a different style, express different ideas, or be of a different value to the rest of an author-translator's writings, the translated texts may not appear to have significant relationships with those other writings. Translations begin to belong to a writer's *œuvre* when readers perceive thematic or stylistic similarities between the translations and the writer's own works. There must be some sort of apparent connection, due to the expectations of coherence inherent in the concept of an *œuvre*.

If there is a connection between a writer's own texts and their translations then translations can be viewed as an extension of a writer's *œuvre* through another writer's texts. Like a graft, they form part of the work but at the same time they are also recognisably distinct. Translations often take a liminal position of belonging and not belonging, because they are part of a writer's textual production but at the same time they also present something which is potentially radically different from the other texts by the author.

The place that translations find in an *œuvre* is reliant on how they are perceived in relation to the other works by their translator. There are three main trends that can be seen in examples from other studies and Davis' work: translations may have no relationship to other texts; or they might be seen as having influenced a writer; or they might form some sort of dialogue with the other texts. In what follows, I sketch out these three main trends in order to give a background to the relationships Davis' translations form with her own texts.

Translations are not always completed as literary projects. They can be simply a way of paying the bills. Literary writers may undertake translations that are technical or commercial in nature, which are *de jure* works-for-hire. Such translations are often unsigned by the writer and consequently extremely difficult to trace through library catalogues or other sources. Due to the lack of signature, such texts would almost never belong to an author's *œuvre*, because they are not associated with that author. Unsigned translations could also justifiably be said not to be part of their translator's *œuvre*, as they are not claimed by the writer/translator as part of their body of work.

Lydia Davis has produced such unsigned translations. According to Thad Ziolkowski (1993), Davis and her then husband Paul Auster 'translate[d] a variety of art books and catalogues for the Galerie Maeght' when the pair were living in France in the 1970s. These translations appear lost: they cannot be found in library catalogues, or were unsigned at the time of publication and consequently are difficult to trace back to either Auster or Davis. Auster mentions the translations in an interview:

> Then I went through a long period where I earned my living doing translations. That was a completely different matter [to his translations of modern French poets]. I had nothing to do with choosing the texts. The publishers would tell me that they needed a translation of such and such a book, and I would do it. It was very draining work and had nothing to do with literature or my own writing . . . You grind out so many pages a day and it puts bread on the table. (Auster 1998: 272–3)

Auster's description of the life of a jobbing translator sounds pretty bleak: 'grind[ing] out pages' suggests a painful, violent process. Translation in this case is a job like banking or cleaning: it is what you do to earn money and it bears no resemblance to an artistic activity. Auster's statement that he was translating to earn a living, and the lack of attribution to the translator on the texts, place these early commissioned translations outside of Auster's authorial *œuvre*: they are excluded from relationships with his other work through his reduction of them to non-artistic activities.

The translations by Auster and Davis from this period that are attributed to them and accessible in library catalogues reinforce Auster's description of the texts as the choice of the publisher rather than the translators. The earliest is a translation of Saul Friedländer and Mahmoud Hussein's *Arabs and Israelis: A Dialogue*, published by Holmes & Meier in 1975. Auster and Davis translated four other books together: two of Chinese history (Chesneaux, Le Barbier and Bergère 1977; Chesneaux 1979), a collection of short essays and interviews with Jean-Paul Sartre (Sartre 1977), and a novel by Georges Simenon, *Aboard the Aquitaine* (Simenon 1979: 229–325). The books of Chinese history and the dialogue between Friedländer and Hussein cannot be considered literary works and there is little in the texts to suggest that they may have literary connections to other writings by Davis or Auster. The texts by Sartre and Simenon that the couple translated are more literary, but are more conventional than the avant-garde authors that Auster and Davis were also translating individually during that period, such as André Du Bouchet (1976) in Auster's case or Blanchot (1975, 1976, 1977) in Davis'.

The co-translations do not reflect the pair's other literary activities from the period. Auster had already published a book of poems, *Unearth*, in 1974, as well as translations of Jacques Dupin's poetry (Dupin 1974). Both books were published by *Living Hand*, a press and magazine that Auster and Davis edited (Ziolkowski 1993). The magazine ran from 1973 to 1976 and the press published another book of translations by Auster, Du Bouchet's *The Uninhabited* (1976), as well as Davis' first collection of short stories, *The Thirteenth Woman and other stories* (1976). Davis also began publishing her translations of Blanchot's *L'Arrêt de mort*, under the title 'Death Halt', in *Living Hand* in 1975. The journal and the two writers' own works at this time were far more avant-garde than the translations they were undertaking together.

In relation to these more avant-garde activities, the co-translations certainly appear to be a means of making money. They were published by large presses – Holmes & Meier for *Arabs and Israelis*, while the China books were published by Harvester in the UK and by Pantheon (a division of Random House) in the USA. Sartre's interviews and essays were also published by Pantheon in the USA, and republished in the UK a year later, with a different title, by André Deutsch (Sartre 1978). *Aboard the Aquitaine* was published as part of *The African Trio* by Hamish Hamilton in London. These books appear not to have been reprinted, but publication with such large publishers meant that they would have been much more widely disseminated than Auster's and Davis' own writing at the time.

It would be difficult to successfully argue that these early co-translations have extensive relationships with Auster's or Davis' later writing. In the interview, Auster explicitly excludes the possibility that translations done at a publisher's behest, even the signed translations, can belong to his *œuvre*. Although Davis has not been so vocal about these early translations, it would also be hard to present them as relevant to her authorial *œuvre*. Davis characterises these translations, as well as many of her other translations, as 'works-for-hire' (Davis 2007b: 7), suggesting she does not see them as artistic undertakings but as professional activities. There is little to relate them to her writing, either formally or thematically. Due to the fact that they were co-translated with Auster, they also become marginal to the body of works that could be viewed as her translatorial *œuvre*. It is impossible to know, without access to drafts or without conducting interviews, how Auster and Davis shared the work of translation.[8] The co-translations are the product of their joint effort. They cannot be relied upon to characterise Davis as a translator because she was not alone in translating them.

Translations, then, do not always interact with an author's other writing. Such translations do not affect how the author's other books are perceived. Auster and Davis both translated books as paid translators. Auster says that his books were commissioned, as were many (if not most) of Davis'. In the examples above, and in many of Davis' other translations, the translator can be thought to put aside their own authorial persona. Susan Bernofsky calls this type of translation 'service translation', which she explains as: 'translation in which the translator strives to subjugate his own authorial intention to that of the author of the original text' (Bernofsky 2005: ix). 'Service translation' may not only be connected with translations that writers have undertaken solely as a means of employment, since a translation that an author has undertaken on their own initiative can also be respectful of the author in this way. For a translation to have a relationship with its writer's authorial *œuvre*, however, there needs to be more of a connection than just the same signature. The translations need to interact in some way with their other writing. One of the typical relationships that has been identified is the relationship of influence, which can be related to the idea of translation as a form of training for writers.

In the same interview as above, Paul Auster mentions other types of translation that he undertook before he began earning his living as a translator in the 1970s. He translated French poetry as an undergraduate at Colombia, while he was also writing his own poetry (Auster 1998:

271). Translation became a form of training for him: 'Translation allows you to work on the nuts and bolts of your craft, to learn how to live intimately with words, to see more clearly what you are actually doing' (ibid.: 272).[9]

The idea that translating can serve as a form of training for young writers is well established. It first appears in Cicero's remarks on translation in *De Oratore*, and has an influence into the present day. Cicero found paraphrasing another writer's poetry or speech limited as an exercise, because 'those words which best befitted each subject, were the most elegant and in fact the best, had already been seized upon' (Cicero 1997: 7). Cicero could therefore not improve the poem or speech by using his own words. Translating from Greek to Latin allowed him not to repeat the same words as the Greek orators, because he had to find new ways of expressing their thought in Latin. Translation became a way of practising rhetoric.

The idea of translation as training changes with the growth in vernacular languages in the middle ages as well as in the nationalistic movements of the late eighteenth and early nineteenth centuries. While Cicero's concern was to perfect his own individual ability as a writer/speaker, vernacular translation in the middle ages 'us[ed] translation to develop and perfect literary skills in the native language' (Copeland 1991: 92). The goal was not just the development of the individual writer, but of the expressive capacities of the vernacular language. Rita Copeland foregrounds the way in which vernacular translations would supplant their Latin models: the translators were trying to 'generate a vernacular canon which will substitute itself for Latin models in the very process of replicating them' (ibid.: 93). Through extending the capacities of the vernacular language, the medieval translators would reduce the privileged position of Latin, because there would be a text in the vernacular that could serve the purpose of a model. The vernacular would therefore grow in power as well as capability. The German Romantics also focused on translation as a means of developing a language, a culture and the individual writer. Antoine Berman sees translation as closely connected to the German concept of *Bildung*, which combines the concepts of culture, education and training (Berman 1984: 72). In the early nineteenth century there was an effort to bring into existence a German culture, specifically a German literature which at the same time undertook 'un retour aux sources' ('return to source') and an 'ouverture de plus en plus "multiple" . . . sur les diverses littératures mondiales' ('more and more "multiple" opening . . . onto world literatures'; ibid.: 28). German literature was formed through its encounters with foreign texts and through translation.

Not only would the national literature be subject to the process of *Bildung* by translation. The individual writer would also be shaped by encountering the foreign text and translating it. Novalis claimed, no doubt hyperbolically, that there had been 'no German writer of any substance who ha[d] not also been a translator, who in fact has not puffed himself up so much over his translations as over his original works' (Novalis 1997: 212). Since any 'writer of substance' would have been a translator, translation would have been important in the training of those writers. The Germans had, like the Romans, 'learned so immensely' (ibid.) from translation, both as a people and as individuals.

The idea of translation as a way of developing the repertoire of literary (often poetic) and rhetorical techniques of a language community and an individual continued into the twentieth century. According to Steven Yao (2002: 6), modernist poets saw translation as a means of expanding 'the range of cultural, linguistic, and generic fields in which they could actively participate'. The expansion of the individual's skills and the possibilities of the language are joined in modernism. Ezra Pound (1954: 7) also counselled young writers to translate, so that their subject matter would not 'wobble', advice that Auster (1998: 272) refers to in the same interview as quoted above. By advising writers to learn their craft through translating, Pound makes translation into an act of *Bildung* for the author. His advice follows a tradition that has been active in European letters since the Romans.

In light of this tradition, it is very tempting to see authors' translations as part of their apprenticeship. There are two effects that follow: first, the translations cannot fully become part of an author's *œuvre* because they are preparation for the writing of it. Translation ends up by being both included in and excluded from the *œuvre*. An author's translations affect how other texts are read, but are also not considered to be equal to those other texts. If translation is viewed as training or practice then it becomes supplementary to the authorial *œuvre*: it is what one does before and as well as writing. Second, the relationship between the translations and the writer's own texts is viewed as one of influence. The texts that an author has translated can be read as having been formative of their own writing, and as such the translations become a record of influence on the translator/writer from the author they have translated. The translated text can be seen as a precursor to a writer's other texts. A good example of this approach is Hiroko Cockerill's (2006) reading of the relationship between the Japanese writer Futabatei Shimei's own writing and his translations from Russian, which places those translations in the position of influences on his own work, especially his novel *Ukigumo* ('*Floating Clouds*') from 1887.

Translation may also be instrumentalised by an author, as the German Romantics and the Modernists thought, to alter the parameters of the literary culture in which they live. Edwin Gentzler (1996) suggests that Robert Bly used translation as a way of exploring a poetics that was outside of the American norm. The Spanish and Latin American writers that Bly translated and published in *The Fifties*, such as Juan Ramón Jiménez, Antonio Machado and Federico García Lorca, offered a different way of writing that allowed Bly to develop his own style of writing in English. Bly's use of translation in *The Fifties* clearly relates to the idea of translation as a way of expanding a literary repertoire that has been common in the European tradition since the middle ages.

While these two examples show that translation functions as training for some authors, for Lydia Davis there are far more complex relationships with her other writing, which can be characterised as dialogic relationships. Moving on from viewing translations as solely a form of training means positing that they enter into a more multilateral relationship with the rest of an author's *œuvre*. A translation may be undertaken because it appeals to the author, or they may view it as an extension of their own artistic project. In such cases, there will be interactions with other writing by the author both before and after the translation, as I will demonstrate throughout this book in relation to Davis' work.

The question of influence becomes less unidirectional in this case, as an author's writing practice can influence how they translate and what they choose to translate.[10] Rather than solely looking for echoes of translations in the translator's writings as an author, as one might when analysing influence, it is necessary to search out echoes of the translator's authorial writing practices in their translations. John Felstiner, for example, sees such echoes of Paul Celan's own poetry in his translations of Emily Dickinson (Felstiner 1998: 169–70). According to Felstiner, Celan's German translation of Dickinson deviates from her poem in meaning and form. These deviations show traces of Celan's own authorial voice, which causes Felstiner to call these translations 'strong' translations (Felstiner 1998: 165). Celan's translations would not be examples of what Bernofsky (2005: ix) has called 'service translation', because he does not subordinate his authorial intentions to the service of the translated text. Bernofsky has her own theory of 'strong' translators, who, she says, '[place] their own unmistakable imprint on the works they translated . . . their translations are marked by the literary concerns that can be found elsewhere in the *oeuvre* of each' (Bernofsky 2005: x).

Such 'strong translation' shows a relationship between translator and original author that is less hierarchical than the one found in conventional, 'service' translation (following Bernofsky's terms). 'Strong' translation may be a signal of the dialogic relationship between an author's translations and their other writing. It locates the translations as an extension of the author's own writing, contiguous with their authorial *œuvre* because of shared concerns and techniques. Susan Bassnett's publication of her translations of Alejandra Pizarnik alongside her own poems as *Exchanging Lives* (Bassnett and Pizarnik 2002) makes visible how translation can form a dialogue with the translated author and the authorial *œuvre* of the translator, highlighting how 'translation may be one of several different literary activities undertaken by the same person' (Bassnett 2006: 174). Translation is, for Bassnett, a form of literary textual production; it can be considered alongside other forms of literary writing as part of an author's *œuvre*. The layout of *Exchanging Lives* leads the reader to believe that Bassnett's poems are in dialogue with Pizarnik's. Her own poems are visually intertwined with the translations, leading the reader to investigate the links between them. The translations cannot be read solely as translations, either: they represent part of a larger poetic project. Bassnett's translations of Pizarnik show a dialogue with her own poetry. The poems and translations echo each other through their placement on the page. Bassnett readily admits that her writing changed under Pizarnik's influence, albeit 'in ways [she] cannot properly explain' (Bassnett 2006: 180).

Dialogue is not just one singular, stable concept but can take multiple forms. The way in which Bassnett's translations from Pizarnik interact with her own poems is different from the way in which Celan's translations interact with his poems, or how Hölderlin's translations of classical authors extend his poetic project (Louth 1998) or how Angela Carter's translations of Charles Perrault's fairy tales reverberate across her work (Hennard Dutheil de la Rochère 2013), or, as I shall show later, how Davis interacts with texts she has translated. Yet they all still produce dialogues with the source text and the author's other writing. Importantly, viewing the translations in dialogue with an author's other writing places the translations within the author's *œuvre*. The translations are given a status commensurate with their other writing, as they are also important for an understanding of the author-function that unites those texts.

Translation becomes an extension of the author's own work in both training and dialogue. The translations allow the author to expand in directions that are not normally open to them in their own work. The difference between training and dialogue lies in how the translations are perceived by author and reader. If the translation serves only to help a writer learn their craft, or develop new techniques, then it is reduced to a supplementary role as training. If the translation exhibits correspondences with an author's own work on several levels, such as style, theme, narrative technique and so on, which do not appear to have developed as a result of the translation but which were already present before writing the translation, then it may be regarded as being in dialogue with the author's own works.

Davis' work presents a complex relationship between her translations and her own writing, which tend to take on some form of dialogue. As she commented in an interview with Larry McCaffery, she enjoys translating because she enjoys 'assuming a disguise' and because translating allows her to write in a way that would be out of place in her own work (McCaffery 1996: 75). Davis here recognises the importance of difference for her as a translator: the translations interest her because they are written in a way which is distinct from her own writing and which would not fit in with her authorial image. The translations allow her to explore a way of writing which is not her own. This can clearly be seen, as I argue in Chapter 3, in her translation of Leiris' autobiography, where the autobiographic element is out of place in Davis' writing, but by translating Leiris it offers her the opportunity to explore that genre without writing her own autobiography.

The metaphor of the graft, introduced earlier, helps explain the relationship of translations to the rest of Davis' *œuvre*. If an apple tree has a branch from another apple tree of a different variety grafted onto it, then it will produce different apples on that branch than on the rest of the tree. For example, a Granny Smith tree may have a Braeburn branch grafted onto it. The new branch would continue to produce Braeburn apples, although it was part of a Granny Smith tree. The graft continues to function as something distinct from the rest of its host. Translations continue to be distinct from the rest of the author's *œuvre*, while still being part of it. The graft will be rejected, however, if it is too different. You cannot graft an apple branch onto a strawberry bush. There must be a degree of initial similarity for the graft to take hold. Translations enter into a relationship with an author's other works when there is some form of similarity, either in outlook or style or theme: some point of contact between the works. Without that point of affinity, it becomes difficult for a reader to see any connection between them.[11]

In some of her public statements, Davis highlights points of contact between certain of her translations and her own work, allowing the reader to begin perceiving the translations as a graft onto Davis' *œuvre*. For example, in an interview with Christopher Knight, Davis remarked:

Proust's approach . . . probably did have a big influence on the way I wrote *The End of the Story*, even though of course I first read him years ago. I guess, for me, Proust was only the first in a line of writers that included Michel Leiris and Maurice Blanchot who all tended to go very deeply, very analytically into an experience. And I can't tell whether I'm drawn to them and happy translating them because I approach things the same way, or whether they have influenced me to do this even more. (Knight 1999: 529–30)

Davis here complicates the idea of influence as unidirectional. She is drawn towards Proust, Leiris and Blanchot because she feels an affinity for them, because she 'approach[es] things in the same way', but this affinity and translating them may have influenced her to write a certain way. Her own work influences her choice of translations to accept, and her translations influence her own work. Talking to McCaffery, Davis remarked that '[w]hatever affinity I have for an author I'm translating is already there in advance. I'm not going to be influenced by translating Blanchot so much as I *already* felt a kinship for him. Otherwise I would not be interested in translating him' (McCaffery 1996: 67–8; original emphasis). Davis clearly suggests she felt that she and Blanchot were working in similar ways and this attracted her to translating his work. As I show in Chapter 2, her translation of Blanchot is not a form of training, but rather an extension of elements of her own work through the work of another writer.

It should be clear at this point that the relationship a translation has with Davis' other works will be specific to that translation. There is not a single relationship that all of the translations have with Davis' own work. It is necessary to read the translations individually to understand how they interact with Davis' stories. My analyses in the following chapters may therefore appear to be discrete, but they are all formed around the same question of how Davis' translations relate to her stories, with each focusing on the dialogic aspects of that relationship. As such, different approaches in each chapter, drawing from a variety of critical discourses (narrative, Lacanian psychoanalysis, rewriting, authority, parody and collage), bring forth the dialogic aspects of the texts.

To read every translation in-depth would make this book an unmanageable size, given that Davis has translated over twenty books. Such a reading would not be warranted for many of the translations, which have no or only very minor links with Davis' own writing.[12] Davis' own comments have, to some extent, pointed out the writers that I focus on: the writers she translated that she mentions often as being important to her as a writer are Proust, Leiris and Blanchot. In 2007 she published a small book of essays related to these writers called *Proust, Blanchot and a Woman in Red*. In it she explicitly states that they have been 'very important in [her] career as a translator' (Davis 2007b: 7). Chapters 2,

3 and 4 therefore analyse the relationships between her work and her translations of Blanchot, Leiris and Proust.

Chapter 2, 'Blanchot and Affinity', analyses Davis' interaction with Blanchot's work in two ways: first, by an analysis of her translation of *Death Sentence/L'arrêt de mort*, which shows how attentive Davis was to the structures of Blanchot's writing, especially to features such as ambiguity. Her translation shows respect for the source text and the ways in which it signifies. The second analysis is a reading of her story 'Story' (Davis 1986: 3–7), which shares formal features with *The Madness of the Day/La folie du jour*, particularly its use of indeterminacy. However, it positions the narrator as the one looking for meaning in a tale that is unstable, where the narrator in Blanchot's text is the one producing such a story; there is a reversal of perspective in Davis' text. The difference comes from the characters' different motivations: Davis' narrator is motivated by jealousy whereas the story requested from Blanchot's narrator is necessary to fulfil a jurido-medical explanation of his affectless state. Both these analyses demonstrate a link of affinity between Davis and Blanchot, though Davis' work also revises and retreads the territory of Blanchot's stories.

Chapter 3, 'Leiris and Dialogue', analyses Davis' translation of Leiris' *La Règle du jeu*, focusing on her unconventional approach: an utmost fidelity that includes leaving words in French to make explicit patterns in the text. This approach echoes Lewis' theory of 'abusive fidelity' or Venuti's 'foreignizing' translation. Importantly, however, it links to stories ('The Letter', 'French Lesson 1: Le meurtre') by Davis where French words are used in the text to distance the reader. These stories precede the translations and it would seem here that Davis' own writing practice influences her translation practice. However, Davis explicitly positions Leiris as a precursor in other texts, which are explored in the chapter. It then goes on to analyse the parallels between Leiris' and Davis' writing. Both can be seen to privilege what Jakobson calls the 'poetic' function of language, i.e. the possibility of making the reader focus on the signifier as much as the signified. Drawing on Lacan's and Kristeva's theories, the second half of the chapter argues through a series of close readings that while Leiris focuses on the poetic function to recover unconscious structures as part of his autobiographical project, Davis uses it to question the symbolic order. As such, the two authors use similar means to reach different goals. Davis can be seen to draw from Leiris' formal experiments, but revises his use of them. Her translations of him therefore act like a graft on her work – part of it but distinct.

Chapter 4, 'Proust and Rewriting', focuses on the two ways that Davis can be seen to be rewriting Proust's work. She openly admits to Proust's influence on her work, especially *The End of the Story*. However, her translation of *The Way by Swann's* comes late in her career, which highlights the arbitrariness of assigning influence to a text that someone has translated, as critics often do (in this case, for example, Knight 1999: 525). Drawing on conceptions of rewriting from both contemporary literature (Moraru) and translation studies (Lefevere), the chapter analyses how Davis' novel rewrites Proust's, shifting the gender of the narrator and questioning the teleological goal of Proust's novel: *The End of the Story* does not aim to tell the story of an artistic awakening as *In Search of Lost Time* does (though Proust's novel does tell other stories too) but rather it aims to tell the story of a relationship. Yet it complicates this goal by fragmenting and questioning its own narration. It therefore rewrites Proust through a postmodern lens. Davis' other rewriting of Proust takes place in her retranslation of *The Way by Swann's*, which she translates in a very literal style. This distances her translation from previous translations by C. K. Scott Moncrieff and James Grieve, both of whom make multiple adjustments to the text at sentence level. Davis and her editor, Christopher Prendergast, both explicitly position their translation in opposition to Scott Moncrieff's in their prefaces. Through a close reading of selected extracts, Chapter 4 analyses just how Davis' translation differs from the other two translations. The precision with which she translates can be related to the care taken to find the right word in her own stories. Once again, her translation can be seen to connect in multiple ways to her own writing, going beyond influence and becoming a part of her work.

I analyse her Flaubert translation in Chapter 5, 'Flaubert and Authority'. The translation was published after Davis' statements about writers important to her in *Proust, Blanchot and a Woman in Red*, however it is refracted in her 'Ten Stories from Flaubert' (Davis 2010), which translate and reshape stories from Flaubert's letters, as well as the essay 'Some Notes on Translation and on *Madame Bovary*' (2011b). Davis' translation of Flaubert's *Madame Bovary* comes after she was awarded a McArthur Genius grant for her own writing; therefore it can be considered that she chose to do this translation for personal reasons rather than from the need to earn a living (as had been the case with many of her translations). It differs from most of Davis' other translations as there is already a wealth of translations of *Madame Bovary* (as opposed to the two of Proust or the lack of previous translations of Blanchot or Leiris). Davis' translation, then, is an intervention in a crowded field. Her translation strategies can be compared with those of other translators (as critics did when it was first published). In one sense undertaking this translation is a test of her philosophy and practice of translation – how does it stand up against other translators' work? – and at the same time it allows her to put her own personal stamp on a classic text. The affinity that she talks of in relation to some of the writers she has discussed resurfaces with Flaubert: the attention to detail and the search for the *mot juste* are shared features with Davis' own writing. In the second half of the chapter, Davis' text 'Ten stories from Flaubert' is analysed: here we have a clear case of Davis using translation in the construction of one of her 'own' stories, much as she does in 'Marie Curie, So Honorable Woman', discussed in the next chapter. The text is analysed in relation to the question of its authorship, as it maintains its links to Flaubert and is explicitly marked as a text by Davis, leaving it with a dual authorship.

Chapter 6, 'Marie Curie and Parody', focuses on another of Davis' refractions. While the previous chapters have focused on the texts that Davis states have been important to her, this chapter focuses on her reuse of a translation that she completed as a 'work-for-hire' assignment, a biography of Marie Curie by Françoise Giroud. This text resurfaces as a source for her story 'Marie Curie, So Honorable Woman' (Davis 2001: 99–119). In this chapter, I argue that 'Marie Curie, So Honorable Woman' is best understood under the rubric of parody. The chapter begins by analysing the paratextual framework for the story, which does not include an acknowledgement of its source text. The story is revealed to contain overly literal translations from Giroud's biography. Yet these translations do not resemble Davis' published equivalents and the story greatly abridges the biography. In this way it resembles other stories based around extracts by Davis, for example 'Extracts from a Life' and 'Lord Royston's Tour'. However, it differs in its use of translation and its lack of acknowledgement of its source. Following a reading of copyright law (which does not question the legal status of the text), parodies do not have to acknowledge their sources and so 'Marie Curie, So Honorable Woman' would need to be a parody, that is, show a critical distance from its source text. This can be seen in its translation style, which is hyperbolic, and also the choice of extracts, which choose the more awkward moments. The text is therefore not a fair representation of its source material and I argue that, in fact, 'Marie Curie, So Honorable Woman' questions the possibility of fair representation by highlighting how representation is always the result of interpretation and so always selective.

Davis' 'Marie Curie, So Honorable Woman' and 'Ten Stories from Flaubert' destabilise boundaries between translation and other modes of writing, collapsing them together. This instability in Davis' work is taken up again in the final chapter, 'Translation as Composition', which offers a wider reading of translation, suggesting that Davis' use of other writers' work in her own stories is related to her translation activity, equally grafting the material of others into her own. The final destabilisation takes place in her stories which take translation as a figure, creating translational texts which are nevertheless not translations. The first part of the chapter examines Davis' use of the works of other writers in her stories, which can take the form of collage or montage, as in the case of 'Marie Curie, So Honorable Woman' and the excerpt stories from the previous chapter, or quotation ('The Walk', 'Once A Very Stupid Man') and pastiche ('Kafka Cooks Dinner', 'Southward Bound, Reading *Worstward Ho*'). It is argued that these techniques mirror translation in their recontextualisation of material from another source and by the way that they associate Davis as a writer with other authors, creating a literary context for her work. The result is a dialogic relationship with these authors which is similar to the dialogic relationship Davis has with writers she has translated. Interestingly, in all these works, Davis never quotes exactly, preferring to alter the text slightly, thus questioning the reader's acceptance of the texts as citational works: there is a parallel here with contemporary art that uses fake found objects (such as Jeff Koons' work) to undermine the viewer's expectations. In the second part of the chapter, two stories which use translation as a theme are analysed. In 'Foucault and Pencil', the reading of a difficult text by Foucault is used as a metaphor for understanding an argument that the narrator is having with their partner. As in other stories by Davis, intellectual problems are worked through in place of emotional difficulties, which can be resolved once the intellectual problems have been. This can also be seen in 'The Letter', where the interpretation of a poem in French substitutes for a message from an ex-lover. These stories are evidence of where translating and writing clearly overlap in Davis' work, but the two modes of creation are mutually implicated throughout Davis' *œuvre*, as she responds to and rewrites texts she has translated as well as incorporating the work of other writers into her own though quotation and pastiche. As such, Davis can be seen to problematise the concept of authorship and the bounded text or work: it is open to multiple voices. Her identity as a writer is tied to her identity as a translator and vice versa. Equally, Davis complicates the role of originality in literary production. In this way her work can be seen to be part of the growth of a translational poetics (Perloff 2010), where writing draws extensively from other texts or from intercultural contact, but it goes further than many of the writers associated with this term (Kenny Goldsmith, Yoko Tawada) as Davis actually produces full translations as well as using translation in her own writing.

Notes

1. I have included references to these works in the bibliography, so that an interested reader can seek them out. Please see Jouve 1995, 1996, 1997a, 1997b; Detrez 1984, 1986; Butor 1986; Jardin 1988; Badinter 1995.
2. As such, it could also be seen to respond to work on transnationalising American literature such as Wai Chee Dimock's *Through Other Continents* (2006). Rebecca Walkowitz's *Born Translated* (2015) analyses the role of translation in Anglophone literature in a slightly different way, by focusing on the presence of translation within novels written in English.
3. See also Laurent Berlant and Lee Edelman's discussion of 'Break it down' in relation to negativity (Berlant and Edelman 2014: 63–117).
4. I am using 'appropriation' here in the sense of taking and using the source text, rather than Julie Sanders' definition of appropriation as 'a more decisive journey [than adaptation] away from the informing source into a wholly new cultural product and domain' (Sanders 2006: 26).
5. While there has clearly been a tradition of the short story in the USA since the late nineteenth century, the very short story, or the short short story as it is also known, is a more recent genre. As Robert Shapard (1986: xiii) notes, readers may ignore them because they think of them as fragments of larger stories. However, even though short stories, and to an extent short short stories, are established as a genre, the novel is the more dominant form in American literature, if not world literature (see Walkowitz 2015: 2).
6. Recent work in the discipline, for example Pérez-González and Susam-Saraeva 2012, has begun to address the lack of research on non-professional translation.
7. Further examples include Block 1981, Kaplan 1989, Gentzler 1996, Heep 1996, West 1996, Stark 1997, Felstiner 1998, Louth 1998, Kristal 2002, Bernofsky 2005, Cockerill 2006, Varney 2010.
8. Even interviews may be misleading, as it is over thirty years since these translations were completed, and both Auster's and Davis' memories of the process may no longer be precise.
9. Auster also says that 'Working on translations removes the pressure of composition' (Auster 1998: 272). This formulation is very similar to Davis' comment that translation is writing 'without the pressure of invention' (Knight 1999: 528). The similarity is not surprising, given the fact that the two writers were married and translated books together.
10. This will not be the case for all translations: some will have no real relationship with an author's other writing, as was the case for the work-for-hire translations that Auster talked about in the interview quoted above.
11. My use of grafts as a metaphor for the place of translations in an author's *œuvre* has similarities to the reading of the graft in Derrida's work and especially in Jonathan Culler's reading of Derrida in *On Deconstruction* (1982: 134–56). Derrida, in Culler's reading, uses the idea of grafts to explain how texts are woven together from multiple discourses (Culler 1982: 135). Derrida's grafts erase the possibility of a single reading of a text, forcing the reader to accept multiple meanings at the same time. My

use of the metaphor of grafts has similarities to Derrida's and Culler's use, because it highlights how translations take a double position of being both within and outside of an *œuvre*. Neither Derrida nor Culler use the idea of the graft at the level of authorship, but always as an internal part of a text. Their grafts affect how meaning is perceived within a text, while I am suggesting that the translated texts themselves appear as grafts within a larger system of the author's work, and offer new possibilities for the reception of other texts by that author.

12. See Evans 2011: 143–68 for a discussion of some of Davis' translations (from Léon-Paul Fargue and Danièle Sallenave) excluded from this book.

Chapter 2

Blanchot and Affinity

Davis' most enduring relationship as a translator is with Maurice Blanchot. She began publishing her translation of *Death Sentence* in 1975 in the magazine *Living Hand*, which Davis and her then husband Paul Auster edited. Over the next eighteen years, Davis translated six books of Blanchot's: *L'Arrêt de mort* (1977, first published 1948) as *Death Sentence* (1978), *Au moment voulu* (1951) as *When the Time Comes* (1985), *Celui qui m'accompagnait pas* (1953) as *The One Who Was Standing Apart from Me* (1993), *Le dernier homme* (1957) as *The Last Man* (1987), *La folie du jour* (2002, first published 1973) as 'The Madness of the Day' (1977) and *The Gaze of Orpheus and other literary essays* (1981). The first four of these are novella-length texts, called '*récits*' by Blanchot. The fifth, 'The Madness of the Day', is a short text that was published separately as a book in 1981, despite only being nine full pages in length in its 1977 English magazine publication and the same when it was reprinted in *The Station Hill Blanchot Reader* (Blanchot 1999: 191–9).[1] Davis' other translation, *The Gaze of Orpheus and other literary essays* (Blanchot 1981b), was the first English collection of Blanchot's critical essays. It contains work from Blanchot's collections *Faux pas* (1943), *La Part du feu* (1949), *L'Espace littéraire* (1955), *Le Livre à venir* (1959) and *L'Entretien infini* (1969). It appeared just before two other translations of Blanchot's essays (Blanchot 1982a and 1982b).

Davis has stated how important translating Blanchot was for her as a translator. While translating him she 'learned to stay extremely close to the text . . . practising an extreme fidelity' (Davis 2007b: 7). She published early versions of her translations in magazines (Blanchot 1975, 1976, 1977) which, with the exception of Michel Leiris' work, is something she has not done with her other translations, although it mirrors her practice with her own short stories. These early publications increased her visibility as a translator and helped to establish her reputation.

While Blanchot's importance to Davis as a translator seems clear, it is harder to establish how important he is for her as a writer; in other words, how her activity translating Blanchot impacted on her writing and how her identities as author and translator are affected by this. Davis has mentioned that she shares some sort of affinity with Blanchot as a writer, which drew her to translating him (McCaffery 1996: 67–8), and the prevalence of the Blanchot translations in Davis' bibliography has influenced many of the critics who have written about Davis. They tend to approach Davis through the lens of Blanchot's critical writings, suggesting that his ideas have influenced Davis. Beverly Haviland noted 'Davis's excellent work as a translator of Maurice Blanchôt [sic] seems to have made her as distrustful of language as he is' (Haviland 1989: 153), an impression that Marjorie Perloff deepens with reference to Blanchot's observation that 'ordinary language' is also full of misunderstanding (Perloff 1989: 205). Likewise, Josh Cohen posits Blanchot's influence when, in an article on irony which is heavily grounded in Blanchot's thinking, he chooses Lydia Davis' work as a way of demonstrating how the 'mode of (non)revelation work[s] within the specific space of individual literary texts' (Cohen 2005: 76), noting that his choice of Blanchot's American translator is not coincidental. Cohen also foregrounds elsewhere (Cohen 2010: 502) how Blanchot's critical writings can be used to understand Davis' work.

Rather than following this path, this chapter focuses on Davis' relationship to Blanchot's fiction. Davis' translations of Blanchot show a respect for his writing as they tend to follow Blanchot's style, although by no means does she practise the 'extreme fidelity' that she claims to (Davis 2007b: 7). This approach is representative of her acceptance of the difficulties that Blanchot's work presents to the reader and reveals an affinity with his approach. Due to limits of space, I focus on her translation of *Death Sentence*, which is important to Davis' *œuvre* of translations as it was the first book she translated alone and she writes that it was her 'extended initiation into translating closely and exactly' (Davis 2007b: 1). Her autonomy as a translator was stressed by Blanchot himself when she wrote to him (Ziolkowski 1997).

After reading her translation, the rest of this chapter questions how Davis responds in her own fiction to Blanchot. I choose to focus on *La Folie du jour*/'The Madness of the Day', the shortest *récit* by Blanchot that Davis translated, and how it relates to Davis' story 'Story' (1986: 3–7). Both stories reject the possibility of a single interpretation of events. This indeterminacy attracted Davis to Blanchot as a writer, although she writes with much more focus on emotional connections than Blanchot, and appears ultimately to question his influence on her.

Translating *Death Sentence*

Death Sentence tells two stories which the reader is left to connect. The point of cohesion between the two parts is the narrating 'I', although it is difficult to be sure that the two 'I's refer to the same character. The first part of the book relates the death of J., a female friend of the male narrator. As she is dying, the narrator receives a call from her sister Louise asking him to come. He does, and J. has a miraculous recovery, or rather a reprieve, as she then dies again, helped by a large dose of narcotics from the narrator. The second part features the narrator and several women; there are repetitions of events (a character entering a room unannounced, for example), and towards the end the narrator tells a cold body in a room 'Come' (Blanchot 1978: 69): this body being the woman the narrator is looking for. Kevin Hart (2004) sees in the first part a retelling of the story of Mark 5:21–34, where Jesus brought Lazarus back from the dead. I would suggest that the second command to come can be viewed as a parallel event to J.'s appeal to the narrator, as it is said to a character who has disappeared and who is dead; as such it brings her back to life. Other than this possible calling back to life, another link between the two parts may be the making of plaster casts of hands, first of J.'s and then the narrator's (Blanchot 1978: 10, 75), an activity which would make an image capable of surviving the death of the person whose hands have been cast. These casts would stop death, just as the deaths in the book are stopped or postponed. But death is never truly stopped, as J. dies after her reprieve, as the casts themselves will disappear too; they will, however, outlast their model.

The apparent lack of relationship between the two parts of the *récit* makes *Death Sentence* into a book that requires careful and multiple readings, and one not likely to have mass appeal. Gilberto Sorrentino (1986) also notes that Blanchot's writing 'is not intended for the anonymous body known as the public', a comment that seems illustrated by the publishers' recollection that while there was an 'avid "cult following" for *Death Sentence* on the Lower East Side of Manhattan . . . a Blanchot readership took its own time in developing' (Quasha and Stein 1999: 512).

Davis' translation was fêted by Sorrentino (1986) in his review, where he said that Blanchot's work had been 'beautifully translated'. The translation seldom proves difficult to read on the sentential level in English, although it remains difficult to follow the narrative of the text. Davis generally replicates Blanchot's paragraphing, with the exception that dialogue is sometimes extracted from the middle of paragraphs into new paragraphs of its own. This could be explained as reflecting the norms prevalent in English publishing, and may have been a decision of an editor, especially since the technique is not applied uniformly.[2] Davis' attention to the shape of Blanchot's paragraphs, with the exception of the changes to the presentation of speech, shows a trust in his storytelling. It makes the translation more source oriented, and suggests that Davis was writing a 'service translation' (Bernofsky 2005: ix), reducing her own authorial presence in the text.

Blanchot's title, *Arrêt de mort*, is problematic to translate. As Jacques Derrida notes, it 'plays with language to the point of stopping [*arrêter*] any translation' (Derrida 1979: 90; original interjection). 'Arrêt de mort' is used idiomatically in French to mean 'death sentence' in the sense of capital punishment. It could also, if read literally, mean a stopping of death, which is mirrored in the events of the stories. Davis used this literal approach for the sample published in *Living Hand*, calling it 'Death-halt' (Blanchot 1975), before reverting to the idiomatic translation for later publications, which follows her overall strategy of idiomatic translation in *Death Sentence*. 'Death sentence' itself generates a certain polysemy, although different from the French: a sentence (phrase) of death. Yet *Death Sentence* has no sentence of death, only a sentence of reprieve from death: 'Come'. The focus on writing in *Death Sentence* could be seen as justifying the possible polysemy in English. The narrator notes '[i]f I have written books, it has been in the hope that they would put an end to it all' (Blanchot 1978: 1), suggesting that writing is related to death, an idea that Blanchot explores in 'Literature and the Right to Death' (Blanchot 1981b: 21–62; 1999: 359–99) and 'The Work and Death's Space' (Blanchot 1982b: 87–159). Davis' translation of the title, then, idiomatically translates the French title and produces ambiguity, although a different ambiguity to the French. Here, as elsewhere, Davis gives a translation of Blanchot that is acceptable to the target audience, but which endeavours to replicate the difficulties of his writing style.

There is an elusive nature to Blanchot's prose, which, as John Updike wrote, 'gives an impression, like Henry James' [prose], of carrying meanings so fragile they might crumble in transit' (Updike 1982: 93). Part of this fragility lies in the narrator's lack of certainty. For example:

> Je pense qu'elle m'annonçait par là qu'elle allait mourir. Cette fois, je decidai de rentrer à Paris. Mais je me donnai encore deux jours. J'annonçai cela par téléphone ou par télégramme. (Blanchot 1977a: 31)

Davis translates this as:

> I think that in saying that, she was announcing that she was going to die. This time I decided to return to Paris. But I gave myself two more days. I let her know by telephone or by telegram. (Blanchot 1978: 17)

The narrator's uncertainty with regard to how he transmitted the information seems difficult to accept, assuming that the narrative is realistic. There are also many referents here that are not mentioned or unclear in relation to 'this' or 'that'. What exactly does the narrator announce in the final sentence – his return to Paris or his decision to stay two more days? Davis' translation also avoids clarification of this point, but she clarifies the recipient of the announcement: 'I let her know'. The addition of 'her' would be unavoidable with Davis' choice of 'let know' for 'annonçai': Blanchot's French here offers an impersonal announcement, whereas Davis' English addresses an interlocutor. The increase of textual cohesion, making explicit who the recipient of the announcement is, does not seriously alter what the reader understands, however, as the interlocutor is arguably implied in French by her appearance in the preceding sentences.

Davis' translation manages to recreate much of the ambiguity of the source text, despite her occasionally making more explicit individual parts of a sentence. The imperfect tense of 'annonçait'/'she was announcing' suggests a continuous action, without any clear reason why. To announce that one is doing anything is a single completed action and should take the *passé simple*. Davis' choice not to repeat 'announce' could be explained by consideration of the norms of English: using an impersonal 'I announced this' might appear excessively formal, and disrupt the reading of an already strange statement. Davis' decision here, contrary to her earlier explicitation of the recipient, reduces the cohesion of the text by removing repetition: the narrator's announcement no longer seems to mirror J.'s.

While Davis (2007b: 31) might have thought that her translation was close and exact, she makes the text more explicit than it is in French. The text is altered on a syntactic level to be more acceptable to the target language reader. Davis' strategy is much closer than in her work-for-hire translations (Davis 2007b), but it still adapts the text for a target language readership. In this example from the second part, Davis makes explicit certain implicit references:

> Ce voyage en métro m'a laissé le souvenir d'une grande tristesse. Cette tristesse ne se rapportait pas à mon peu de mémoire. Mais quelque chose de profondément triste était en train de se passer là, avec tous ce gens de midi. Il y avait, à deux pas, un malheur important, aussi silencieux qu'un vrai malheur peut l'être, étranger à tout secours, inconnu, que rien ne pouvait fair apparaître. (Blanchot 1977a: 63)

> This ride on the metro left me with the recollection of a great sadness. The sadness had nothing to do with my short memory. But something profoundly sad was happening there in that car, with all those people going home to lunch. Very close to me was a great unhappiness, as silent as a real unhappiness can be, beyond all help, unknown, and which nothing could cause to appear. (Blanchot 1978: 37; Davis' translation)

Davis does several things here to make the text more explicit: for 'les gens de midi', which implies people going home for lunch but which does not state it, and which could be translated as 'the midday rush', she explains that they are going home to eat. Her 'there in that car' adds the element 'in that car' to the French 'là' ('there'). Finally, she adds an 'and' to the last part of the final sentence, which increases the cohesion of the sentence, although the 'que' [which] alone would also connect the final description to its noun.

Davis' word choice often reproduces the formality of the narrator's diction, while remaining idiomatic. For example, the repetition of 'sadness' and the use of 'sad' in the third sentence mimics the French 'tristesse' and 'triste', as the repetition of 'unhappiness' does for 'malheur' in the last sentence. The use of the cognate 'profoundly' for 'profondément' sounds formal here, but not out of place. Davis' strategy in this example combines reproducing the register and feel of the text, while at the same time making the connections between sentences more explicit.

Davis' tendency toward using formal language in this translation is a sign of her approach to Blanchot as a writer: it mimics the diction of his narrator, creating a similar style. Throughout the text there are examples of words or expressions which appear formal or slightly antiquated, for example 'I was seized by a great tenderness for her' (Blanchot 1978: 5) for 'je fus pris pour elle d'une grande tendresse' (Blanchot 1977a: 14), or 'with the fervor of hopeless desire' (Blanchot 1978: 8) for 'avec l'énergie d'un vœu désespéré' (Blanchot 1977a: 18). The elevated register of these terms, as well as others throughout the text, is similar in both English and French, and characterises the narration as formal. They also reflect the detached state of mind of the narrator, who is writing the tale of an event that he thinks should not be written (Blanchot 1977a: 8; 1978: 2), which also explains the lack of certainty that I discussed earlier. The sentence structures offer a similar formality. In the following example, Davis recreates the pausing, reflective sentence which allows the verb 'touched' to have two subjects (the will and the thought).[3]

> Ce minuscule testament, à la mesure de son existence sans bien, déjà dépossé-dée, cette dernière pensée d'où j'étais exclu, me touchait infiniment. (Blanchot 1977a: 14)

That tiny will, in keeping with her propertyless, already dispossessed existence, that last thought, from which I was excluded, touched me infinitely.
(Blanchot 1978: 6)

Davis' 'propertyless', for Blanchot's 'sans biens', and 'infinitely' both
appear quite elevated in register, as does the placing of the preposition at
the beginning of 'from which I was excluded'. Yet Davis does not over-
formalise the text. Despite using several cognates, for instance existence/
existence, dispossessed/dépossédée, touched/touchait, she translates
Blanchot's 'miniscule testament' as 'tiny will'. She produces an idiomatic
translation that fits with her general strategy of accuracy and adapting
syntactic structures to follow English language norms.

Davis' own early writing in *The Thirteenth Woman and other stories*
(1976) and *Story and other stories* (1983), as Edie Jarolim remarks, also
tends 'to be conservative in its formality' (Jarolim 1985: 144). The story
'The Housemaid' begins:

I know I am not pretty. My dark hair is cut short and so thin it hardly hides
my skull. I have a hasty and lopsided way of walking as though I was crip-
pled in one leg. When I bought my glasses I thought they were elegant – the
frames are black and shaped like butterfly wings – but now I have learned
how unbecoming they are and am stuck with them, since I have no money to
buy new ones. (Davis 1976: 42)

The sentences here are conservative in their construction, offering
nothing out of the ordinary. There are similarities in diction of the
speaker in the story and the narrator of *Death Sentence*. The description of the glasses as 'elegant' and 'unbecoming' sounds slightly formal
and slightly outdated, as if the speaker had been kept from the outside
world. As the story develops, this turns out to be the case: she is a maid
in a house where her mother is the cook. Her relationship to her mother
is one of quiet antagonism: 'I can hardly bear to sit across from her at
dinner and I can tell by the look on her face that she feels the same way
about me' (ibid.). The narrator's feeling of exclusion is subtly shown
through her language, in a similar way to how Blanchot's narrator's
detachment is shown in his choice of lexis and sentence structure. Other
stories by Davis in this collection share a similar formality, although
they do not always have a first person narrator. Her writing is conserva-
tively well written, and does not play with unconventional English as her
later work will: for example, in 'Marie Curie, So Honorable Woman'
(Davis 2001: 99–119) which I analyse in Chapter 6, or even 'Foucault
and Pencil' (Davis 1997a: 10–12), which is written in note form (see
Chapter 7). Her translation of Leiris (discussed in Chapter 3) also questions convention, as it is peppered with French words and often follows

his complex syntax. However, for the younger Davis, Blanchot's characters' linguistic formality would have seemed a familiar element, and adds to the impression of affinity between the two writers.

Davis' translation of *L'Arrêt de mort*, then, is respectful of Blanchot's text regarding form and narrative. Where her translation differs from the original is in cases where she translates in such a way that she makes the text more cohesive. There is a move towards literalism in her translation style, especially when compared to her 'work-for-hire' translations,[4] but she does not translate in a word-for-word manner. The changes she makes are generally quite minimal and often affect the level of syntax. Her translation style shows a respect for Blanchot's particularity as a writer, such as his use of uncertainty and formal tenor, which positions this translation as a form of 'service translation' (Bernofsky 2005: ix): Davis does not stamp her own imprint as a writer on the text.

While they are not radically literal, the Blanchot translations represent for Davis a step towards realising her own style as a translator. As she says in an interview with Francine Prose, she likes to translate 'keeping, as much as possible, the same word order and same words' (Prose 1997), an approach that would be more apparent in one way in her translations of Michel Leiris and in another way in her translations of Proust, and which would also influence her translation of Flaubert. For this reason, the Blanchot translations, especially *Death Sentence*, are important in Davis' *œuvre* as a translator.

It is harder to read from the translation the importance of Blanchot to Davis as a writer. There is some similarity with her own writing in her use of formal diction in both her own work of the time and her translation, which suggests an affinity between her and Blanchot. Nevertheless the connection cannot be read from the translations alone as the evidence is insufficient. It needs support from other elements of Blanchot's writing and Davis' relation to them.

Authorial Response

Blanchot has become best known in the English speaking world for his literary criticism,[5] but Davis translated more of his *récits*. While there is certainly some connection with Blanchot's theories of literature in Davis' work, I propose that it is possible to read elements of Davis' work as a response to Blanchot's fiction. I refer specifically to Davis' story 'Story' (1983: 27–30; reprinted in Davis 1986: 3–7), and Blanchot's *La Folie du jour*/'The Madness of the Day' (2002), which are the focus of this section.

La Folie du jour was one of the first texts Davis translated on her own, showing an early interest in Blanchot and especially his narrative form. Davis published an early translation in *Tri-Quarterly* in 1977. A revised translation was published in 1981 as a small book by Station Hill Press and reprinted in *The Station Hill Blanchot Reader* (Blanchot 1999: 191–9). Davis' translation can be considered as one aspect of her response to the text and her revision suggests a continuing involvement with it. Both versions tend to follow the source text closely, replicating the sentence and paragraph structures of the French. The revised version is very similar to the first translation, with most of the changes being minor stylistic alterations which restore ambiguities present in the French that were smoothed over in the first translation. For example, 'ce jour' (Blanchot 2002: 10) is first translated, quite plausibly, as 'this daylight' (Blanchot 1977b: 168) and then revised to 'this day' (Blanchot 1999: 191). The translation is therefore very similar in style to her translation of *Death Sentence*, discussed above, and shows a similar respect for the source text's author and his writing style.

'Story' can be considered as Davis' more authorial reaction to Blanchot's *récit*. The history of *La Folie du jour* suggests one reason to compare it with 'Story': it was first published in 1948 in *Empedocle*, under two possible titles: 'Un récit?' and 'Un récit', a fact that Derrida comments on several times in his book about Blanchot (Derrida 1986: 130–6, 245–6, 275–7), even going so far as to reproduce the cover, contents page and first page of the *Empedocle* publication of 'La Folie du jour' on pages 132–4. These earlier titles could be translated as 'A story?' and 'A story', giving Blanchot's and Davis' texts almost the same title. Even if Davis were unaware of this fact, it suggests a similar narratological focus.

La Folie du jour also appears to be ideal for reading Davis' response to Blanchot, not only for its questioning of narrative, but because it is, as Manola Antonioli remarks, 'peut-être le récit le plus enigmatique de Blanchot' ('perhaps the most enigmatic of Blanchot's *récits*').[6] Both Blanchot's and Davis' texts problematise the possibility of ever deciding on a single interpretation of events, or even in Blanchot's case of being able to narrate a tale that satisfies that demand. Such indeterminacy is theorised by Blanchot. It is worth considering his theory of the *récit* and how it may have influenced Davis. The rest of this chapter then questions how Davis' story can be read as a response to Blanchot's. I argue that the indeterminacy in his fiction attracted Davis to Blanchot as a writer, although she writes with much more focus on the interpersonal, emotional elements of narrative than Blanchot does, as he focuses in 'The Madness of the Day' on the institutional use of narrative.

Both Davis and Blanchot question the possibility of narrative within their narratives. Blanchot's *récits* are difficult to read as they evade normal characteristics of narrative: none really concludes; none has a traditional three-part story arc with beginning, middle and end. Davis herself has written of how difficult it was for her to produce an adequate summary of *The One Who Was Standing Apart From Me* (2007b: 32–3). The texts require a different, deeper type of reading than other works, as Brian Fitch notes: 'toute approche superficielle est vouée à l'échec: elle ne saurait déboucher que sur un constat d'incompréhension' ('any superficial approach is bound to fail: it can only result in a statement of incomprehension'; Fitch 1992: 7). Deborah Hess calls these texts 'non-Aristotelian' (Hess 1999: 1) as they appear to eschew Aristotle's three poetic unities of place, time and action. This means that the reader struggles with the texts, as their 'literary competence' (Culler 2002: 131–52) is likely to be based in Aristotle's unities, which form the backbone of Western poetics.

Blanchot himself suggests a way out of Aristotelian narrative poetics in his theory of the *récit*, which he compares to the singing of the Sirens (1959: 9–17). It is: 'un mouvement vers un point, non seulement inconnu, ignoré, étranger, mais tel qu'il ne semble avoir, par avance et par dehors de ce mouvement, aucun réalité' ('a movement towards a point which is not only unknown, unheard of, strange, but such that it seems that it is not real before or outside of this movement'; all quotations in this paragraph from Blanchot 1959: 13–15). The *récit* thus creates itself, at the same time pushing towards a place that is, like the Siren's song, outside of the reach of conventional conceptions of reality. The *récit* is not the narration of the event; the narration is the event. Rather than producing a narrative that has a unity of time, place and action, the *récit* can enter into another time, 'qui est le passage du chant réel au chant imaginaire' ('which is the passage from the real song to the imaginary song'). It is this irregular and unreal relationship to time that defines the *récit*: it is narration which produces its own time, as well as its own event. Blanchot also notes that it avoids the trappings of fictionality – it does not develop in the conventional way, but within its own framework. It is a text which is not assimilable to generic conventions other than its own. The *récit* is therefore a text where narration is more significant than narrative; reading the text is more about the experience of reading than being able to ascribe a causal sequence to the events described.

This theory of the *récit* appears to have been attractive to Davis. Her stories also represent a departure from the accepted understandings of what a story might be, avoiding or complicating ideas of plot, character and setting. For example, her novel *The End of the Story* (1995) interrupts its own narration to discuss and question the plausibility of that narration, disrupting the functioning of the plot. Some of Davis' stories are very reductive in what they include – in several instances, they are only one line long. In such stories, there cannot be more than just a name or a pronoun for a character. For example, in 'Suddenly Afraid' (Davis 2007a: 189), all the character information given is the gender pronoun, 'because she couldn't write the name of what she was'. The reader is forced to supply the rest of the information, which means that each reader will envisage this female character differently. Stories like 'A Mown Lawn' (Davis 1997a: 2) tell no story, but present a text which reads more like a poem with development that follows an association of ideas rather than a narrative progression. It is its own event rather than the narration of any event. Blanchot and Davis have an affinity as their texts disrupt narrative conventions, especially that of closure. However, the link between them is more complex, with Davis responding in her own text to Blanchot's.

'The Madness of the Day' can be split into two movements. The first is a first person account of a man's life. He says he has lived in different circumstances: 'J'ai été pauvre, puis plus riche, puis plus pauvre que beaucoup' (Blanchot 2002: 9), or in Davis' translation, 'I have been poor, then richer, then poorer than many people' (Blanchot 1999: 191).[7] Various events are recounted in this half of the narrative, such as the narrator being placed before a firing squad, being buried in mud in some sort of medical treatment, having his hand stabbed, falling into poverty and spending time in a 'bas-fond surchauffé' (overheated basement) of a library, and seeing a man in a doorway giving way to a baby carriage. None of these incidents seems to lead to the next, and there are moments of reflection between them. Antonioli notes how '[l]e "récit" pourrait sembler ... recommencer à chaque nouveau paragraphe' ('the "récit" could seem ... to start again with each new paragraph'; Antonioli 1999: 33), and indeed there is a feeling that the text is discontinuous, but at the same time the text does seem to present some sort of narrative development, with events noted as coming 'après' (11) or 'afterward' in Davis' translation (191). The structure of the text, with reflective passages between narrative passages, suggests that the narrator is looking back over their life and trying to establish some sort of positioning for the later events. The beginning does not, however, explain the rest of the text.

The second movement of the text begins with the narrator recounting that '[j]e faillis perdre la vue, quelqu'un ayant écrasé du verre sur mes yeux' (18 – 'I nearly lost my sight, because someone crushed glass into my eyes'; 194). Yet this information, which becomes central to the development of the rest of the narrative, is not foregrounded by being placed at the beginning of a paragraph, but rather appears two sentences in. The casualness of that placing in what is effectively the pivotal moment of 'The Madness of the Day' means that the reader almost misses its significance. It is as if the narrator wants to reduce the importance of the event. However, the rest of the text recounts a narrative that unfolds as a consequence of the damage to his eyes; the narrator is hospitalised and treated for the injuries and is questioned about how he could have come to have glass ground into his eyes. He is given a job in the institute, but the doctors and nurses find his acceptance of his circumstances unacceptable. It seems he should want to 'rendre justice' (24 – 'see justice done'; 197), and he sees the silhouette of the law, a feminine figure (just as 'la loi' in French is a feminine noun), who speaks to him directly. He is locked up in what appears to be a mental hospital, as the doctor thinks he is 'bien fou' (25 – 'truly crazy'; 198). The doctors continue to ask questions of him, which he says come back to the question of who threw glass into his face. He finds it difficult to tell his examiners the story they want to hear, and it seems that the narrative he tells them may be the narrative the reader is reading, as it begins: 'Je suis ni savant ni ignorant. J'ai connu des joies' (29 – 'I am not learned; I am not ignorant. I have known joys'; 199), which is the same as the first line of *La Folie du jour*/'The Madness of the Day'. The narrator concludes 'Un récit? Non, pas de récit, plus jamais' (30 – 'A story? No. No stories, never again'; 199).

Any summary of 'The Madness of the Day' reduces the complexity of the narrative, giving a coherence that the text itself does not have. While the 'story' of the text seems to centre on the narrative of the man who has had glass ground into his eyes, the refusal of the narrator to prioritise that event means that the centre of the story is shifted or dispersed. At the same time, as Leslie Hill (1997: 99) notes, it is only after that event that the text begins to follow any continuous narrative, effectively making it the centre of the story. Thus the glass attack seems to be both central and not central at the same time. It is tempting to try to resolve this duality, yet the text does not allow it.

Indeed, the text further complicates matters, as the narrator, just before recounting that someone crushed glass in his eyes, remarks that 'Je n'avais pas d'ennemis. Je n'étais gené de personne' (17 – 'I had no enemies. No one bothered me'; 194). This causes the reader to find it difficult to know how to value the statement that someone crushed glass into his eyes, which appears in the same paragraph. Hess (1999: 52) sees the glass grinding as 'a symbolic episode', arguing that this would deprive the narrator of sight permanently. Hess' argument highlights the fictional nature of the text: in fiction apparently unrealistic moments need not perturb the reader's suspension of disbelief, and may be accepted for the very reason that they appear in a fictional text. Blanchot's narrative works are not exempt from such moments – for example, J.'s miraculous reprieve from death in *Death Sentence* (Blanchot 1977a: 36; 1978: 20). The narrator of 'The Madness of the Day' may be able to recover his sight in the story, precisely because it is a story, although even then he does not fully recover – '[m]ême guéri, je doutais l'être' (19 – 'Even after I recovered, I doubted I was well'; 195) – suggesting that Hess' reading of the incident as symbolic reduces its effects within the narrative. The event both foregrounds the fictionality of the narrative and produces realistic consequences, a paradox that would seem not to be extraordinary in Blanchot's work.

The difficulty for the reader lies in the disjunction between someone who says that he had no enemies and that no one bothered him and then, almost immediately, says someone ground glass into his eyes. The apparently motiveless nature of the crime is disturbing. It is not only the reader who has difficulty in accepting the narrator's account of the incident: the doctors keep asking him as well. When he does tell them, they dismiss his account, calling it nothing more than 'ce commencement' ('this beginning') and exhort him to 'en viendrez au faits' (29 – 'get down to the facts'; 199). This might be taken as proof of the narrator's unreliability, as when other characters do not accept the narrator's word it becomes hard for the reader to do so, but in 'The Madness of the Day' the doctors' questioning seems rather to originate in a position where it is impossible to accept that there may have been no motive, or no 'story'.

In French the word used for 'story' in the last three paragraphs of the text is 'récit' (29–30), causing Derrida (1986: 251–87) to question the narrative's generic status. For Derrida the text problematises the genre of the *récit*, as it does not recount a story, but rather questions the possibility of telling a story (ibid.: 268). He even suggests that the 'I' of the text may not necessarily refer to the same character throughout (ibid.: 269), although there is little evidence either way of this in the text itself.[8]

Derrida points out that one of the ways that 'The Madness of the Day' problematises a traditional sense of story is through the moment where the text seems to fold back on itself and quote the beginning: 'ce bord supérieur ou initial, ce qu'on appelle la première ligne du livre, vient faire une poche à l'intérieur du corpus' ('this superior or initial edge, what is called the first line of the book, comes to make a pocket at the interior of the work'; ibid.: 271). This repetition of the beginning threatens to repeat the whole text, although it continues for only three sentences before the narrator returns to the point in the narrative where he is being questioned: 'Un récit? Je commençai: Je ne suis ni savant ni ignorant. J'ai connu des joies. C'est trop peu dire. Je leur racontai l'histoire tout entier' (29 – 'A story? I began: I am not learned; I am not ignorant. I have known joys. That is saying too little. I told them the whole story'; 199). Davis' first translation from 1977 places the repeated beginning of the text in quotation marks: 'A story? I began: "I am neither learned nor ignorant. I have known joys. That is saying too little." I told them the whole story' (Blanchot 1977b: 176). The quotation marks contain the repetition, clarifying its status as a citation, which neutralises the destabilising effects that Derrida (1986: 270–3) attributes to it. Davis' removal of the quotation marks in the revised translation restores the ambiguity of whether or not the repetition is a citation.

Derrida's comments focus on the narratological elements of the text, but it is not enough to focus solely on these: the disturbance of narrative that takes place in the text is in keeping with the diegetic situation of the narrator trying to respond to the question of who threw glass into his face. For instance, Derrida sees a second fold, or 'invagination' as he prefers to call it (Derrida 1986: 272), in the repetition of 'Un récit?'/'A story?', which comes before the narrator starts telling his story to the examiners and then again after, in the text's last line. Derrida views this as excluding possibly the last line of the text from the *récit*, situating it as an append-age. This speculation is not warranted, as the concluding line of the text follows from the narrator's protests that he cannot tell a story: 'je n'étais pas capable de former un récit de ces événéments' (29 – 'I was not capable of forming a story out of these events'; 199). In one way this inability to tell a story is also a continuation of his withdrawal, which becomes clear when he remarks: 'Cependant quelque chose en moi cessait assez vite de vouloir' (21 – 'Yet something inside me quickly stopped wanting'; 196). He stops wanting in general, and it seems that this withdrawal is at least partially responsible for his being locked up; he no longer follows con-ventions and thus seems mad within the order of reason represented by the medical profession. His inability to tell a story is met by incredulity, although the incredulity is attributed to what may be a hallucination of the narrator (and therefore an externalisation of his own incredulity):

Mais, étant deux, à cause de cela ils étaient trois, et ce troisième restaient fermement convaincu, j'en suis sûr, qu'un écrivain, un homme qui parle et qui raisonne avec distinction, est toujours capable de raconter des faits dont il se souvient. (Blanchot 2002: 29–30)

But because there were two of them, there were three, and this third remained firmly convinced, I am sure, that a writer, a man who speaks and reasons with distinction is always capable of recounting facts that he remembers. (Blanchot 1999: 199)

While the text plays with the impossibility of telling a story and to some extent does not tell a story, it also tells a story. This appears contradictory, but the logic of the text is one of contradiction. The text does not provide a unified narrative; in this sense it does not tell a story. Yet at the same time, the text presents a narrative, albeit one with gaps and uncertainties: the narrative of a man who chooses not to bring to justice someone who ground glass into his eyes, a man who cannot tell the story of how that happened. Moreover the man can only provide a non-Aristotelian narrative, which is unacceptable to the medical and juridical questioners, who require motive and narrative causality. Readers are placed in the same position as these examiners, trying to tie up the loose ends. Yet readers can choose to accept the non-logic of the narration, unlike the examiners who are trapped in their institutional setting which requires a certain form of logic. Readers do not have to rationalise the story; they can accept it with its contradictions.

Lydia Davis' 'Story' presents a perspective that almost mirrors that of 'The Madness of the Day'. Instead of the narrator producing a contradictory narrative that is unacceptable in the institutional setting where it is told, the narrator is told a story by her lover and cannot decide whether or not it is true. The narrator in 'Story' is therefore in the position of the examiners in *La Folie du jour*, but she is not so bound by institutional logic. In 'Story' the reader is made to identify with the narrator's position and follow her interpretation of events with the hope of arriving at a conclusion. Davis therefore shifts the perspective on Blanchot's *récit* away from a narrator trying and failing to tell a story, to the narrator being told a story she cannot accept. The perspective is reversed, suggesting that Davis' story is performing some sort of response to the text she had previously translated.

'Story' is a story of two parts. The first (Davis 1986: 3–6) is narrated in the present tense by a female narrator and describes an evening when her lover, whom she does not live with, has stood her up to see his old girlfriend, the argument over the phone which ensues and the narrator's visit to her lover's house and the confusing discussion there. The narrator finds the explanation given by her lover unsatisfactory and thinks that '[e]verything he says is a contradiction'. A second part (ibid.: 6–7) entails the narrator trying to 'figure it out'. This section involves her recounting to herself (and the reader) the tale her lover has told her and questioning it:

> So they went to the movies and then came back to his place and then I called and then she left and he called back and then I called back twice but he had gone out to get a beer (he says) and then I drove over and in the meantime he had returned from buying beer and she had also come back and she was in his room so we talked by the garage doors. But what is the truth? (Davis 1986: 6)

She continues to question his story, unsure of whether or not he has told the truth. She knows he does not always tell the truth, and this makes her unsure of him at other times. In the end she is unsure of whether the truth matters, although it would allow her to 'come to some conclusions' about some questions she has of the relationship:

> whether he is angry at me or not; if he is, then how angry; whether he still loves her or not; if he does, then how much; whether he loves me or not; how much; how capable he is of deceiving me in the act and after the act in the telling. (Davis 1986: 7)

It seems impossible that she should be able to answer these questions just from knowing the truth about that one evening; even knowing where her lover had been, it would be difficult to tell if he was angry, or how much he loved either the narrator or his old girlfriend.

The two-part structure of 'Story' is reminiscent of the two-part structures of Blanchot's *Death Sentence* and *The Last Man*; however, the relationship between the two parts of Davis' story is a lot clearer than the relationship between the two parts of *Death Sentence* as the latter part is clearly set up as a thinking through of the earlier part. The combination of reflection and narration also echoes 'The Madness of the Day', although there they are mixed throughout the text. The reflective passages in 'Story' serve to help the narrator to try to understand the encounter, whereas in 'The Madness of the Day' they seem rather to disperse any decidable meaning or narrative: the reflections on books (Blanchot 2002: 15; 1999: 193), for example, seem unrelated to the rest of the text. However, Perloff notes that incomprehension is also the function of the second part of 'Story': 'the narrator's re-recounting of what she has already told us ... gradually blocks all possibility of interpreting the signs' (Perloff 1989: 207). By questioning all the parts of the preceding narrative, and the permutations of their possibilities, the narrator arrives at a position where the multiple possibilities cannot be reconciled or the most likely chosen. As Perloff describes it, '[t]he "story" cannot reach closure' (ibid.: 208). She also notes that the narrator appears to lose interest in the events of the narrative, 'for it is the puzzle itself which has become the narrator's obsession' (ibid.). This also appears to be Karen Alexander's view of 'Story': '[t]he events she relates prior to her concluding calculations serve only to make those calculations possible' (Alexander 2008: 170).

Yet those calculations are not 'possible' per se, as the narrator cannot arrive at any answer. The narrator's 'obsession' may not be the puzzle either, but rather the concluding line of the story: 'how capable he is of deceiving me in the act and after the act in the telling' (Davis 1986: 7). The threat of betrayal motivates the narrator's attempts to understand, rather than an intellectual interest in the possibility of truth. The beginning of 'Story' suggests her anxiety over her lover:

> I get home from work and there is a message from him: that he is not coming, that he is busy. He will call again. I wait to hear from him, then at nine o'clock I go to where he lives, find his car, but he's not home. I knock at his apartment door and then at all the garage doors, not knowing which is his – no answer. I write a note, read it over, write a new note, and stick it in his door. (Davis 1986: 3)

This opening sets up the idea that something has been planned, and the narrator is upset by her lover's cancellation of the date. She goes over to look for him at 9pm leaving a note, which she is careful enough to redraft only after exhausting the possibilities for finding him at home. The narrator seems to be thorough, almost to a point of obsession, and her knocking on every garage door in attempts to find her lover can be related to her later attempts to decipher the truth: she is capable of entertaining several possibilities, but only in the hope that one of them might be true.

The narrator's suspicions of her lover are revealed later on, when they are talking: 'I am waiting for him to say that she is there also that it's all over between us', and when he does not she notes 'I have the feeling he did intend to say something like that' (ibid.: 5). Here the possibility for what he can say or might say encroaches on what he does say. The narrator is not able to accept what she is told: unlike the questioners in *La Folie du jour*, who are bound by an institutional need for motive, her jealousy causes her to be cautious and mistrustful. At the same time she knows he is withholding information from her, as they are standing outside and not in his room, as one might expect. He admits that his old girlfriend is there, but assures the narrator that she was not when they spoke on the phone. His acts and his statements seem difficult to reconcile and it would appear that the narrator's suspicion is justified. She is haunted by what she cannot know, which relates to what her lover and his old girlfriend have been up to, whether or not he has been unfaithful, and so forth. As Perloff asks, 'is "old" equivalent to "former"?' (Perloff 1989: 207). The lover's relationship with his old girlfriend is never clear.

'Story' then, is about jealousy: the question is not about finding out some truth, but rather, more specifically, finding out if the lover has deceived her, and how. The attempt to 'figure it out' at the end of the story is an attempt to overcome this jealousy, yet it perversely has the opposite effect of making it impossible to find the truth and so allay the jealous fantasies. Freud (2006: 163) notes that a child may repeat unpleasurable experiences in an attempt to master them, and it seems that the narrator here is trying to master the narrative through repeating it, yet she cannot because she does not know, and so repeats with different possibilities. The effect is not mastery but rather a dissipation of control: she cannot know what happened and cannot control it or her lover. This is reminiscent of Marcel's struggles with Albertine in Proust's *À la recherche du temps perdu*; the unknown, in the spectre of Albertine's possible lesbianism, haunts him.

The relationship between the lovers needs trust for it to work. Suspicion means that not only is the lover's word put into question, but also the relationship: she expects him to say it is over, she questions if he loves her and how much. As Josh Cohen notes, in relation to 'Story': '[t]he everyday interaction of lovers is built on the shaky foundations of one or other "story" whose correlation with "the truth" can be neither confirmed nor refuted' (Cohen 2005: 77). All loving relationships rely on accepting a narrative: by not accepting that narrative the conditions of the relationship are questioned.

The narrator in 'Story', like the doctors in 'The Madness of the Day', thinks that it should be possible to arrive at a story, but she cannot. There is a hint she may stop trying to make sense of it: she notes '[m]aybe the truth does not matter' (Davis 1986: 7). The narrator of 'The Madness of the Day', on the other hand, begins to repeat only to stop the repetition after a few words (Blanchot 2002: 29; 1999: 199). He seems not to want to control the events or to revisit them. The difference lies in the relationships the narrators have with other people: the narrator of 'The Madness of the Day' is alone, whereas the narrator of 'Story' is involved in an amorous relationship. For her, interpreting the story is connected to her acceptance of her lover, whereas Blanchot's narrator is being asked to find a story to fulfil the abstract notion of justice, rather than an emotional goal. The motivation for the story is therefore very different. One is unavoidably facing a failure to reach a conclusion; the other cannot entertain the basis on which any conclusion could be based. Blanchot's narrator is not interested in or not capable of clearing up any ambiguities, whereas Davis' narrator would like to, but cannot. The effect in both narratives is, however, a failure to find any closure and a questioning of narrative's possibility to provide a complete 'story'.

The narratological similarities between the two texts show evidence of an affinity of approach in Davis' and Blanchot's work. However, there are also important differences in motivation of the narrators of the texts, suggesting that Davis moves away from the terrain covered by Blanchot in her own writing. She creates characters and situations that are much more down to earth than Blanchot's – 'Story', for instance, focuses on a woman not trusting her boyfriend, rather than the elaborate mental deterioration of the narrator in *La Folie du jour*. She writes in 'Story' in a way that is more immediately based in emotional reactions, compared to the emotional blankness of Blanchot's narrator in *La Folie du jour*. Blanchot's influence on Davis, then, cannot be considered in simple terms of similarities appearing in their works or the influence his theories have had on her. Rather, Davis stages the same narrative impasse in 'Story' that Blanchot explores in 'The Madness of the Day', but twists and reconfigures it. Davis' story can therefore be read as a response to Blanchot's because it investigates the emotional territory that the narrator in Blanchot's fiction will not or cannot.

If Davis' story can be read as her fictional response to a text that she translated, it is also possible to say that her translation of 'The Madness of the Day' offered her another way of responding to that text by rewriting it in English. In fact, the translation is one level of response and her story is another. She has mentioned that she translates because she enjoys 'assuming a disguise' (McCaffery 1996: 75), but her translation of Blanchot does not appear to be only a disguise: by translating *La Folie du jour*, she worked through a text that questioned narrative in a way that she herself was interested in. Her attraction to Blanchot's writing, as I noted earlier, stems from this shared questioning of narrative and the affinity she felt for that writing. Susan Bassnett remarks that 'frequently writers translate other people's works because those are the works they would have written themselves had they not already been created by someone else' (Bassnett 2006: 175), and the similarity in the questioning of the possibility of a 'story' in Blanchot's and Davis' text seems to bear this out, especially as Davis translates *La Folie du jour* in a way that shows a respect for the French source text. However, it is equally important to recognise that Davis' story focuses more on the personal aspects of narrative than Blanchot's: her concern is for the emotional response that stories evoke, while Blanchot focuses more on the institutional need for narrative as a form of understanding. The difference between them allows Davis' work to be read as a response to Blanchot's; in her story she asserts her own authorial persona in a way that she does not in the translation.

Rather than the affinity that Davis claims she feels for Blanchot, and which other critics have suggested, there is in fact a sort of rejection of his influence in her writing. Davis writes in a way that mirrors some of the structures and narrative techniques of Blanchot, and which draw on his theory of the *récit*. On the other hand, she creates characters and situations that are much more down to earth than Blanchot's by focusing on the emotional lives of her characters.

Her initial attraction to his writing leads to a more complex relationship between Davis' and Blanchot's writing: there is a form of dialogue between their works. Davis' own texts appear to respond to Blanchot's, and her translations of Blanchot resonate with her own writing. The translations encourage a reading of Davis' work in relation to Blanchot, and therefore they appear to be a part of her work, influencing how the other texts in her *œuvre* are received. At the same time, they are not assimilated into Davis' writing. They can still be read independently, as translations of Blanchot. They retain a double status, which allows the dialogue, as they offer something different to Davis' own stories. Her 'Story' can be seen to respond to the indeterminacy present in Blanchot's *récit*, but this response is part of a conversation, showing Davis' own perspective which has affinities with Blanchot's writing but at the same time produces something new.

Notes

1. According to Paul Buck (personal correspondence), Davis had also translated Blanchot's essay 'Traduire' ('Translating') for his magazine *Curtains* in 1974.
2. On page 16, for instance, there is dialogue in the middle of a paragraph and separated out.
3. The sentence has similar rhythms to Henry James' sentences, especially in *The Turn of the Screw* (James 1946), a narrative that Blanchot admired (Blanchot 1959: 155–65). This similarity may lie at the root of Updike's (1982: 93) comparison of the two writers.
4. See Evans 2011: 143–68 for a discussion of some of these translations.
5. See, for example, introductions to his work by Gill (1996) or Haase and Large (2001).
6. Antonioli 1999: 32. All unacknowledged translations in this chapter are my own.
7. All references to Davis's translation of *La Folie du jour* are to the most recent version, found in *The Station Hill Blanchot Reader*, unless otherwise noted. There are some differences between the two versions. It is assumed that the later version should be taken as the definitive translation. Page numbers in the following discussion refer to Blanchot 2002 for the French and Blanchot 1999 for the English translation.
8. Derrida's reading of *La Folie du jour*/'The Madness of the Day' as a text

about genres and the problem of the limit that the concept of genre includes is echoed by later commentators: Hill (1997: 98) brings up the question of the limit while Antonioli remarks that the text is about 'l'impossibilité du récit' ('the impossibility of narrative'; Antonioli 1999: 32).

Chapter 3

Leiris and Dialogue

Davis translated three books by Michel Leiris: *Brisées: Broken Branches* (1989), a collection of occasional essays, and two parts of his four-part autobiography, *Rules of the Game: Scratches* (1997a) and *Scraps* (1997b). As mentioned in the Introduction, Davis wondered if Leiris was the 'real pinnacle' of a translator's career (Davis 1999: 87), given the complexity of his style and its close ties to the sound and sense of French. This chapter explores how Davis' translations of Leiris produce a dialogue between the two authors, focusing, because of its centrality in Leiris' *œuvre*, on Davis' relationship with *La Règle du jeu*. Leiris wrote in many genres, from surrealist poetry to ethnography, but for many critics his most important works are in the field of autobiography.[1]

I begin with analyses of Davis' translations of Leiris.[2] Her approach to his work is uniquely radical, as Davis broke norms of translational procedure in responding to an unorthodox, poetic text. The recreative form of translation she practises here suggests a productive dialogue between the translation and Davis' stories, which is also suggested by two texts by Davis with an intertextual link to Leiris, 'Swimming in Egypt: Dreams While Awake and Asleep' (Davis 2007b: 35–44) and 'To Reiterate' (Davis 1997a: 83). The second section of this chapter argues that these texts position Leiris as a precursor and influence, and the final section reads *La Règle du jeu* in relation to Davis' writing, focusing on how Davis and Leiris have an affinity in their privileging of what Roman Jakobson (1960: 356–8) calls the 'poetic function' above narrative development in their texts. The poetic function is where language brings attention to itself, 'focus[ing] on the message [i.e. the verbal text] for its own sake' (ibid.: 356). This is not only relevant to poetry, but to any verbal text that is self-reflexive, folding the reader's attention back onto the text and the formal construction of that text.

Scratches and *Scraps* in Translation

In a 1997 interview Davis remarked that she was working on the third volume of Leiris' autobiography. This translation has not been published and it would appear that Davis was interrupted by the work required to translate Proust, which she began in 1997 (Davis 2007b: 11). In the same interview she expressed her concerns that she had 'gone too far' in her preference for literal translation, afraid that she might be 'creating a language that [was] going to read as a stilted difficult language in between French and English' (Prose 1997). Her translation of Leiris represents a further development of the increasingly source-oriented style that she had practised in translating Blanchot, but also shows parallels with techniques used in her own stories. Beginning with *Brisées* (Leiris 1989), Davis' Leiris translations, I will argue, show a unique relationship with that writer, one that blends influence and response.

The title of Davis' translation of Leiris' essays, *Brisées: Broken Branches*, announces a new approach in Davis' translation work, moving away from the assimilative commercial translations and even the directness of her translations of Blanchot. Keeping the French word in the title suggests something untranslatable about the word 'brisées'. The French blocks comprehension for the English reader. *Brisées* are literally, as the subtitle states, broken branches. There is no clue as to how or why they have become broken and the subtitle does not really help the English reader understand what is meant by the French term. A definition from Littré's *Dictionaire de la langue française* is given in the opening pages of the English translation of *Brisées*, in French:

> **Brisées** (bri-zée), s.f. plur.
> 1. Branches cassées par le veneur
> pour reconnaître l'endroit où est la
> bête . . . 3. Marques fait aux
> arbres par le passage d'un bête.
> 4. Branches taillées pour marquer
> les bornes d'une coupe de bois.
> (Leiris 1989: unnumbered page)
> (**Brisées** (bRize), n{oun}. fem{inine}. pl{ural}.
>
> 1. Branches broken by the huntsman
> to recognise the place where the animal
> is . . . 3. Marks made on
> trees by the passage of an animal.
> 4. Branches cut to mark the
> limits of a felling area. (my translation)

'Brisées', while being broken branches, also have the characteristic of being markers in some way; another possible translation might have been 'tracking marks', which would cover several of the meanings. Davis chose to leave *brisées* in French, which is more suggestive in its lack of significance to the English reader. Providing the definition in French in the book itself, with no translation, sends a message to the audience that this is a French book, despite being translated into English. Indeed, many of the essays in *Brisées* are about topics that require a wide knowledge of French culture to understand and the choice of a French title would alert the reader to the cultural background of Leiris' writing.[3]

The title alerts the reader to the translation strategy in the book. It does not contain as many French words and expressions as *Scratches* or *Scraps*, but there is far more than in almost any of Davis' other translations.[4] In *Brisées*, there are occasions where French is used not because of its semantic specificity, but to show connections between words, for example *baclé* ('bungled') and *débâcle* (Leiris 1989: 36–7), which also receive a translator's footnote to explain their etymology. Most of the titles of works referred to by Leiris are kept in French, for example *Le Piège de la méduse* ('Medusa's trap'), a play by Eric Satie, which requires later references to traps to have a backwards gloss relating the word trap to *piège* (Leiris 1989: 57), showing Leiris' wordplay. Davis uses long, convoluted sentences in her translation, following the syntax of the French, which sometimes leaves the reader a little lost, looking for the subject of the sentence after a long digression. This fidelity to Leiris' style shows a trust in its ability to create effects for the reader, and an understanding that these effects (including boredom) are relevant.

Yet the translations in *Brisées* look conservative next to those in *Rules of the Game*. Leiris' autobiography is not typical of the genre. The titles of the individual parts, rather than describing the stages of life (such as childhood), are abstract and seemingly unrelated: *Biffures* ('crossings out'; Davis' translation is *Scratches*), *Fourbis* ('gear/equipment', but in a mess; Davis translates this as *Scraps*), *Fibrilles* ('fibrils, small fibres') and *Frêle bruit* ('fragile noise'). The titles of the parts of *Rules of the Game* suggest a piecemeal approach to autobiography, reducing the importance of the self to small things (*Fourbis, Fibrilles*) or to faint or hidden things (*Biffures, Frêle bruit*). Davis' translated titles *Scratches* and *Scraps* are alliterative. The alliteration is suggested by the repetition in 'biffures' and 'fourbis', although Davis does not, and could not, reproduce the way these words almost reverse each other, changing only one vowel: /bifYR/ and /fuRbi/. Leiris repeats the sounds /f/, /b/ and /R/ across the series of titles in a variety of permutations, but it is doubtful that Davis' decision to repeat /skRæ/ would work across the last two titles.

The difficulty in translating Leiris lies in his style, which is baroque and digressive. Davis comments on Leiris' style in her translator's introduction, calling it a 'deliberate overload [that] tempts the translator to go too far in the direction of a similar deliberate awkwardness' (Davis 1997b: xi). This can be seen in the beginning of *Scratches*, which starts with a paragraph-long sentence which is full of digressions, questioning the recollection of the narrator and providing a wealth of detail:

> Sur le sol impitoyable de la pièce (salon? salle à manger? tapis cloué auz ramages fanés ou bien tapis mobile au quelconque décor dans lequel j'inscrivais des palais, des sites, des continents, vrai kaleidoscope dont mon enfance jouait, y agençant des constructions féeriques, tel un canevas pour des mille et une nuits que ne m'ouvraient alors les feuillets d'aucun livre ? [. . .] le soldat était tombé. (Leiris 2003: 3)

> On the pitiless floor of the room (lounge? dining room? fixed carpet with faded leafy designs or even loose carpet with some decoration into which I inscribed palaces, sites, continents, real kaleidoscope that my childhood made use of, creating there fairytale constructions, like a canvas for the thousand and one nights that no book had yet opened up to me? [. . .] the soldier had fallen. (my literal translation)

> Onto the pitiless floor (of the living room or the dining room? onto a fitted carpet with faded floral patterns or a rug with some other design on which I inscribed palaces, landscapes, continents, a true kaleidoscope delightful to me in my childishness, for I designed fairytale constructions on it as if it were a canvas for some thousand and one nights that hadn't yet been revealed to me by the pages of any book in those days? [. . .] the soldier had fallen. (Leiris 1997a: 3; Davis' translation)[5]

The conclusion to the sentence feels somewhat disappointing when it is finally reached by the reader, who by now feels a little confused and disorientated. This is not the sort of construction one expects to find in a genre which is supposed to be informative, such as autobiography. This sentence looks as though it might belong more to a prose poem, where a narrative flow is not expected, than to a supposedly narrative genre.

The translation follows the digressions of Leiris' French, without following a translation strategy of slavish literality. Davis occasionally alters and anglicises word order, as well as clarifying the meaning of the sentence. Davis increases the cohesion of the text: she adds a second 'onto' before mentioning the carpets, bringing them back into the narrative of the sentence, where Leiris' mention of them is more of a reflection, questioning his memory of the room. Davis also relates the rug to the fixed carpet with 'some other design', whereas Leiris only mentions 'some [quelconque] decoration', in a form of enumeration that seems only to suggest his thinking of the carpet, rather than its relation to the rest of the sentence. The addition of an alliteration in 'faded floral patterns' (where Leiris writes 'ramages fanés') is in keeping with Leiris' poetic style, and increases the literariness of the text. Davis' translation is, therefore, not as extremely literal as it first appears to an English reader: it is willing to adapt the text in minor ways towards coherence, while at the same time recreating major stylistic features. Davis balances a commitment to the style of the text with a need for the text to be understandable for the target audience.

Davis' other solutions are not always as helpful to the English reader. She remarks in her translator's note that 'certain of Leiris' words must remain in French', because of the 'historic truth' inherent in the auto-biographical nature of the work (Davis 1997b: xi): the sounds and words relate to Leiris' own childhood, and it would be inauthentic to try to recreate that childhood in English. Her solution is to use many French terms throughout the text, leaving many of the puns in French with either glosses or footnotes to explain them. Of the 255 pages in *Scratches*, 126 contain French words. Thus the text is visually peppered with French words, which can sometimes produce a disrupted, uncomfortable reading experience for the English reader. For example, the following list appears as quoted here, with the French terms all followed in brackets by Davis's glosses:

> *coup de foudre* [lightning bolt], *coup de théâtre* [dramatic turn of events], or *coup de ciel* [blow from heaven] – one can speak of a *coup de dés* [throw of the dice] . . . from *coup de sang* [apoplectic fit] to *coup de vent* [gust of wind], from *coup de mer* [heavy sea] to *coup de feu* [gunshot], from *coup de tête* [head butt in wrestling] to *tout à coup* [all of a sudden] (Leiris 1997a: 33)

The text shows the graphological pattern of the French around '*coup de*'. Davis' glosses allow the reader to follow the French, but their positioning makes the text difficult to read, as the reader is forced to code-switch while reading. Yet the French disrupts the reading process, offering an excessive possibility for meaning creation that was not in the source text as the words are now doubled. The reader hesitates between a sound pattern and the meaning of the words.

Similarly, the songs in the section 'Songs' (Leiris 1997a: 7–17) are all given in French with an English translation that does not attempt to reproduce rhyme or metre but does give the meaning of the words. There are a number of lexical items in 'Songs' which pose particular problems for the translation, as they are words that can be easily confused in French. Leiris explains how, when he was too young to read, he would mishear the lyrics, creating a whole different meaning for the song. For example, in a song sung by a friend of the family, he misunderstands the word 'clairet' as being addressed to the singer's parrot, rather than modifying the preceding noun: 'Quand je bois du vin clairet' ('When I drink pale red wine'; Leiris 1997a: 8). The young Leiris thus understood the song as 'Quand je bois du vin, Clairet' ('When I drink wine, Clairet'), where Clairet was the parrot, even though the narrator, who is looking back on the event, would know that this was not what it meant. Further on, the young Leiris understands the name of a family, '*les Tréforts*' as the '*Très forts*' ('very strong'; ibid.: 9–10). The problem for the translator here is that these words are inseparable from their French setting: while it is conceivable that a parrot could be called 'Clairet', because English adjectives are almost always placed before nouns, the end of the song's line would be 'pale red wine', losing all hint of an apostrophe and as such the possibility of confusion. The translation needs to reproduce Leiris' confusion: by keeping the French it becomes possible to show how that confusion can arise.

I include a table of some other examples of Davis' use of French in the English text of *Scratches* (Table 3.1). It is not exhaustive, but it illustrates the type of usage and the various strategies Davis uses to allow the English reader to understand the French.

In some cases there are only isolated instances of French words or expressions; these are less problematic to the reading of the text as an English text than the cases where French and English are interwoven, as in the example above from page 33 or the examples from pages 15, 22, 36 and 237 in the table. Davis' choice of footnotes or in-text glosses does not alter the effect of strangeness that such a heavy presence of French has. For footnotes, there is a part of the text which is opaque to the target language reader which is clarified by finding the extratextual gloss. Glosses interrupt the reading process but simultaneously allow the reader to continue reading the text without changing eye position.

As Davis writes in the translator's note: 'Certain words, phrases, labels or remarks which fell upon his ears . . . are, for him [Leiris], not only sounds of sentimental importance but also so many knots where the threads of his remembrances and associations, ideas and moods, come together' (Davis 1997b: xi).[6] These 'knots' in the text are often untranslatable puns, such as those relating to the songs mentioned, or patterns of sounds, such as 'ver' (Leiris 1997a: 109), which could be '*vert, verre* or *ver*' ('green, glass or worm'), as well as relating to Véronique and *vert-de-gris* ('verdigris'). While the way these words are written would not allow there to be any ambiguity between them, the repetition of sound across them all allows the meanings to become entangled for Leiris. To reconstruct these phonological patterns in English may not be impossible, but doing so would almost certainly

Table 3.1

Page	Phrase(s) in the text	Davis' means of explaining the term
7	*pleurer comme une madeleine*	A footnote explains the ambiguity: 'a *madeleine* is also a cookie.'
15	an *étable*, a *retable*, a *totem*, a washbasin with water that is either *potable* or *non potable*	Footnote: 'Stable; altarpiece; totem; drinkable; and non-drinkable'
19	"*Un bar-e-bier . . . de qualité, de qualité, de qualité!*"	Gloss: [a ba-er-ber of quality]
20	*guérites*	In text: 'sentry boxes – *guérites*'
21	*Passer au falon, au tourniquet*	Footnote, giving both idiomatic meaning (to be court-martialled) and literal meaning
22	*patois patoisant* and *ouailles* from the *paroisse* of *Fouillis-les-Oies*.	Footnote: 'Babbling dialect and minister's flock from the parish of "Middle-of-Nowhere"'
27	King Pétaud	Footnote: explanation of the term, as well as relation between Pétaud, *pet* and fart
36	M the majesty of *mort* [death] or *mère* [mother]; C the concavity of *cavernes*, *conques* [conchs], or the *coquilles* [shells] of breakable eggs	Gloss after French words.
66	the *tu* is *tué*	Gloss after expression: [the intimate you is killed]
83	Just as a violin has its *âme*	Gloss: [sound post, lit. "soul"]
102	Salpêtrière hospital ("*salle Pêtrière*," as I called it)	No explanation of the phrase 'salle Pêtrière' ('Dirty Pêtrière')
143	*ça me serre le cœur*	Gloss: [it gives me a pang, lit. "squeezes my heart"]
199	*cri de Coeur*	No explanation.
237	between *idole* [idol] and *plâtre* [plaster], for example, by way of *idolâtre*[idolatrous]	Gloss after the word
258	*Tantôt*	Gloss: [later, presently]

not reconstruct the same semantic pattern. In a novel this might be an option, depending on how important the semantic meaning of the words was for the narrative, but in an autobiography there is more of an obligation to retain the existing networks, as they refer to a life actually lived in that language, and to translate them would distance the text significantly from its moorings in the references of that life. The text ends up full of French words and expressions, but it does retain many of the networks of words that exist in the source text and ties the target text to the source text at those moments when the source text itself plays with the French language. Interestingly, Davis' use of French reduces in

Scraps, where only 61 pages out of 241 contain French words, a reduction from one half to one quarter. This mirrors a shift in the emphasis of Leiris' autobiography from his relationship to words to his relationship with people, which I explore further in the next section.

Davis does not so much try to recreate in English Leiris' creative use of French, but reproduces the French alongside English. This non-translation is also a failure of translation because it highlights the non-equivalence between the French and English terms. Davis' translation is transgressive in this respect. Davis' position in the literary world at the time of the translation may have given her the possibility of translating in such a way, although Leiris' status as a well-known surrealist poet may also have contributed to the willingness of the publishers to accept such an unconventional translation. Despite growing acceptance of using French terms in academic texts (Gaddis Rose 2000: 298), it is still uncommon for a translation to use a significant amount of foreign words in fiction or other literary genres like autobiography. Davis had already published eighteen books in translation before *Scratches*, including her translation of *Brisées*, which although it tends towards literalism never strays too far from what is acceptable. Davis had also published three books of short stories, including one for the major publisher Knopf, *Break It Down* (1986).[7] She would thus be no longer the little-known writer/translator that she had been for earlier translations, especially those she wrote with Paul Auster: her status put her in a position to be able to break norms.[8]

However, Davis' strategy in her translations of Leiris did not become the norm for her translations. Her four books of translations of Pierre Jean Jouve are much less experimental in translation strategy. She does, however, reproduce Jouve's unconventional use of shifting perspectives (from first to third person) and changes in tense (from past to present) in her translation of *Le monde désert* (Jouve 1926, translation 1996), suggesting that the focus on style that begins in her work on Blanchot was still present. Even her translation of Proust, for which her aim was 'to stay as close as possible to Proust's original in every way' (Davis 2002a: xxxi), did not resort to the same practices, and arguably did not produce such a difficult and foreign text as her translations of Leiris.[9]

Davis' strategy of using French words in an English text in *Scratches* and *Scraps* is in fact suggested in some of her own writing which predates the Leiris translations. Two stories in *Break It Down* rely on the use of the two languages: 'The Letter' (Davis 1986: 49–56), and 'French Lesson 1: Le Meurtre' (Davis 1986: 128–36). 'The Letter', which I analyse more fully in Chapter 7, tells the story of a female translator who receives a handwritten French poem from her former lover. The story revolves around the translator's attempts to understand the meaning of the poem/letter, which is not the meaning of the French poem itself but her former lover's reason for sending it to her: a central expression is '*nous nous retrouvions*, we found each other again' (Davis 1986: 55), which she thinks may refer back to their agreement to meet again, although she isn't sure. The French in 'The Letter' is provided with an English gloss, allowing a monolingual reader to follow it, but at the same time producing an alienating effect.

'French Lesson 1' contains much more French.[10] It resembles some of the passages from *Scratches* that I analyse above in its combination of French and English. The story is shaped like a primer used for teaching language:

> *Les chiens* cringe in the presence of their master, *le fermier*, and bark at *les chats* as *les chats* slink mewing to the back door, and *les poulets* cluck and scratch and are special pets of *le fermier*'s children until they are beheaded by *le fermier* and plucked by *la femme* of *le fermier* with her red-knuckled hands and then cooked and eaten by the entire *famille*. (Davis 1986: 129; original emphasis)

This appears to be a parody of the primer genre, which would not give such information as the dogs' fear of their master, nor the morbid (though entirely normal) end of the chickens. As a parody it mirrors other stories by Davis, which similarly take existing texts and alter them (see Chapters 6 and 7). Davis does not give English glosses in the story, partly because the French words are fairly basic and partly because a primer would not either: the point is to learn the meaning of the words in context. A reader could determine that 'les chiens' referred to dogs, as they bark, or that 'les poulets' are chickens as they 'cluck and scratch' and become dinner.

The use of French in the stories creates an atmosphere of distance, stalling the reader's comprehension and enacting a movement of interpretation in the case of 'The Letter' and recreating, albeit with a twist of adult knowingness, a childhood experience of learning a language in 'French Lesson 1'. The reason for using French in the translations is different, as it ties the translated text back to its source and recounts the story of Leiris' initiation into language and life, reproducing the moments that his French childhood produced that a childhood in English could not. The textual effect of French in English in both the translations and the stories is to increase the difficulty for the English reader, who now has to read the French, even if there is an English gloss or explanation. Only a translator who was confident of herself would propose such a procedure, which would be likely to be rejected by more conservative publishers.

Davis' use of French in her own stories and in her translations of Leiris shows a link that is unique in her *œuvre*. Techniques that are present in her own writing reappear in the translations and those earlier stories could be read as training for her translations. There is much more evidence of a dialogue at the level of style between her works and her translations than is the case with Blanchot. The translations suggest an important link between the two writers, which is further strengthened by Davis' writing which refers to Leiris.

With Reference to Leiris

Two texts by Davis based on intertextual references to Leiris suggest that Leiris has influenced Davis' writing in ways that go beyond stylistic or thematic influence. 'Swimming in Egypt: Dreams While Awake and Asleep' (Davis 2007b: 35–44) narrates a sequence of dreams and dream-like moments that appears to be almost a rewriting of Leiris' *Nuit sans nuit et quelques jours sans jour* (1961). In this work, Leiris records, in chronological order, a sequence of dreams and waking moments that appeared like dreams. In her text, on the other hand, Davis decided to recount dreams and dreamlike moments, but not identify which were which, and to 'sequence them according to a logic that was not necessarily chronological', as well as 'shaping the dreams as [she] liked' (Davis 2007b: 38).

The relationship between Davis' text and Leiris' here seems at first glance to be one of direct influence. Indeed, Davis notes that the text 'illustrates the way in which a work of literature . . . can exert an influence that produces a concrete result years later on' (Davis 2007b: 7). Davis' project is directly inspired by Leiris' book, which she records having 'acquired . . . many years ago, soon after it was published in Richard Sieburth's translation' (ibid.: 37). The genesis of 'Swimming in Egypt' was not, however, immediately related to her reading of *Nights as Days, Days as Nights* (as Sieburth titled his 1987 translation), but to an experience that appeared extremely dreamlike to Davis, of driving up what should have been a road, according to her map, but which turned out to be a forest path. This experience made her 'contemplate Leiris' book with fresh interest and devise a project of [her] own' (Davis 2007b: 37).

The explanation of how 'Swimming in Egypt' came to be written is included in the text itself, which was published in *Proust, Blanchot and a Woman in Red*. It seems that Davis needed a piece of writing for that volume which could represent her Leiris translations. The other two essays in the volume, which deal with Davis' relationship to her translations of Maurice Blanchot and Marcel Proust, are based on previously published material. Davis (2007b: 38) notes that the experience took place 'recently': the piece could have been written for the pamphlet.[11] While the rest of *Proust, Blanchot and a Woman in Red* deals directly with works Davis has translated, 'Swimming in Egypt' refers to a text translated by Richard Sieburth (and read in translation by Davis), complicating any supposedly simple relationship between translation and influence.

The second text is a lot more tenuous in its connection to Leiris and does not refer to Leiris himself, but to Michel Butor. 'To Reiterate' (Davis 1997a: 83) was first published in the magazine *Pequod* in 1986, before Davis published her translation of *Brisées*. It begins: 'Michel Butor says that to travel is to write, because to travel is to read.' This appears to refer to a footnote in Leiris' essay on Butor's *La Modification*, reproduced in *Brisées*, which quotes Butor as saying 'words on a page are only markers on a road the reader himself is traveling' (Leiris 1989: 212n). If this is the quote that Davis is referring to, then she has reversed his metaphor from 'reading is a form of travelling' to 'travelling is a form of reading'. 'To Reiterate' develops this analogy further, linking translating to writing, reading and travelling, until 'to read is also to read, and even more, because when you read you read, but also travel, because traveling read, therefore read and read' (Davis 1997a: 83). The text folds in on itself, doubling meanings and questioning a received understanding of the relationship between writing, translating, reading and travelling. Its connection to Leiris remains slim, but it shows a usage of language that brings attention to itself which suggests an affinity between the two writers, even before Davis had started to translate *Brisées* or *Rules of the Game*.

Davis' writings that make a reference to Leiris, albeit a submerged one in the case of 'To Reiterate', avoid direct interaction with Leiris' work: they do not quote or otherwise integrate Leiris' writing into Davis' own. They place Leiris as a source of inspiration; a writer to emulate, although with variation, in 'Swimming in Egypt', and as the (probable) source of a quote that provided the stimulus for 'To Reiterate'. Both texts position Davis in relation to Leiris, making him into a precursor, although at the same time demonstrating Davis' difference from him.

Breaking the Rules of the Game

The point of contact between the two writers is not only apparent in these texts, however, but also in the affinity they have for writing in a way that privileges the poetic function of language. This section reads how Leiris uses language in *La Règle du jeu* to question his unconscious, playing with misreading and mishearing in order to develop his autobiography, then it questions how Davis manipulates language.[12] I suggest that she reflects formal elements of Leiris' writing, but does not have the same autobiographical motivation. There is a form of dialogue between the two writers, which again plays out in how Davis responds to Leiris' work.

Throughout *Rules of the Game* Leiris interrogates the role of words in his life, and nowhere more so than in the first volume, *Scratches*. The first section, '. . . Reusement!', describes the entry into the world of words of the young Leiris. While the child Leiris described in this section is already a speaking subject, capable of forming sentences and talking, he begins to be able to contemplate words in relation to each other, and to some extent as objects in themselves rather than just carriers of meaning, suggesting Leiris' later poetic vocation. The process could be read as an entry into Lacan's symbolic order, which represents the social aspect of language. Slavoj Žižek (2006: 8) likens the symbolic order to the rules of a game of chess. The symbolic order represents the rules of the 'game' of social interaction, and Leiris' understanding of this 'game' grows in '. . . Reusement!'

The young Leiris shouts out 'reusement', only to be corrected, told that he should say 'heureusement' (Leiris 2003:5; 1997a: 5). The effect is one of revelation:

> Appréhender d'un coup dans son intégrité ce mot qu'auparavant j'avais toujours écorché prend une allure de découverte, comme le déchirement brusque d'un voile ou l'éclatement de quelque vérité. Voici ce vague vocable – qui jusqu'à présent m'avait été tout à fait personnel et restait comme fermé – est, par un hasard, promu au rôle de chaînon de tout un cycle sémantique. (Leiris 2003: 6)

> Suddenly to perceive in its entirety a word that I had always mangled before felt like a discovery, as though a veil had suddenly been torn away or some truth exploded. This vague utterance – which until now had been private and in some sense closed – had suddenly and fortuitously been promoted to the role of a link in a whole semantic cycle. (Leiris 1997a: 5)

Leiris' awareness of the word as a word increases. Through the knowledge of the word 'heureusement', he can connect it to the word 'heureux' ('happy'), a connection that allows Leiris to go on to note the change from a personal expression (. . . reusement) to a more socialised and shared expression (heureusement) which is understandable by other people and also connected to a series of other words.

Yet 'heureusement' is not the only word around which this section revolves. The object that causes the child's exclamation is a toy soldier, and the word 'soldat' ('soldier') is repeated in each of the first six paragraphs, although Leiris notes how little importance the fact that it was a soldier had for him, being more interested in the fact that one of his toys had fallen and could have broken: 'soldat, cela n'évaillait aucune résonance définie en moi' ('I had no definite response to the word "soldier"'; Leiris 2003: 4; 1997a: 4). Yet 'soldat' dominates the first half of the section. It is the only thing in the first few paragraphs which the reader can be sure of: all other descriptions are questioned or multiplied – 'Un soldat neuf ou ancien' ('A new soldier or an old one'), 'Un soldat vraisemblement français' ('Probably a French soldier'; Leiris 2003: 4; 1997a: 4). The theme of soldiers, and the image of manliness that they represent, becomes more important later in the latter two sections of *Scratches* which describe Leiris himself as a soldier: the word soldier is by no means arbitrary.

The whole '. . . Reusement!' section forms an introduction to *The Rules of the Game*. The opening provided by the word 'heureusement' into a more social view of language is mirrored by the movement in the first two volumes away from the personal to a more social vision; from Leiris the child to Leiris the adult, engaged in a war. Seán Hand in fact sees *La Règle du jeu* as 'playful variations on the theme of producing self-representation' (Hand 2002: 86), although he goes further and bases his analysis of the whole work on his reading of '. . . Reusement!'. In Hand's reading, 'we find that *Biffures*'s opening ". . . Reusement!" scene encapsulates the general drama of the whole autobiography' (ibid.: 172). Not only is the question of the social introduced here, but also the figure of the soldier and the question of language. Leiris' fascination as a child with the way the word 'heureusement' connects to the word 'heureux' allows him to picture a social world, 'd'obscurément sentir . . . en quoi le langage articulé . . . me dépasse, poussant de tous côtes ses antennes mystérieuses' (Leiris 2003: 6 – 'to sense obscurely . . . how articulated language . . . went beyond me, thrusting mysterious antennae in all directions'; Leiris 1997a: 6).

All the sections of *Scratches*, apart from 'Sunday', are constructed around readings or misreadings of words, clearly shown in the confusion between 'Je bois du vin clairet' and 'Je bois du vin, Clairet' in the section 'Songs'. This form of misreading (or mishearing) and the subsequent confusion that ensues appears often throughout *Scratches*, which is called *Biffures* in French. Leiris explains his intention to use the word 'bifurs', meaning bifurcations or railway junctions and sounding almost the same as 'biffures' ('crossings out') to describe the material he was using. His attention is focused on what he calls

> [les] trébuchements ou glissements de pensée se produisant à l'occasion d'une fêlure, d'un miroitement ... ou d'une quelconque singularité ... se mani-festant dans le discours (Leiris 2003: 262–3)

> trippings or slippings of thought occurring as a result of fracture, a dazzling flash ... or some singularity or other ... manifesting itself in speech (Leiris 1997a: 238)

Hand describes this as 'the *astonishment* of the subject-in-language' (Hand 2002: 89; original emphasis), which he sees as grounding *Biffures* in a 'graphological' scheme; it follows Leiris' development in language rather than his biological development. Lejeune agrees when he notes that Leiris' work considers 'son histoire comme celle d'un *être de langage*' ('his story as that of a *being of language*'; Lejeune 1975: 7; original emphasis). The development in language does not exclude his social development – rather it situates Leiris' autobiography on the level of the symbolic, despite its continual returning to what Julia Kristeva (1974: 19) calls the pre-Oedipal semiotic elements of language.

Sections like 'Alphabet' (Leiris 2003: 33–68; 1997a: 31–63) and 'Il était une fois ...' (Leiris 2003: 128–68) ('Once Upon A Time ...'; Leiris 1997a: 117–53) use the sound of the word as a starting point for further reflection. In 'Once Upon A Time ...' this reflection is mainly at the beginning, with isolated moments later on, but in 'Alphabet' it continues throughout the text, with various words and sounds provid-ing the impetus. Thus Leiris manages to associate the word 'alphabet' with horses, expressions like 'coup de foudre' [love at first sight], dice, letters, sensual impressions. He goes on to include biblical names, which often cause him to pause because of the diaereses in the French versions of the names Caïn and Moïse (Leiris 2003: 50–2; 1997a: 47–8). Finally he moves on to French history. The shifting pattern of association is the formative principle of the text, rather than narrative or argument.

This development by association is what Hand (2002: 86) refers to as the 'musical form' of *Scratches*. The text appears to be constructed more like a symphony, with recurrent themes that intimate and reference each other, rather than a narrative text. This is strange in autobiography, which Bran Nicol (2006: 105) describes as 'a really rather conserva-tive form of prose writing'. However, as Blanchot (1949: 239) notes in relation to another text of Leiris', autobiography is always in a state of flux; its subject is not constant, but always in a state of becoming. Leiris' writing mirrors this constant movement, and the recourse to the semiotic and phonological elements of language overshadows a more strictly logical and rhetorical development. Lejeune (1975: 160) sees the autobiography as being written like a poem and notes how Leiris will search for the centre of a series of associations, while also allowing himself to develop secondary chains of association (ibid.: 164). This can be seen in the ranging from the alphabet and letters to the diaereses in biblical names (in French), which then lead on to French history in the section 'Alphabet': it is possible at the same time to read a chronological movement hidden behind the chain of associations, as one learns the alphabet first and then other things.

The form of sections in *Scratches*, then, tends towards a description of the effect of language on the young Leiris and allows the movement of each section to develop around a chain of associations. In the second volume, *Scraps*, the focus on language is reduced, although not absent. Indeed, while words continue to play an important role in 'Mors' (Leiris 2003: 289–356; 1997b: 1–71), they lead here into a discussion of death, ranging from thoughts of his own mortality to the death of others, to the theatricality of death and even zombies, which represent a suspension of death. Yet the central theme of the section, death, is not mentioned for sixteen pages. Before then there are reflections on the theatre, a trip to the Antilles, the theme of waking, his family, self-reflexive passages about writing, and even corrections to *Scratches*. These latter take the form of actual corrections, where Leiris had misquoted songs, and reflections on the sound of words. All these subjects lay the groundwork for themes that will reappear throughout 'Mors'.

While 'Mors' seems more focused than the earlier sections, it still proceeds by association, sometimes leaving the reader wondering how Leiris has moved from one theme to another. He tries to explain the process in the text:

> J'opère une série de glissements, d'obscurité à sommeil, de banlieue à désert, d'oubli à Zuyderzée, d'insecte à somnambule, de solitude à mort (Leiris 2003: 310)

> I am performing a series of shifts: from darkness to sleep, from suburb to desert, from oblivion to the Zuider Zee, from insect to sleepwalker, from solitude to death (Leiris 1997b: 23)

Yet he never really explains the process of association; he only asserts that that is what he is doing. The effect, again, is that the text reads more like a prose poem than a narrative.

'Mors', like much of *Biffures*, tends towards a privileging of what Kristeva (1974: 83) calls the *géno-texte*, that is, the part of the text which is filled with the pre-Œdipal drives of the semiotic, manifested as phonological and graphological patterns. In the early parts of Leiris' *La Règle du jeu*, the *pheno-texte*, or the communicative aspect of the text, tends to be submerged under the *géno-texte*, although both are present, and both are, as Kristeva makes clear, essential to the meaning of any text. The writing operates like a controlled version of free association: it aims to recover Leiris' unconscious through the return to the semiotic.

The privileging of the semiotic over the symbolic in Leiris' autobiography represents the return to childhood implicit in the first part of *Biffures*, but in the later parts and 'Mors' in *Fourbis*, the theme is no longer of childhood and the semiotic aspects of the text seem more like an attempt to reunite individual (child) and social (adult) selves. However, the final two sections of *Scratches* involve less wordplay. The sections 'Les Tablettes Sportives' and '«Vois! Déjà l'ange . . .»' in *Fourbis* even follow generally linear narratives. The first describes Leiris' interest in sports as a child and leading up to his time in the army, at the beginning of the second world war, while '«Vois! Déjà l'ange . . .»' describes an affair he had with a prostitute called Khadidja, also when he was a soldier. These last two sections can be seen as a development of the tendency in the first two volumes of *The Rules of the Game* to move towards social interaction and the symbolic order (already hinted at in '. . . Reusement!'), away from a child's unconnected world of individual language.

Davis also explores language use and the social order, questioning the established order by demonstrating how language is used to build it. Where Leiris uses language as a means of self-exploration, Davis invites readers to question their assumptions about the symbolic order of language. For example, in the story 'They Take Turns Using A Word They Like' (Davis 2001: 98) the different stresses of words are emphasised:

"It's *extraordinary*," says one woman.
"It *is* extraordinary," says the other.
[Quoted in full; original emphasis]

Davis' story seems like a caption for a non-existent *New Yorker*-style cartoon: one that is tinged with a surprisingly metaphysical question, with the focus on being in the second woman's utterance. The almost-repetition is discomforting; from the title the reader would expect something different. The repetition of the words comes as a surprise; the change in emphasis is the difference between them, but it is left to the reader to interpret what that difference may mean. The story provides the impetus for thought. The difference between the two utterances causes the reader to imagine what the two women might look like, how they would sound, why one would like the word 'is', and so on. Here Davis stages Jakobson's 'poetic function' (discussed above, p. 46), making the reader of the text focus on the words themselves. The reader is confronted with the words as words, facing a revelatory moment in a similar way to the young Leiris in '. . . Reusement!', but Davis differs from Leiris in that she does not give an interpretation, leaving it up to readers to question their own expectations and understanding.

Other stories by Davis are also structured around what seem to be minor grammatical features, such as 'Examples of *Remember*' (Davis 2001: 28), 'Honoring the Subjunctive' (Davis 2001: 71) and 'Example of the Continuing Past Tense in a Hotel Room' (Davis 2007a: 201).[13] These stories, each of which is no more than two lines long, focus the reader again on the structures of language involved, but do not explicitly interpret them. In 'A Double Negative' the grammatical construction demonstrates the character's ambivalence towards having children: 'she does not want to not have had a child' (Davis 2001: 66).

In the story 'Grammar Questions' (2007a: 27–9), a grammatical structure is similarly used as cover for an emotional development. The question of how to refer to a dying or dead person in the present or past tense allows the narrator to explore, albeit obliquely, how she will react to her father's imminent death. Through the questions it unfolds that the father is in hospital, cannot eat, and is not conscious. Here it is not so much grammar itself that worries the narrator, but rather what it is used to refer to – a person to whom she has an emotional connection. Language may exist as a symbolic system, but 'Grammar Questions' reminds the reader that it is referential: the way one uses language is important because it refers to people.

'Letter to a Funeral Parlor' (Davis 2001: 74–5) similarly takes the language used to refer to the dead as its starting point, specifically a complaint over the word 'cremains'. The narrator/letter-writer notices several instances in which the language of professional undertaking is distanced from the experience of the bereaved: 'your representative used the words *loved one* to refer to him. That was comfortable for us, even if the ways in which we loved him were complicated' (ibid.: 74; original emphasis). The word 'cremains', though, is uncomfortable for the family and the narrator explains why, referring to its status as a portmanteau word and how it makes them think of 'some kind of chipped beef dish' (ibid.: 75). Here, again, sensitivity to language is used to explore the relationship between the narrator and their dead father. There is still an element of humour in both these stories, but rather than being solely humorous they develop a narrative of mourning around the (mis)use of language.

In these stories, Davis reminds the reader that words do not just refer to other words, but rather to people and things outside of language. Marjorie Perloff has noted this tendency in Davis' fiction, which she says 'renew[s], however elliptically, the contact words make with their referents' (Perloff 1989: 212), although she does not highlight the interpersonal nature of this renewal. The referent in 'Letter to a Funeral Parlor' is the narrator's father, who is now dead. While there is language to refer to the father, he also exceeds language: he is more than how he can be described. As people (and things) exceed language, they are not wholly assimilable to the symbolic order. Lacan calls 'réel' ('real') that which lies outside of the agreed illusion of the symbolic order (Lacan 1973: 53–4). This real he says appears with the force of an encounter (Lacan 1973: 54) – an encounter which is always traumatic. The narrator of Davis' story turns away from the symbolic order, which reduces their father to 'cremains', preferring the trauma of their encounter with their father, in all its difficulties.

Where 'Letter to a Funeral Parlor' refuses the play of language and so the symbolic order, 'A Mown Lawn' (Davis 2001: 2) playfully combines a privileging of the poetic function which echoes Leiris' writing and an explicit criticism of the symbolic order. The text was published in *The Best American Poetry 2001* (Hass and Lehman 2001: 67) as a poem, although Davis prefers the designation story, which she says she finds 'more elastic' (Manguso 2008). 'A Mown Lawn' begins, 'She hated a *mown lawn*' (original emphasis in all quotations from this story); the italics distance the words from their communicative function. The reader is therefore unsure whether it refers to an actual area of grass that has been cut, or the words 'mown lawn'. The second sentence places words as combinations of symbols (letters) and phonemes, but also reverts to semantic meaning at the end: 'Maybe that was because *mow* was the reverse of *wom*, the beginning of the name of what she was – a *woman*.' The words 'mow' and 'wom' are anagrams of each other, foregrounding their material nature and suggesting the sort of play that is possible in language. The return of semantic meaning, 'woman', at the end of the sentence brings back a connection between phonemes/graphemes and a signified. The signified in this case is part of the symbolic order: by describing 'woman' as 'the name of what she was', Davis separates the word from the entity (or possibly state) of woman.

This questioning of the word 'woman' is also present in another of Davis' stories, 'Suddenly Afraid' (Davis 2007a: 189), which I quote here in full: 'because she couldn't write the name of what she was: a wa wam owm owamm womn'. 'Suddenly Afraid' echoes the phrasing in 'A Mown Lawn', separating the name 'woman' from the condition of being a woman, but also foregrounds an anagrammatic play in the way the words after the colon approach asymptotically the word 'woman' – the reader can infer this word from the failed attempts at writing it. In both texts, then, the word seems to exist in itself, separate from what a woman is.

The two texts highlight how the symbolic order, where words are accepted as having a meaning, is separate from a real existence. Lacan notes that the real is 'cela qui gît toujours derrière l'automaton' ('that which always lies behind the automaton'; Lacan 1973: 54), the automaton here being the acceptance of standard meanings for English words, especially the word 'woman': Davis shows how the word itself need not mean anything and how a woman is always distinct from the word 'woman'. This could be related to an experience of translation, where there is constant confrontation with different words that apparently refer to the same object, state or condition, thus highlighting the arbitrary connection between signifier and signified. Davis' foregrounding of 'woman' is also similar to the way that Leiris interrogates his reactions to words throughout *Scratches*, although here, as in the earlier examples, Davis does not fully develop the exploration of the word's meaning, rather leaving the reader to question their own understanding.

'A Mown Lawn' resembles Leiris' autobiography in the way that it develops through a series of associations, as do the sections of *Scratches*. From 'lawn' it goes to 'man' to '*Nam, a bad war. A raw war*', then back to 'lawn', which the narrator notes 'was a contraction of *law man*'. The question of law then holds for several sentences before meeting resistance from the narrator, who appears not to like the conformity involved in mowing a lawn: '*A lawn not mown grows long* she said: better a *long lawn.*' The obvious alliteration and assonance here, as well as a staccato rhythm of single stressed syllables, make the text sound like a tongue-twister, but again it does not quite let go of semantic meaning – as the best tongue twisters do not, either. The text has moved from considerations of sound to feelings of claustrophobia caused by surburban conformity in America and intimations of the connection of surburbia to neo-colonial wars, with the two references to (Viet)Nam. Here there is a connection between the mown lawn of the title, the conformity it represents, and imperialism.

'A Mown Lawn' advocates for a resistance to conformity, a refusal to play by the rules of the game, not only in its semantic content, but in its form: the anagrammatic play foregrounds the arbitrary connections between word and meaning, signifier and signified. As the Lacanian symbolic order is intimately connected to language (Lacan 1966: 155–7), this undoing of language questions the symbolic order. It does not return to a real referent, as 'Letter to a Funeral Parlor' does, but it opens a space, like Davis' other stories, for the questioning of received ideas.

Davis' undoing of the fabric of language in some of her stories reflects Leiris' method of analysing words in *Scratches*. They both use an investigation into language to structure their texts. In the case of the shorter stories, though, Davis does not perform the analysis herself, but rather creates a space of confusion that requires the reader to analyse the text. Leiris, on the other hand, seems to be interested in analysing for his own sake: the reader is left outside of the process, following along but not required to analyse words for themselves. Where Leiris excludes readers from the text, Davis' stories include them.

The difference can be explained by the difference in the projects of the two writers: Leiris is writing autobiography, and wants to develop an understanding of events and words in relation to his own life. Patrick Sauret describes the construction of *Scratches* as a 'série d'exercices de lecture ainsi qu'une description du mode de lecture employé' ('series of reading exercises as well as a description of the way of reading that is used'). He calls what Leiris is reading 'autogramme[s] . . . la traduction verbale d'un fragment d'existence' ('autograms . . . the verbal translation of a fragment of existence'; Sauret 1995: 46). The material in *Scratches* is therefore intimately linked to Leiris' actual existence. The text cannot really exist without reference to the life of Michel Leiris, even if it only refers to certain aspects of that existence. Leiris' foregrounding of the poetic function, then, focuses his analysis on the words in his life, and so he needs to analyse those words himself, in order to come closer to an understanding of his relationship to them. Leiris is expressly trying to learn about himself, writing that *La Règle du jeu* 'visait, originellement, à être moyen de m'éclairer pour une conduite plus cohérente de ma façon de vivre' (Leiris 2003: 296 – 'was originally intended to be a means of enlightening me for a more coherent conduct of my way of living'; Leiris 1997b: 9). The text is, in Blanchot's words, 'un acte réel' ('a real act'; Blanchot 1949: 238): it is not only supposed to be literary, but also an intervention in Leiris' life. Leiris therefore fills in interpretations, explains how certain words are meaningful to him, as he is searching for a meaning that belongs to him.

Davis, on the other hand, is writing fiction. Her stories need not be referred to her own life, although several can be, such as 'Letter to a Funeral Parlor' (Davis 2001: 74–5), which refers to a father who was an English professor, as was Davis' (Knight 1999: 525). Yet here Davis distances the story from her own life by casting it in the form of a letter of complaint and not including details or names. When questioned about the autobiographical nature of her fiction by Christopher Knight, she commented that some of her work has a basis in her life 'but there are always fictional elements' (Knight 1999: 547). The example of 'Swimming in Egypt' (Davis 2007b: 35–44), which emulates a text by Leiris, demonstrates how Davis distances herself from the text: Davis copies Leiris' basic process, recording dreams and dreamlike moments, but changes them so they have a fictional form, rather than one which is autobiographical.

Even the narrator of Davis' novel *The End of the Story* (1995) writes in a way that divorces what she writes from herself. As she notes: 'I began to wonder how the things I was writing could be formed into a story, and I began to look for a beginning and an end' (Davis 1995: 198). The narrator is thus transforming the writing from autobiographical to fictional, by making the material follow the dictates of narrative form. There is, therefore, a refusal of the autobiographical in favour of fictionalisation. The text is never confessional, but takes elements from the life of its writer.

Davis says that this is what she also does: 'I still define myself as a fictional writer for lack of another term, but I'm not really inventing. I'm taking what I see, the material I'm given, and arranging it, and really doing very little invention' (Stewart Atwell and Espach 2009). Davis' writing frames and shapes 'the material [she is] given', through a focus on formal elements, into literary texts. This echoes a process of translation, which also arranges existing material; however, translation involves another process of recreation from one language to another. Not all writing is translation, as the process of writing involves a level of selection and choice that is not open to the translator: the writer can do whatever they want, whereas a translator must produce a text that can stand in for a text in another language.

Davis chooses strange instances of word use and grammar to write about, but she leaves the reader to find their own interpretations for them because the work is not about the author, unlike Leiris' autobiography, but about those strange instances. If Davis interpreted them for the reader, then the work would be more about her. By leaving the reader to fend for themselves, the texts allow the reader to question meaning and the symbolic order that shapes meaning. Yet at the same time she returns to a sense that meaning is not just linguistic or symbolic: there are people and things that language refers to. To reduce them to linguistic devices is to ignore their reality. Hence the horror at the word 'cremains' – it reduces the remains of the body of a loved person to a neologistic trade term.

The texts that are mostly based around language are mainly from *Samuel Johnson is Indignant* (2001) and *Varieties of Disturbance* (2007), both of which date (mainly) from after Davis' translation of Leiris. It would be hasty to ascribe the way she questions words and language to her experience translating Leiris, however. Davis has her own project in questioning language that differs from Leiris' exploration of the self: Davis' questioning focuses on the social, interpersonal aspects of language use. Leiris does explore both social and linguistic aspects of his life, but the two are less intertwined through *La Règle du jeu* than they are in Davis' stories. Leiris can be read as a precursor, as he uses a similar technique, but Davis develops and refines this technique in her own way. Davis' own textual productions, in the form of 'Swimming in Egypt' and 'To Reiterate', which I discussed earlier, reinforce the reading of Leiris as a precursor for Davis' work. In both these texts, though, as in the stories discussed in the latter half of this section, Davis' application of Leiris' techniques is always veiled: either by fictionalisation or other forms of displacement. Davis can be said to take formal elements from Leiris, but not content.

It is equally possible to read their relationship as a form of extension of Davis' writing. By approaching the autobiographical in Leiris' work, she can write in a way that is outside of her own usual style. She said in an interview with Larry McCaffery that she liked translation because translating allowed her that ability to write like someone else (McCaffery 1996: 75). Translating Leiris would allow her to explore his lyrical autobiographical mode without writing something that is openly autobiographical. Her translation therefore offers the chance to write as if writing autobiography, but as the autobiography belongs to someone else, it becomes fictional. It cannot have the same intended purpose for Davis as it does for Leiris: it will not act as intervention in her life. What it does become is an exercise in writing, a literary game. It is like a found text that has been reworked by Davis, echoing her other stories which incorporate the work of others that I analyse in Chapters 6 and 7. As a text by Davis, it loses the seriousness and purposefulness that Leiris accorded it and it becomes similar to Davis' other works in its literariness. It becomes part of Davis' work, but the possibility of reading it in the context of Leiris' work never vanishes. Both readings are possible at the same time. The oscillation between the two is indicative of any translation by Davis: they can be part of her work and the work of someone else.

Notes

1. See, for example, Lejeune 1975, Leigh 1978, Sauret 1995, Hand 2002. Strangely, English language writers on autobiography (for example, Anderson 2011; Eakin 1999) do not refer to Leiris, despite their reliance on the work of his commentator Lejeune. Leiris is mentioned briefly in Marcus 1994, but only as an example of 'Freudian-inspired autobiography' (Marcus 1994: 215). Seán Hand regards all that Leiris wrote as connected to autobiography, 'seizing the rule of its own singular game' (Hand 2002: 4), so even the essays in *Brisées* could be viewed as part of the same project.

2. While Davis' translation of *Rules of the Game* is incomplete, it is worth noting that originally Leiris intended *La Règle du jeu* to be just two volumes (Leiris 2003: 1285), *Biffures* and *Fourbis*, titles which reverse each other in sound and thus mirror each other in a closed system. Patrick Sauret sees *Fibrilles*, the third volume, as 'd'une manière le dernier volume' ('in a way the last volume'; Sauret 1995: 112), with the fourth volume *Frêle Bruit* being almost an arbitrary continuation of the text.

3. Davis' translation of *Brisées*, and Leiris' work more generally, by keeping French words in the English text offers a way of displaying and drawing attention to the issues of untranslatability that Apter (2013) feels are often elided in world literature in translation.

4. Possible exceptions here are the Tocqueville biography (Jardin 1988) and Badinter's *XY* (1995), both of which are academic books and where the French is often only used when there is no English equivalent.

5. The full sentence is 250 words in length.

6. Davis' translation strategy in *Rules of the Game* practises a form of what Philip E. Lewis (2004) calls 'abusive' translation. He explains that 'the abusive work of the translation will be oriented by specific nubs in the original, or points or passages that are in some sense forced, that stand out as clusters of textual energy' (Lewis 2004: 263) – those moments in the text when there is an abuse of the norms of the source language. Davis' 'knots' recall what Lewis refers to as 'nubs'. Apter (2013), writing after Davis' translation was published, calls similar moments 'untranslatables'.

7. *Break it down* received a special citation from the PEN/Ernest Hemingway Foundation award, a recognition that may have led to Davis receiving a Whiting Writer's Award in 1988 (Ziolkowski 1993).

8. Gideon Toury (1995: 169) notes that certain translators may be able to successfully break the norms of translation in a given language if they have sufficiently high status.

9. Given that Penguin, a large commercial press, was the publisher of the Proust translation, rather than a small or university press as had been the case for the translations of *The Rules of the Game*, Davis' *The Way by Swann's* would have had to appeal to a larger public and so would not have been able to use the same strategies.

10. Larry McCaffery (1996: 59) sees this use of French as an example of translation influencing Davis' writing, yet there is not necessarily any connection to translation; any writer who has used a French primer and has a reasonable knowledge of French could have written a story that mimics a primer.

11. Two sections of 'Swimming in Egypt' were published as a broadside by Kore Press of Tucson in 2007, according to the copyright notice for *Proust, Blanchot and a Woman in Red*.

12. The importance of language is a regular feature in writing on Leiris (see Thomas 1975).

13. Laurent Berlant and Lee Edelman discuss how Davis' 'Break it down' focuses on the relationship between pronouns (Berlant and Edelman 2014: 72–6).

Chapter 4

Proust and Rewriting

Davis' relationship to Proust's *In Search of Lost Time* is the most complex of her relationships with texts she has translated. Davis's move towards a more literal, source-oriented form of translation, which began with Blanchot and was developed in her translation of Leiris, continues with her translation of Proust. She has stated how her 'aim in [this] translation was to stay as close as possible to Proust's original in every way, even to match his style as nearly as [she] could' (Davis 2002a: xxxi). This approach allowed Davis to focus on Proust's word choice and syntax, which is mirrored by her own careful selection of words in her translation as well as in her own stories.

Davis has discussed Proust's influence on her writing of *The End of the Story* (Knight 1999: 529). Given that her translation of *The Way by Swann's* was published later in her career, the process of translating Proust is not a determining feature of that influence. On the other hand, Davis' reading of Proust was influenced by C. K. Scott Moncrieff's earlier translation (Proust 1960). She describes Proust as 'going deeply into the impression that a thing made on him as a child or as an adult, exploring the nuances of the effect of an experience on the narrator' (Knight 1999: 529). This is a process that can also be seen in Davis' *The End of the Story*, which explores the narrator's relationship with an unnamed man and its aftermath. *The End of the Story* contains several intertextual references to *In Search of Lost Time* which position it as a Proustian novel. As this chapter shows, similarities of form and technique also make Proust a precursor for Davis: *The End of the Story* begs to be read within a tradition that stems from Proust. But, I will argue, Davis subverts the teleological goal of Proust's novel in her own, writing a narrative that has no goal to reach other than its own telling.

The End of the Story could be considered to rewrite elements of Proust's novel. This is not the only rewriting of Proust that takes place in Davis' work, however, as her translation of *The Way by Swann's* can also be considered a form of rewriting. This retranslation had to differentiate itself from the previous English versions, notably Scott Moncrieff's canonical 1922 *Swann's Way* but also James Grieve's lesser-known 1982 translation. The difference, she claims, lies in its being a 'close' translation, aiming at a more source-oriented rendering of the text (Davis 2004: 57). Davis therefore effects two rewritings of Proust: first as an author, second as a translator.

Using the word 'rewriting' to refer to both her translation and her novel draws on André Lefevere's (1992) as well as Christian Moraru's (2001) concepts of rewriting. Lefevere argues that translation is one among many forms of textual manipulation, others including the editing of anthologies, literary criticism and literary history. Each of these rewritings re-presents the text to an audience, affecting how that audience will perceive it. Moraru sees rewritings somewhat differently: as 'a "flagrant" retelling of identifiable literary tales', or 'novels that "repeat" other novels' (Moraru 2001: 17). Moraru focuses on contemporary American literary texts which critically rewrite earlier narratives, primarily in the American canon. Importantly for their difference from translations, they are recognised and sold as literary works by the later author. For example, Moraru argues that Auster rewrites Poe's detective stories in *City of Glass*, transposing the narrative to contemporary New York and explicitly making reference to Dupin (ibid.: 69–74). Auster's rewriting takes place in a novel that is identified as his, with Poe's name not being connected to it in terms of authorship. The relationship to Poe's stories is signalled in the text, but a reader unfamiliar with those stories will not recognise the rewriting. Nor is Auster's novel only a version of Poe's stories, as it constitutes an original literary text in its own right.

There are differences, then, between the translatorial rewriting that Lefevere discusses and the authorial rewriting that is Moraru's subject. Moraru expresses his reservations about collapsing the divide between the two, and this is not what I propose: the two forms of rewriting are distinct in their outward forms and in the licence they have to manipulate the text. It would be equally false to propose that editing, literary criticism and translation are all the same (which is not what Lefevere suggests), but all are forms of rewriting. Lydia Davis' case is interesting because it offers two forms of rewriting of a single text by the same writer, the links between which can shed light on how translation and other forms of rewriting relate to each other. This chapter will first analyse *The End of the Story* as a rewriting – a translation in the metaphorical sense – of *In Search of Lost Time*, then show how her retranslation of *Du côté de chez Swann* performs a rewriting of Proust in English.

An Authorial Rewriting

My concern in this section is how *The End of the Story* presents itself as a Proustian novel. In effect, I am using Proust as a lens through which to read Davis' novel. The two works dance around each other with multiple points of correspondence and Davis' can be read as a dialogic rewriting of Proust's, using but revising elements from the earlier novel. *The End of the Story* tells the story of the end of a love affair, punctuated by the author's reflections about writing the narrative. The narrative she is telling is one of obsession, with the narrator seeking out her former lover over a year after the relationship has ended. Her writing is a way of investigating the past, putting into words a process of remembering. As she recounts, 'I used to like to go over every moment of that first evening' (Davis 1995: 22). The narrator seeks out her former lover after the end of the affair, driving over to his house at night to look in through the windows. She is reluctant to let go of the relationship, even though it is over. This love affair is reminiscent of Swann's love for Odette in 'Un Amour de Swann', as well as the way the narrator of the *Recherche* falls obsessively in love with Gilberte and, later, Albertine. Indeed, the visiting of the former lover at the garage can be seen as an echo of Swann's visit to Odette's at night (Proust 1954: I, 274–5), where Swann's obsession has led him to question Odette's excuses for going home, thinking she may be meeting someone else.[1] Thematically and structurally, then, *The End of the Story* offers echoes of and parallels with Proust's novel.

Davis' novel contains numerous more or less explicit references to Proust. Karen Alexander (2008: 171) rightly mentions the tea that both begins and ends the narrative as a point around which the novel rotates, just as the moment with the madeleine and the tea is pivotal for the narrative of the first part of *The Way by Swann's*, 'Combray'. For Proust this moment is a point of entry into a new layer of memory. Eventually it is recognised as a moment of what could be called resonance, and it is these moments of resonance that the narrator recognises as joyous (Proust 1954: III, 873). For Davis, however, it serves as the end of the story: 'I think one reason the cup of tea in the bookstore seems like the end of the story even though the story went on afterward is that I did stop searching for him at that point' (Davis 1995: 230). Davis' tea answers Proust's: no longer the source of a revelation, but rather a consciously chosen moment of an ending. This element of reflexive choice, especially in relation to memory and narrative, in many ways distinguishes Davis' novel from Proust's, as I will go on to show.

There are several obvious moments of intertextuality that neither

Alexander nor Christopher Knight (2008) mention. One of the characters in *The End of the Story* is called Madeleine, in what could be read as a reference to the *Recherche*'s most famous moment. This reference seems not to signify much other than its own referentiality, suggesting it may be a joke: the Madeleine character is not particularly central to the story, as she is the narrator's flatmate (Davis 1995: 24), although she does reappear often and does stop the narrator from visiting her love object at work (ibid.: 164). Another apparent reference to Proust is a section that begins 'For a long time, there was the same pattern to our days and nights' (ibid.: 67), which cannot but remind the reader of the famous opening of *The Way by Swann's*: 'Longtemps, je me suis couché de bonne heure' (Proust 1954: I, 3), or in Davis' translation: 'For a long time, I went to bed early' (Proust 2002: 7). The section develops into a narration of their habits rather than a reflective passage as in Proust, but the echo reminds the reader of Proust. These explicit references serve the purpose of allying the novel to the *Recherche*, which allows it to be read as part of a Proustian tradition, and as a rewriting, in Moraru's sense, of the *Recherche*. This foregrounds certain elements of the text, such as memory and relationships, both clearly present in *The Way by Swann's*.

Memory is a significant trope in *The End of the Story*, along with the novel's questioning of narrative possibility. Critics have remarked on this: Alexander notes that 'memory plays a prominent role' in the novel (Alexander 2008: 171) while Knight explicitly compares the two writers: 'as with the French novelist, memory is central to her work' (Knight 2008: 210). I would argue that while memory is important at the beginning of *Swann's Way*, it becomes less central as the novel develops. The question of the prominence of memory in the *Recherche* is one taken up by many critics: for example Walter Benjamin, who thought that the novel describes 'nicht ein Leben wie es gewesen . . . sondern ein Leben, so wie der, der's erlebt hat, dieses Leben erinnert' (Benjamin 1977: II, 311 – 'not a life as it actually was, but a life as it was remembered'; Benjamin 1999: 198). This stress on memory and remembrance has affected how the novel has been received, giving an impression that the novel is only about memory.

Part of the problem of the perceived importance of memory in the *Recherche* lies in the way the volumes are split up, and the relation of the first volume to the rest. Many of the main themes of the novel as a whole are rehearsed or prefigured in the first volume: Swann's love for Odette is almost a model for Marcel's for Albertine; the musical phrase by Vinteuil makes its first appearance; many of the characters are mentioned very early on (albeit obliquely); the question of art appears, not only in the form of Swann and his collections, but also in the young

Marcel's first piece of writing, about the steeples of Martinville (Proust 1954: I, 181–2). Early readers of *Du côté de chez Swann*, including Jacques Madeleine, the reader for the publishers Fasquelle, seem to have had difficulty with the shape of the novel. Madeleine's reader's report begins by noting that 'au bout des sept cent douze pages de ce manuscrit . . . on n'a aucune, aucune notion de ce dont il s'agit' ('at the end of these seven hundred and twelve pages . . . you have no idea whatsoever what it's about'; Madeleine 1972: 13).[2] The novel does provide the reader with a key to its interpretation, but only in *Le Temps retrouvé*, where it is explained that it all leads to the possibility of writing. This is why Gilles Deleuze describes the novel as an 'apprentissage d'un homme de lettres' ('apprenticeship of a man of letters'; Deleuze 1970: 8). Deleuze's viewpoint, though, is from a time after the whole of the *Recherche* was published; Madeleine had seen only the manuscript of *Du côté de chez Swann* and Proust's covering letter, which he admitted 'apporte quelque éclaircissments' ('does bring some clarification'; Madeleine 1972: 13), although he also noted that the reader of the novel would not have access to that letter and so would not be able to benefit from those clarifications (ibid.: 13–14). I would contend that it is problematic to read *Du côté de chez Swann* without reference to the rest of the novel. Malcolm Bowie argues that reading the novel through *Le Temps retrouvé* is reductive, losing 'a whole range of paradoxes, dissonances and unusual consonances' (Bowie 1998: 5). While I do not disagree with Bowie, focusing too heavily on individual details will also lead to a limited reading: a balance needs to be preserved between part and whole. Going beyond the first volume, the reader realises that Proust's novel is about many more things than just memory, which is the focus only for the first part of 'Combray'. Gérard Genette's (1972: 83–8) analysis of the structures of narration in the *Recherche* shows how the narrative actually tends toward chronological development (with analeptic and proleptic sections) after the end of 'Un Amour de Swann' and the beginnings of the narrator's love for Gilberte (which takes place in the last section of *The Way by Swann's*). This later, more linear narrative structure reverses the impression given by the first pages of the *Recherche* that it is a novel solely about memory and childhood, which play less of a role in the developing story.

Importantly for how Proust's work is to be read in relation to Davis', the two writers' approaches to memory differ. As Knight (2008: 201) points out, memory in Davis' work is haunted by the possibility of other choices. Memory, for Proust, is something other than this: even within *Du côté de chez Swann* memory is more of a catalyst for creation than something to be interpreted. The 'Combray' sequence, for instance, does not question the possibilities other than the narrator's mother not kissing him goodnight when Swann visits (Proust 1954: I, 23–36), but rather narrates the occasions as Marcel remembers them. At the beginning of *Swann's Way*, the first section of 'Combray' has an intertwining of memory and narration that shows the difficulty the narrator is having in remembering, but it does not question the multiple interpretations of that remembrance. The narrator writes that during his nights of insomnia, he would remember his past in Combray, Balbec, Doncières, Venice and elsewhere (Proust 1954: I, 9).[3] From here the description of his life in Combray begins, including the description of Swann's visits and the emotional turmoil they would cause the narrator. The narrative soon returns to the present moment, or at least the moment of narration, and the narrator writes that he remembers nothing of Combray other than this 'pan lumineux' (I, 43 – 'luminous panel'; 46) of Swann's visits. 'Cela était en réalité mort pour moi' (I, 43–4 – 'It was really quite dead for me'; 46), he writes, because the only memory he has of it is furnished by voluntary memory. The narrative then proceeds to the moment of involuntary memory, caused by the madeleine and the tea, before beginning the second section of 'Combray', which carries on without further substantial reference to the narrator's present until the paragraph beginning 'C'est ainsi que je restais jusqu'au matin' (I, 186 – 'Thus I would often lie until morning'; 146), and which also introduces, although it is not part of, the narrative of Swann's affair in 'Un Amour de Swann'. In this movement back and forth to a central, indeterminate position, that of the nights of insomnia, Genette sees a mimicking of the '*difficulté de commencement*' ('difficulty of beginning'; Genette 1972: 88; original emphasis). Once the novel has reached the section after 'Un Amour de Swann', 'Nom de pays: le nom' (I, 383–427), it begins to settle into a more linear narration. Once the narrator has found a way of remembering, the question of how to remember retreats to the background.

The back-and-forth movement of beginning is also present in *The End of the Story*, which also eventually settles into a generally linear narrative. The novel begins with a description of the last time the narrator saw the lover, then it tells the story of his poem-letter, before telling the story of the last time she went looking for him. A metafictional section follows which explains the tea as the end of the story, and the narrator's idea that 'the beginning didn't mean much without what came after, and what came after didn't mean much without the end' (Davis 1995: 11). Then the tale of the relationship begins with their first meeting and continues in a linear though fragmented way until it ends, with the tea in the bookshop. One way in which Davis differs from Proust is that her narrator continues to interrupt the story to discuss the possibility that she might not be remembering it correctly. Proust's narrator seldom openly doubts the efficacy of his memory, especially after the madeleine incident (which, it should be remembered, takes place very near the beginning). *The End of the Story*, on the other hand, vocally questions its own reliability: 'Have I got that particular incident right?' asks the narrator (ibid.: 231). The narrative is about the possibility not only of remembering but also of recounting that memory; the narrator is trying to remember how those events happened for her, and is struggling with the difference between her ability to narrate them and what actually took place.

For the narrator of the beginning of the *Recherche*, the difficulty of remembering lies in the fact that he is trying to remember, that he is relying on 'la mémoire de l'intelligence' (I, 44 – 'the memory of intelligence'; 46). This too is what the narrator of *The End of the Story* is using: for her there are no moments of revelation. She is forced into using material supports, such as phone bills or photographs that her friend Ellie has sent, yet she finds that these material supports undermine her memory:

> I did not know those faces, I did not recognize them. I did not know those prominent cheek bones. I did not know the man who belonged to them . . . Looking at the pictures made me think that I don't really know what sort of person he was, either, because I never saw him from the outside. (Davis 1995: 171)

Here the narrator faces the problem of the subjectivity of memory; when confronted with something as apparently objective as a photograph, she cannot equate that with her memory of the person. As she says later, however, 'I wrote about him so much that he was no longer quite real' (ibid.: 196) – the act of writing makes him into something other than he was. As she continues to write, she begins to wonder if what she had written can be made into a story: memory gives way to narration, or memory and narration become confused. The narrator does not seem able to decide which is more important to her: 'I have been telling the story as accurately as I can, but I may be mistaken about some of it, and I know that I have left things out and added things, both deliberately and accidentally' (ibid.: 228). Here she wants her story to be accurate although she also questions her memory and her narration. The last scene of the novel is a revisiting of the cup of tea in the bookstore, where the narrator questions the accuracy of her memory of that event, but at the same time highlights its place within a well-formed narrative:

> And since all along there had been too many ends to the story, and since they did not end anything, but only continued something, something not formed

into any story, I needed an act of ceremony to end the story. (Davis 1995: 231)

Davis' storytelling is shaped by the need to tell a story and the difficulty of doing so. *The End of the Story* therefore has more of a self-conscious narratological focus than Proust's novel.

The narration of *The End of the Story* is complicated by its division into multiple timeframes, one of which is the time of the events of the story, another of the writing of the story. The latter features the narrator's current husband Vincent. He is separated from the time period of the central relationship; he becomes a figure external to that narrative, yet he remains within the narration of the novel. The narrator mentions that Vincent wants to read the novel (ibid.: 39), which draws attention once again to the novel's self-consciousness. The metafictional aspect of *The End of the Story*, the regular reminders to the reader that this text is a novel, that it could have been written differently, rivals the story of the relationship with the young man. Knight (2008: 214–15) notes that rather than one level 'displacing the other ... [they] seem to inhabit one another'. Davis' novel is therefore centred on two elements: the relationship, and how to tell the story of that relationship. The two are inextricably intertwined, for without the relationship there is nothing to narrate, but without the narration there is no novel of the relationship. The actual events of the narrative have faded into the narrator's memory. Davis' self-conscious narrative questions the truthfulness of storytelling, highlighting the processes of selection and interpreting involved in recounting events from memory.

Proust's novel does signal its own constructedness, but in a more subtle way than Davis'. One of the central features of Proust's novel is what Genette calls 'récit *itératif*' ('*iterative* narrative'). He points out that often 'une seule émission narrative assume ensemble plusieurs occurrences du même événement' ('a single narrative utterance brings together several occurrences of the same event'; Genette 1972: 148; original emphasis). In other words, a single point in the narration of the story brings together several occurrences of the one action. One marker of this multiplicity is the use of the imperfect tense, which allows a single sentence to describe multiple past events ('he would go out every day at five'). This use of the imperfect, notes Genette, is not uncommon in narratives and it is also found on many occasions in *The End of the Story*, where it is used for the description of repeated events. For Genette, where Proust differs from other writers is in his use of iterative verb aspects in scenes presented only once, as found in certaines longues conversations entre Léonie et Françoise (tous les dimanches à Combray!), entre Swann et Odette, à Balbec avec Mme de Villeparisis, à Paris chez Mme Swann, à l'office entre Françoise et «son» valet de chambre, ou de la scène du calembours d'Oriane (Genette 1972: 152)

certain long conversations between Léonie and Françoise (every Sunday at Combray!), between Swann and Odette, with Mme de Villeparisis at Balbec, at the house of Mme Swann in Paris, at the office between Françoise and 'her' valet, or the scene of Oriane's pun (my translation)

Proust writes as though these scenes are recurrent, yet the scenes themselves describe what should be unique events. In the episode of Oriane's pun, which recounts a scene at a dinner where Oriane tells a joke, the dialogue between Oriane and Basin is reported in the imperfect tense: 'Ecoutez, Basin, disait la duchesse' ('Listen, Basin, said the duchess'), or 's'écriait M. de Guermantes' ('would cry M. de Guermantes'; Proust 1954: II, 464). The effect is to turn a one-off conversation into a repeated event: this joke 'would be told' in the same way every time; Oriane would react one way, her husband another.

The confusion between singularity and repetition can be read into many of the themes of Proust's novel. The moments of involuntary memory, be they the madeleine or the paving stones, as well as the response to the steeples at Martinville or Vinteuil's little phrase, are all moments where the singular event becomes resonant with other events. It is repeated and singular at the same time. The response to such moments takes place, therefore, out of time. The experience of involuntary memory is an experience which brings together chronologically distant moments. As Blanchot notes, 'ces instants privilégiés ne sont pas des points immobiles' ('these privileged moments are not fixed points'; Blanchot 1959: 30). The moments can take place anywhere. They connect the narrator to any and all similar points in the past.

Davis' impression of Proust's technique, which, as I noted earlier, she relates to the exploration of an experience and its effect on the narrator (Knight 1999: 520), seems superficial in the light of his use of iterative narrative and the focus on the moments which connect the narrator to other moments. Proust does not go deeply into a single moment, but is searching for those moments which resonate across time. They are therefore not singular, but always iterative. The narrator's protestation against the misunderstanding of his work in *Le Temps retrouvé* – 'là où je cherchais les grandes lois, on m'appelait fouilleur de détails' ('where I was seeking great laws, they called me a scourer of details'; Proust 1954: III, 1041) – seems to clarify the narrator's relation to the singular: he is more interested in finding grand schemes than focusing on the unrepeatable event.

The confusion of singular and iterative, not only in the narrative but also in the presentation of relationships as a series, each similar but different to the previous, tends towards a collapsing of the singular into the general. As the narrator remarks in *Le Temps retrouvé*, what he experiences in a moment of involuntary memory is not just a moment of the past, but 'quelque chose qui, commun à la fois au passé et au présent, est beaucoup plus essentiel qu'eux deux' ('something which, common to both the past and present, is much more essential than either'; Proust 1954: III, 872). What the narrator is searching for are essences, which Deleuze describes as the 'unité de signe et de sense, telle qu'elle est révélée dans l'œuvre de l'art' ('unity of sign and meaning, such as it is revealed in the work of art'; Deleuze 1970: 51). Here is also the root of the apprenticeship that Deleuze (ibid.: 9–20) sees in the *Recherche*: the narrator must develop his understanding of signs until he arrives at this possibility for the signs of art.

Davis' narrator's aim is far less grandiose: she is trying to tell a story that might answer her questions (Davis 1995: 198). It could be read as demonstrating the 'incredulité à l'égard de métarécits' ('the disbelief in meta-narratives') that Jean-François Lyotard (1979: 7) sees as defining the postmodern: there is no overarching narrative to which she is trying to find answers, just a local and personal one. The conclusion of *In Search of Lost Time* can be read as giving the novel a unity and a teleology, making it the narrative of the artistic development of the narrator – although this unity can also be contested, as it has been by Blanchot (1959: 33), Bowie (1998: 5), Deleuze (1970: 149) and Margaret Gray (1992: 115–37). The ending of *The End of the Story*, on the other hand, more forcefully questions and disrupts any teleological reading of the novel. Nikolai Duffy (2005: 188–90) views the increasing fragmentation of Davis' text as an attempt to escape the temptation to be completist, to say everything, as the fragment form itself reveals the possibility of always saying something else. The meaning of an event is not fixed by the narrator and is open to interpretation. As the narrator says, 'he [the unnamed lover] may think that many parts of this story are wrong, not only the facts, but also my interpretations' (Davis 1995: 228).

Rather than telling just one story, the narrator is faced with the difficulty of any story. Indeed, Knight regards *The End of the Story* not as a conventional, linear novel, but as a 'novel conceived architectonically – a set of juxtaposed elements rather than a series of unfolding events' (Knight 2008: 209). Yet he also remarks that the narrator feels she should be able to solve the puzzle, that she 'never quite gives up the notion – that gives point to the investigation – that there must be a right way of doing things' (ibid.: 215). While she may never give up that notion, nor does she arrive in the novel at any one solution, with uncertainty dogging her to the last, where she both accepts the tea at the bookstore as an end – 'I still feel that it is the end, and I think I know why now' – and questions her perceptions and memory of that event – 'Have I gotten even that particular incident right?' (Davis 1995: 230). The one story is deferred, questioned, but still searched for. It is as if the narrator of *The End of the Story* would like to arrive at the epiphanic conclusion that Proust's narrator does, but at the same time cannot. There is a complex and contradictory relationship to narrative in the novel that fits Linda Hutcheon's (1988: 4) idea of postmodern art as a 'critical revisiting' of previous art forms: the novel is structured around narrative, but at the same time questions the possibility of narrative.

A la recherche du temps perdu and *The End of the Story* are linked, then, by certain affinities. Both novels defy easy classification or straightforward reading, even if Proust's novel tries to provide itself with a key to such a reading. The novels meet at various points, such as their questioning of memory and their narration of the stories of failed relationships. The references to Proust in *The End of the Story* would present *In Search of Lost Time* as a sort of model, or, more correctly, a precursor. But at the same time Davis' novel has a very different *modus operandi* to Proust's. Davis' narrator seems obsessed by the (im)possibility of narrating the events, while Proust's narrator is more interested in what the events will lead to, although he also becomes obsessed with the minutiae of events. The intertextual relationships alert the reader to Davis' use of Proust's work, but a comparative reading offers an understanding of what their relationship is. Davis does not imitate Proust, but rather places herself in a Proustian tradition, which she also questions, develops and rewrites.

Retranslating, Rewriting

In Davis' translation, her rewriting is on a different footing. What she can do to the text is more limited than in the case of authorial rewriting, because the product must be recognisable as a translation of the source text. Her *The Way by Swann's* is presented as a translation of a text by Proust and not as Davis' own novel. However, the translation is also a rewriting of the image of Proust in English: it is read against the earlier translations as well as the source text.

The Penguin/Allen Lane translation of *A la Recherche du temps perdu* edited by Christopher Prendergast, of which Davis' translation of *The Way by Swann's* is the first volume, is a retranslation. Davis' previous

translations had all been first translations, so this translation marks
a departure for her as a translator. Retranslations, Antoine Berman
claims, serve a different function to first translations in that they offer
a new approach to an already translated text: 'lorsque la traduction est
re-traduction, elle est implicitement ou non "critique" des traductions
précédentes' ('when the translation is a retranslation, it is, implicitly
or not, a "criticism" of the previous translations'; Berman 1995: 50).
Gideon Toury (1995: 166) also emphasises that even though all translations are 'always something that hasn't been there before', this is
especially the case for retranslations: they must produce something not
already present in previous translations (or else what would the point
be in publishing them?). In this section, I first question how the status
of retranslation – and therefore rewriting – affects Davis' practice in
The Way by Swann's, before analysing how Davis' translation differs
from those of her predecessors C. K. Scott Moncrieff and James Grieve.
I argue that she tries to replicate more features of the source text – what
she calls 'translating closely' (Davis 2004: 57) – which stems from her
belief in the importance of lexical choice in Proust's work. This distinguishes her version from the earlier translations.

Christopher Prendergast's General Editor's preface places the 2002
translation in opposition to the previous versions, explaining why a new
rendering of Proust is necessary in English, even though he concedes that
'the more sceptically minded' might doubt the need (Prendergast 2002:
xiv). This statement is, however, falsely modest: Prendergast spends
much of the preface demonstrating how Scott Moncrieff's translation
distorts Proust's writing, 'shower[ing it] with cascades of Edwardian
purple prose' (ibid.: xi), and how Terence Kilmartin's revision, which
tried to produce 'a less ornately garlanded, more direct mode of writing'
still falls short of that objective. Prendergast argues for a less recognisable Proust, one that is 'often strange to even French ears' (ibid.);
he speaks of 'the sheer strangeness of *A la recherche*' and of Proust's
'making-it-strange' (ibid.: xx). His view of Proust rests on the Russian
Formalist notion of art as something that makes us view things anew,
and his 'making-it-strange' is a reference to the concept of *ostranenie*,
'making strange'. This Proustian strangeness, if we follow Prendergast,
has been obscured by the Scott Moncrieff version and Kilmartin's revisions of it. He states that throughout the new translation he is introducing, 'the foreignizing conception has prevailed' (ibid.: xv), pointing the
reader to Lawrence Venuti's discussions of foreignisation. However,
Venuti proposes a 'practice of writing' that increases the strangeness of
the text: he argues for a level of textual manipulation in which 'translators can introduce discursive variations, experimenting with archaism,

slang, literary allusion and convention' (Venuti 1995: 310). This is quite different from the type of 'foreignization' Prendergast supports, which is really a kind of literalism. Prendergast prefers an approach with less intervention on the translator's part than Scott Moncrieff's or Kilmartin's.

It is tempting to think that all retranslations aim to provide a closer, more accurate translation. Jenny Williams and Andrew Chesterman (2002: 72) characterise this supposition as the 'retranslation hypothesis', although the idea does not originate with them. Goethe suggests that whereas first translations will produce more assimilative versions which acquaint the public with the work, a later stage will be an extremely literal translation which 'nähert sich zuletzt der Interlinearversion' (Goethe 1962: II, 258 – 'comes close to an interlinear version'; Goethe 2012: 66). However, in Grieve's 1982 rendering of *Swann's Way* Davis discerns 'a syntax which might have been that of an author writing in English' (Davis 2002a: xxxi), that is, a translation involving more intervention than its predecessor.[4]

Both Davis and Prendergast in their introductions say little about Grieve's translation, preferring to foreground their difference from the standard Moncrieff/Kilmartin translation. Their reticence may well be a matter of tact: Grieve was the translator of the second volume of the Penguin translation. Grieve, on the other hand, complained about the ambitions of the Penguin undertaking in an article in *Meanjin*, provocatively entitled 'Working with the Demented', which was published after the translation in 2005. Grieve observes: 'there's a lot of [foreignisation] about these days – there always was, though it used to be called bad translation' (Grieve 2005: 101), and he complains about the lack of uniformity across the volumes. Grieve's conception of translation is based more on adapting the text to the target culture than Davis'.

Davis' own ideas on translation are outlined in her writings associated with *The Way by Swann's* as paratexts or post-hoc meditations. In contrast to her two- or three-page prefatory notes for her translations of Maurice Blanchot and Michel Leiris, this volume contains a fifteen-page translator's introduction as well as explanatory notes.[5] An article entitled 'A Problem Sentence in Proust's *The Way by Swann's*' appeared in the *Literary Review* in 2002 and was included in a slightly different form, along with other material, in 'A Proust Alphabet' (Davis 2007b: 11–27). A further article discussing the translation, 'Loaf or Hot-Water Bottle', appeared in 2004. She also wrote a story about the translation, 'The Walk' (Davis 2007a: 72–82), which includes extracts from both her own translation and Kilmartin's revision of Scott Moncrieff's translation. This final text partakes more clearly in the breaking down of borders between her work as a writer and as a translator, which I shall return to in later chapters, as it takes part of translation work as part of her own writing.

The translator's introduction for Penguin appears to be series policy. Allowing the translator to explain the translation creates more apparent transparency in the translation process, which should gain the reader's trust and help generate the credibility required for this version to supplant the established translation. The other related essays, however, were written on Davis' own initiative. In 'A Problem Sentence in Proust's *Swann's Way*', 'The Proust Alphabet' and 'Loaf or Hot-Water Bottle', Davis works through the difficulties she had with the translation and explains her working process and decisions. There is a great deal of reflection about the French text, and how to achieve her goal of 'stay[ing] as close as possible to Proust's original' (Davis 2002a: xxxi). The use of a scene from the *Recherche* in 'The Walk' also cites both her translation and Scott Moncrieff's, performing an implicit comparison between the two.

These related writings suggest a self-conscious approach to translation that echoes Davis' self-conscious approach to narrative in *The End of the Story*. She considers that her practice in this translation was yet more literal than in her translations of Leiris: 'in my work on Proust, I tried to take that close fidelity a step further, reproducing, when I could, even the sounds and the punctuation of the original' (Davis 2007b: 7). Yet her Proust does not have recourse to the use of French in the body of the text as her translations of Leiris do.[6] The result is that her English must now try to follow Proust's sound as well as sense, as if Davis were translating a poem. As she remarks, Proust was also extremely attentive to sound. Davis gives the example of the word 'contigu', translated as 'contiguous', which, although it may sound strange in English, carries the contamination of the word 'contagion', which she also saw hinted at in Proust's French, and with which it shares a Latin root, *contingere* (Davis 2007b: 13–17). In the introduction she mentions her attention to Proust's punctuation, and explains how she tried to match it 'comma for comma' (Davis 2002a: xxxv), a practice that Grieve (2005: 101) thought unnecessarily literal.

As Davis (2011b: 88) notes, she worked on *The Way by Swann's* from 1997, and continued to revise the manuscript until 2004, when the American paperback was published. She estimates that she made about 1,500 changes between the British and American hardcover editions, and a further 'several hundred' for the American paperback. Her attention to detail here shows a continuing effort to find the best solution, to differentiate her translation from the previous ones and so rewrite

Proust in English. Davis herself has analysed in some detail how her translation differs from Scott Moncrieff's, especially in 'Loaf or Hot-Water Bottle' but also in her translator's introduction. She finds, like Prendergast, that there were 'gratuitous additions and embellishments [and] misreadings' in Scott Moncrieff's translation (Davis 2004: 54). A short passage will show at the micro-level the differences between their translations and Grieve's. This comes from the end of the first section, as the narrator is having his first, revelatory experience of involuntary memory, an experience he is finding difficult to hold on to. It offers a variety of sentence structures as well as various elements of alliteration and other patterns:

> Arrivera-t-il jusqu'à la surface de ma claire conscience, ce souvenir, l'instant ancien que l'attraction d'un instant identique est venue de si loin solliciter, émouvoir, soulever tout au fond de moi? Je ne sais. Maintenant je ne sens plus rien, il est arrêté, redescendu peut-être ; qui sait s'il remontera jamais de sa nuit? Dix fois il me faut recommencer, me pencher vers lui. Et chaque fois la lâcheté qui nous détourne de toute tâche difficile, de toute œuvre importante, m'a conseillé de laisser cela, de boire mon thé en pensant simplement à mes ennuis d'aujourd'hui, à mes désirs de demain qui laissent remâcher sans peine. (Proust 1954: I, 46)

Scott Moncrieff's translation was first published as early as 1922, while Proust was still alive, and effectively set the standard for how Proust was received in English. Both Grieve and Davis are translating against this early version, and it is against Scott Moncrieff's Proust that their renderings will be measured by the reading public. This is how Scott Moncrieff translates the passage; words in bold have no discernible equivalent in the source text.

> Will it **ultimately** reach the clear surface of my consciousness, this memory, this old, **dead** moment which the magnetism of an identical moment has travelled so far to importune, to disturb, to raise up out of the very depths of my being? I cannot tell. Now **that** I feel nothing, it has stopped, has perhaps gone down again into its darkness, from which who can say whether it will ever rise? Ten times over I must essay the task, must lean down over **the abyss**. And each time the natural laziness which deters us from every difficult enterprise, every work of importance, has urged me to leave the thing alone, to drink my tea and to think merely of the worries of to-day and of my hopes for to-morrow, which let themselves be pondered over without much effort or distress **of mind**. (Proust 1960: 60–1; Scott Moncrieff's translation)

Scott Moncrieff's translation is 144 words long, compared to 116 in the source text – a substantial increase, most of which comes from elaborations and ornamentations. His translation tries to domesticate the French for a target audience, tailoring it to a more ornamental taste.

He follows the French in its sentence structures, but he does add extra meanings, some of which contradict the meaning of the French text: memories for Proust are emphatically not 'dead' moments, as Scott Moncrieff would have us believe. There is also what appears to be a mistake in this translation: Moncrieff translates 'lâcheté' ('cowardice') as 'laziness' – again, seemingly against Proust's meaning. Kilmartin corrects this in his revision (Proust 1981: 50). Kilmartin also revises 'gone down again' to 'sunk back', and removes the 'that' from 'Now that I feel nothing', an addition by Scott Moncrieff that obscured Proust's meaning in the first place: Proust is describing a state, not a causal sequence of events. The 'clear' in the first sentence, which Scott Moncrieff transfers from 'consciousness' to 'surface', Kilmartin leaves alone (ibid.).

Grieve translates differently, reformulating the text to fit target-language expectations of sentence structure and syntax:

> I could not tell now whether this memory, this old moment that had been sought out inside me and set in motion at such a long distance by an identical moment, would ever surface into the daylight of my consciousness. I could feel nothing. It was stationary, or might have sunk back to the bottom, never to climb up out of the dark again. I had to go back to the beginning and try to concentrate on it many more times. And each time I tried, the pusillanimity that distracts one from any difficult task or work of importance kept whispering to me to forget it, just drink my tea and think of my present problems and my wishes for the future, which I could mull over without any trouble. (Proust 1982: 34; Grieve's translation)

Grieve changes syntax around, avoiding structures where a pronoun refers to a noun that has not yet been mentioned, as in the first line of the French ('Arrivera-t-il . . .'). He loses the precision of the French text: his narrator says he feels nothing, but the French narrator no longer feels anything ('je ne sens plus rien'); where the French narrator has to begin again ten times, Grieve's must try many times. Grieve's register is consistent apart from 'pusillanimity', a word whose formality draws attention to it in a way that is not the case with the more neutral 'lâcheté'. On the other hand, Grieve does not produce errors nor add extraneous information that alters meaning, as Scott Moncrieff did. Grieve has rewritten the text so as to be understandable in the new (target) culture, with the 'naturalness of expression' that Eugene Nida (2004: 156–7) recommends translations should have.[7] Grieve's translation has very different aims from both Scott Moncrieff's and Davis', both of which to some extent strive to retain Proust's style.

However, Grieve shifts the tense of the paragraph into the past from Proust's present. Given that much of the novel is narrated in past tense, this implies the proximity of the event to the narrator. It is as if he is (re)living that moment. This is the first example of involuntary memory in the novel and it sets the tone for the others: the use of the present tense is an indicator of how the past is made present in these moments. Grieve's translation overlooks this aspect of the text in order to make the passage more congruent with the surrounding material, but this loses the marked quality of the present tense in the passage.

Davis' translation looks quite different from both Scott Moncrieff's and Grieve's:

> Will it reach the surface of my limpid consciousness – this memory, this old moment which the attraction of an identical moment has come so far to summon, to move, to raise up from my very depths? I don't know. Now I no longer feel anything, it has stopped, gone back down perhaps; who knows if it will ever rise up from its darkness again? Ten times I must begin again, lean down towards it. And each time, the timidity that deters us from every difficult task, from every important piece of work, has counselled me to leave it, to drink my tea and think only about my worries of today, my desires for tomorrow, which may be pondered painlessly. (Proust 2002: 49; Davis' translation)

Davis uses 119 words; much closer in length to the source text than Scott Moncrieff. She makes no additions of words, and keeps adjectives connected to their corresponding nouns. Most of the time she uses cognates, which makes the translation sound similar to the French: for example 'counselled' for 'conseillé', or 'painlessly' for 'sans peine'. Yet she translates 'claire' as 'limpid', even though 'clear' would appear to fit her strategy, and retain the alliteration on 'c' that is present in the source text. 'Claire' is, however, placed before the noun, in an inversion of the normal order in French, which foregrounds it slightly. Davis' choice of 'limpid' enacts a similar foregrounding, but this falters because 'limpid' would have a less obvious meaning to many readers than 'clear'. Alternatively, she may have chosen 'limpid' to avoid the connotations of lack of guilt that 'clear consciousness', with its echo of 'clear conscience', has in English. Davis chooses much plainer, less markedly literary verbs at the end of the first sentence than Scott Moncrieff, in keeping with her perception of Proust's style as unaffected. Her 'attraction' is also less ornamental than Scott Moncrieff's 'magnetism'.

Her choice of 'timidity' for 'lâcheté' at first seems to be out of keeping with her strategy of translating closely, as 'lâcheté' is a stronger notion than 'timidity'. Yet it does fit in with her idea of translating the sound of Proust's sentences. In her introduction, she remarks that there is an 'ABBA structure of vowel sounds in this [phrase]: *lâcheté qui nous détourne de toute tâche*' (Davis 2002a: xxxi; original emphasis). The repetition of vowel sounds is more complicated than ABBA, since five different vowel sounds are used, but it does appear almost palindromic, beginning and ending on the 'â' of 'lâcheté' and 'tâche' (the 'e' being silent). The connection of *lâcheté* and *tâche* is also made through the rhyme on /ʃ/. Another important structure of repetition is on /t/ and its voiced counterpart /d/. 'Timidity' plays into the sound structure of the phrase in English: 'the timidity that deters us from every difficult task'. My bold type shows the pattern of alveolar /t/s and /d/s, linking 'timidity', 'deter' and 'difficult'. There is also a weaker rhyme on /i/ in 'timidity' and 'difficult', a connection not present in the French, but which does not seem out of place: the cowardice is over the difficulty of the task, rather than the task itself. Scott Moncrieff seems to plough over the sound system of this phrase, although one might hear a faint connection on the /z/ of 'laziness' and 'enterprise', and Kilmartin flattens the phrase entirely with 'cowardice'. Grieve's choice of 'pusillanimity' also seems to ignore any sound patterns in the text. Davis' translation here is much more attentive to how Proust's sentences affect the reader, and recognises that there is more to the text itself than just its locutionary meaning: it affects the reader through sound as well as the meanings of the words.[8]

Davis gives an explanation for the close attention she pays to the phonic qualities of Proust's writing. In the section of her introduction on Proust's style she suggests that, for Proust, form and content coalesced – 'the shape of the sentence was the shape of the thought' (Davis 2002a: xxx). The key to understanding Davis' translation practice in *The Way by Swann's* lies in this conjoining of form and content. She dismisses Scott Moncrieff's beautification of Proust's style, which she sees as 'essentially natural and unaffected' (ibid.), because to beautify Proust is to derail the sense of his sentences: Proust wrote certain words because those words best expressed his thought. Davis acknowledged in an interview that she too would be extremely careful in her choice of words when writing her own fiction, even 'putting an X instead of a word if [she couldn't] think of what the word should be' (Ziolkowski 1997). Her translation of Proust, then, mirrors a mode of writing that is already present in her own stories: that of exactness in expression. One reviewer of *Varieties of Disturbance* noted that Davis' Proust seemed 'much more aligned with the aesthetic practised by the translator herself' (Marcus 2007) than the more ornamental Proust of Scott Moncrieff, highlighting a similarity between Davis' writing and her translation.

While this similarity is there, the translation retains its status as a translation, being identified as such by a copyright notice and other paratextual features. There is a trace of Davis' authorial presence in the self-consciousness of the translation, but she never takes over the novel to rewrite it in the way she does in *The End of the Story*. Her rewriting here is of Proust in English – of the canon of Proust translations – with her goal being to present an accurate, unadorned Proust rather than the beautified version that was already in circulation. The self-conscious attention Davis pays to recreating Proust's literary effects and distancing herself from the previous translations, both in her practice and in the essays that surround it, makes her translation a form of extension of her own writing. Davis' translation of Proust, like her translation of Flaubert that I analyse in the next chapter, therefore problematises the distinction made in Susan Bernofsky's work between 'service translation' and 'strong translation' (2005: ix–xi). Davis produces a translation that provides a close representation of the source author and at the same time echoes Davis' own writing practices, but does not become a full authorial rewriting. The boundaries between Lefevere's and Moraru's rewritings are highlighted in Davis' rewritings of Proust. While the borders between them may be blurred in this case, they do, however, remain in place. We see this again in Davis' work on Flaubert, where the distinction between translation and writing is further blurred in her 'Ten Stories from Flaubert'.

Notes

1. I am indebted to one of *Translation and Literature*'s anonymous readers for reminding me of this parallel in response to an earlier version of this chapter.
2. All unacknowledged translations in this chapter are my own.
3. Further references to *À la recherche du temps perdu* in this section give page numbers from Proust 1954 for the French and Davis's translation, Proust 2002, for the English translation, unless otherwise specified.
4. Grieve saw his work as an effort to dispel the myth that Proust was 'abstruse'.
5. Davis' later translation of Flaubert's *Madame Bovary* would also be accompanied by an introduction and notes.
6. Except for passages in verse, which are left in French and given translations. This was a general editorial decision (Prendergast 2002: xvi).
7. Indeed, Grieve's translation could be read as a clear example of Nida's 'dynamic equivalence' (see Nida 2004: 156–7).
8. The translation is literal in the sense Antoine Berman gives the term: 'attention portée au jeu de signifiants' ('paying attention to the play of signifiers'; Berman 1999: 14), rather than a naïve definition of word for word.

Chapter 5

Flaubert and Authority

Davis' translation of *Madame Bovary: Provincial Ways* (2010) is her most recent translation from French and one that was written in her maturity.[1] The perception of translation as a form of training for writing, which I discussed in the Introduction, seems least applicable here: at the point of writing her translation of *Madame Bovary*, Davis had already been awarded a MacArthur Fellowship in 2003 and had already published six collections of short stories, four of which were with major presses, and her novel. By the time the translation was published in 2010, Davis' *Collected Stories* was also in print. It is safe to say that at this point she was an established writer.

Yet she chose to continue translating. The hierarchy of writing and translation, where the former is seen as more valuable, is always questioned by Davis' work, but here it seems most problematic. As with her other, later translations, Davis was working on stylistically complex writing. Where Leiris and Proust may be less commonly read, even if Proust is well known, Flaubert's *Madame Bovary* is popular and regarded as 'an important landmark in the history of the novel' (Davis 2011b: 66). Indeed, in her introduction to the text, Davis argues that '*Madame Bovary* permanently changed the way novels were written thereafter' (2011a: xi). Davis (2011b: 67) found eighteen different previous translations of it, suggesting that it had been popular since its first translation by Mary Neal Sherwood (published in 1881).[2] The narrative of *Madame Bovary* is itself banal: a young woman marries a country doctor and dreams of a more exciting life. She reads magazines and novels by Eugene Sue, Balzac and Georges Sand to inform herself about Paris (Flaubert 2001: 111; Flaubert 2011a: 49–50). She conducts affairs first with Rodolphe, then with Léon. Neither affair really satisfies her craving for a more exciting life. Her inability to deal with financial matters leads to her owing 8,000 francs to Monsieur Lheureux and the bailiffs coming to sell off the Bovarys' possessions. Emma commits suicide by taking arsenic. Her husband is left destitute and dies soon afterward, leaving their daughter Berthe to be looked after by a poor aunt who sends her to work in a cotton mill. One of the Library of Congress categories for *Madame Bovary* is 'Physician's spouses – Fiction', which is accurate, if a little reductive, and encapsulates the ordinariness of the action in the novel. Of course, there is much more to the novel than the plot. *Madame Bovary* appears to be a realist novel, but at the same time further attention to the stylistic and narratological devices reveal its artificiality and how it draws attention to its own form as much as it tells a story.[3]

Davis' own reaction to the text, as reported in her essay 'Some Notes on Translation and on *Madame Bovary*' (2011), reflects the multiple possible readings of Flaubert's novel. Her initial reading, from when she was 23, gave an 'impression [. . .] that was more negative than positive' (Davis 2011b: 71). She goes on to write that '[she] did not like the heroine, the story was depressing, and where was the style for which Flaubert was so famous?' Her later readings picked up on '[Flaubert's] irony, his poking fun at what he considered the stupidity of the bourgeoisie, the priesthood, the self-styled enlightened rationalist' (ibid.). The former reading may be the result, as Davis herself notes, of having the wrong expectations and thinking that the novel would be a love story. Her later impression makes Flaubert into a more modern writer, one who sounds more similar to Davis. Indeed, Flaubert's own search for the *mot juste* and the seriousness with which he wrote the novel, as shown by his frequent complaints about the novel's slow progress in his letters to Louise Colet (Flaubert 1980), recalls Davis' own careful language choices. These similarities were also highlighted by Julian Barnes in his review of Davis'*Madame Bovary* in the *London Review of Books* (2010), where he noted: 'Davis' work shares the Flaubertian virtues of compression, irony and an extreme sense of control.'

Davis' translation of *Madame Bovary* offers an interesting intersection between her practice as a translator and her practice as a writer. This intersection is deepened by her piece 'Ten Stories from Flaubert', first published in *The Paris Review* (2010). This piece is what it says it is: stories taken from Flaubert's letters to Louise Colet, translated by Davis. Here we see the blending of translation and writing. The authorship of 'Ten Stories from Flaubert' is difficult to discern: are these Davis' stories, or Flaubert's? The stories were republished in Davis' *Can't and Won't* (2014), but here they were spread throughout the collection. Each was categorised as a 'Story from Flaubert', just as some other stories were categorised as dreams. While the stories are not from *Madame Bovary*, there is a clear connection between them and Davis' work as a translator of Flaubert, similar in some ways to how she interacted with her translations of Proust, although not as developed as her use of Françoise Giroud's *Marie Curie*, which I will return to in the next chapter.

This chapter will first analyse Davis' translation of *Madame Bovary*, especially in relation to the theorisation of her practice that can be found in her related essay and introduction. It then moves on to discuss her 'Ten Stories from Flaubert', examining how they question authorship.

Translating *Madame Bovary*

Unlike all Davis' other translations, *Madame Bovary* had been translated multiple times before. The only other retranslation that Davis had undertaken was Proust's *Du côté de chez Swann*, which only had two previous translations: the canonical Scott Moncrieff translation (and its Kilmartin update) and the lesser known and harder to access James Grieve translation. As I discussed in the chapter on Proust, Davis' translation there was clearly oriented, through her own preface as well as the project editor's, against the Scott Moncrieff translation and aimed to surpass it. The lineage of *Madame Bovary* is much more diffuse: there are multiple different translators since Mary Neal Sherwood in 1881.[4] Indeed, Sherwood was not the first translator of the book into English at all, as Barnes reports that there was an earlier translation made by Juliet Herbert, who was governess to Flaubert's niece Caroline (Barnes 2010). Barnes quotes a letter from Flaubert to Michel Lévy, where he states that 'an English translation which *fully* satisfies me is being made under my eyes' (ibid.; original emphasis). This differs from the version of the letter in the published edition of Flaubert's correspondence, which reads 'On confectionne sous mes yeux une traduction anglaise de la *Bovary*' ('An English translation of *Bovary* is being made under my eyes'; Flaubert 1980: 712). Jean Bruneau's editorial notes to this letter go on to quote a later letter from Flaubert to Ernest Duplan, where he argues that the translation is a 'chef-d'œuvre' (ibid.: 1371). Bruneau states 'L'auteur de cette traduction est certainement Juliet Herbert' ('the author of this translation was Juliet Herbert'; ibid.: 1372). Herbert's translation is, however, lost to history at this point.

Davis' essay 'Some Notes on Translation and on *Madame Bovary*' sprang out of her translation of Flaubert and offers much information about her process of translation and, importantly, about her reaction to Flaubert's novel and its previous translations. In it, she recalls that her first experience of reading *Bovary* was in English, but she is not sure whose translation she read. She thinks it may have been translated by

Francis Steegmuller (Davis 2011b: 72). Steegmuller's American translation was first published in 1957 by Random House and was reused by the Everyman's Library in 1993. It remains current and Barnes recommends it as a 'freer' version in his review of Davis' translation (Barnes 2010). Davis argues that it, like the other translations of *Madame Bovary*, does not '[reproduce] Flaubert's style' (Davis 2011b: 72). In her introduction to the translation, Davis makes a similar, though less categorical statement: 'many of the translations do not try to reproduce that style, but simply tell this engrossing story in their own preferred manner' (Davis 2011a: xxiii).

Here it begins to become clearer why Davis would want to retranslate Flaubert. Rather than having a canonical translation to fight against, there is a more nebulous crowd of translations, none of which Davis perceives as accurate as they are not written in Flaubert's style. However, how is the style of a text in French reproducible in English, or in any other language? The choices that a writer makes in French are affected by the history of the language and the poetics in place at the time, just as writing in English is affected by past uses of English and the current poetics. Style is therefore intertextual, based on a writer's relationship to other texts (and perceived by the reader through their own knowledge of other writers' work).[5] An English text will never quite have the same style as Flaubert in this sense, as it can never take place in exactly the same conditions as the French.[6] This leads to an endless proliferation of translations, as each is always contingent (see Hermans 2007: 26) and may be considered in need of revision, updating or rewriting by another translator at a later time. As Brooke Allen writes in his review of Davis' *Bovary*, 'there is *no such thing* as a definitive translation' (Allen 2010: 10; original emphasis).

The motor for retranslation is often this sort of dissatisfaction with a previous translation. In the essay, Davis elaborates on reasons why one might want to retranslate a text: (1) as the first edition of the source text may contain typos and other mistakes, or may have been later revised by the author; (2) earlier translators may have needed to adapt the translation to fit the poetics of the target language; (3) earlier translations may be in need of improvement (Davis 2011b: 66). The first one of these suggests the instability of the source text, which is especially true of books like Proust's *À la recherche du temps perdu* which has two different Pléiade editions. This reason is not based on the previous translations' failings, but rather on the evolution of the source text as a published work. That said, there is still an assumption of a 'correct' or 'definitive' version of the source text here. The second reason calls to mind André Lefevere's discussions of poetics and the changing translations of Brecht in America (Lefevere 2012), where earlier translations were adapted to fit cultural expectations and later translations were closer in form to the source texts.[7] Davis does open up a final category of reasons for retranslation which is very open and can be read as a sort of 'etc.' in the list: it covers any other sort of deficit perceived by the retranslator (or the interpretive community [Fish 1980: 171] that the retranslator belongs to). Davis therefore allows any number of possible reasons for a retranslation, though it is clear that the sense of dissatisfaction with the existing translations is at the heart of all of them.

The translation which holds a more canonical role in the history of *Bovary* translations appears to be Eleanor Marx-Aveling's translation of 1886. It is the first British translation of Flaubert's novel and has been republished a number of times, as Emily Apter (2013: 265–97) discusses.[8] The claim to canonicity is related to the continued republishing, but also the fact that much of the discussion of *Madame Bovary* in English returns to the Marx-Aveling translation. Davis herself feels that it is important enough to discuss in her essay. As part of her research for her translation of *Bovary*, Davis consulted Vladimir Nabokov's teaching copy in the New York public library (Davis 2011b: 77–8). As Apter writes, '[Marx-Aveling's translation] gained its greatest notoriety when Vladimir Nabokov referred to it as an exemplary instance of bad translation' (Apter 2013: 268). But Nabokov's complaints are part of the canonisation of the Marx-Aveling translation: by discussing it, Nabokov contributes to the critical framework around it and encourages, therefore, later translators to read it, if only to see what to avoid doing themselves. Yet this has the effect of making it a text that is discussed and referred to, both of which are central to the idea of a canonical text (Wollen 2002: 221). Further canonisation occurs through the fact that Marx-Aveling's translation was used as the basis of Paul de Man's version for Norton in 1965 (Davis 2011b: 73–4; Apter 2013: 268–70). This was a scholarly edition, aimed at a student market and accompanied by a critical apparatus. De Man's introduction includes passages where he highlights the deficits of Marx-Aveling's translation (cited in Apter 2013: 273), in a manœuvre that is similar to Davis' comments about former translations in her introductions to her translations of *Du côté de chez Swann* and *Madame Bovary*. The function of this disparaging of previous translations is to foreground the new translation, highlighting how it surpasses (in whatever way) the previous translation(s). In de Man's case, his arguments are in favour of his revisions (or the revisions of his edition, as Apter [2013: 269] points out that much of the work on the translation was undertaken by Patricia de Man, his wife). Similarly, Davis also argues in favour of her translation: as none of the others have managed to recreate Flaubert's style in English, then implicitly her translation will do this and thus be more acceptable (to Davis) as a translation.

Reflecting on the various translations of Flaubert, specifically in relation to de Man's version, led Davis to list the important skills needed for a translator:

> The translator's knowledge of French language, history, and culture; his or her conception of the task of the translator; and his or her ability to write well in English. (Davis 2011b: 72)

Davis argues that the first of these is least important, as mistakes based on lack of knowledge may be easily fixed in editing (2011b: 73), but mistakes due to a poor conception of translation or to poor writing will affect the translation throughout. She gives her opinion that de Man had been chosen as a translator/reviser for the Norton edition not because he was a good writer in English, nor for his experience as a translator, but rather because he brought a scholarly reputation to the edition that would give it weight in the academic world. The cultural capital that de Man would bring to the project was therefore the reason for choosing him as a translator.

Davis' comments on the other translators' work should, I think, be read as a justification for her own translation that positions it as an aesthetic undertaking. While Steegmuller, Marx-Aveling and the others do not reproduce Flaubert's style, Davis' translation intends to focus on the style and try to recreate it in English. Focusing on the aesthetic aspect of the text also distances Davis' translation from scholarly editions (though it does come with notes) such as de Man's. It is important to remember that, as Deane-Cox (2011) comments, the translations all compete with each other in the English language marketplace. The calm replacement that was suggested by Goethe's theory of the three epochs of translation (1962, translation 2012) does not take place in the case of *Madame Bovary*, nor in the case of *À la recherche du temps perdu*: there remain several versions accessible and in use (being read, referred to and so on). As such, the positioning of a translation through paratexts (the introduction) or other means (in this case Davis' essay, though in other cases interviews and other means of publicly discussing a text) is an essential part of the retranslation process. This can even be seen in the reviews of Davis' *Madame Bovary*, which compared her version to the existing versions (for example, Barnes 2010 and Allen 2010).

Davis gives herself authority in this way to write a reader's version: one that offers privileged access to the source text and will therefore allow the English-speaking reader to experience the translation in a similar way to how the French-speaking audience would. Davis goes on to argue that a translation should not be written in faultless English if the source text is not written flawlessly (Davis 2011b: 78) – it should remain 'graceless or peculiar' (ibid.) where the original is. Davis' theory of translation is in many ways similar to the 'abusive fidelity' that Philip E. Lewis (2004) theorised: for Davis, if the source text transgresses the rules of good writing at points, then so should the translation. Davis' theory has not really changed since her translations of Leiris in the early 1990s. The difference with her practice in the case of *Madame Bovary* can be found in the less experimental writing style of Flaubert and in the fact that this is a novel, not an autobiography. The genre of autobiography, as I discussed in Chapter 3, meant that she was constrained to keep a certain amount of words in French in order to maintain the links to Leiris' own childhood.

At the heart of Davis' translation theory is a trust in and a reverence for the source text author, especially in terms of style. In many of her translations, however, she does not follow the style of the author, but rather adapts the writing to English language expectations. She calls these translations her 'work-for-hire' translations (Davis 2007b) and does not really discuss them in interviews. Only her translations from Blanchot, Leiris, Proust and Flaubert are translated with the closeness she discusses in her reflections on translation. These are also the same writers, with the exception of Flaubert, that she discusses in interviews and in her pamphlet *Proust, Blanchot and a Woman in Red* (Davis 2007b). Her translation of *Madame Bovary* was written after this pamphlet was published, but from her writing about the translation, it appears that it fits into the pattern with this group of writers. As I shall show in the second half of this chapter, Davis also responded to this translation in her own writing (in the 'Ten Stories from Flaubert'), as she did for the other writers she admired.

It is important to look at Davis' translation at this juncture to see if her theory was in fact applied in practice and how her translation of *Madame Bovary* relates to her other translations. While there are multiple different styles in the book – one only needs to think of the various letters and Homais' articles – the opening of the book is a good place to start as it offers the only first person narrator in the novel:

> Nous étions à l'Étude, quand le Proviseur entra, suivi d'un *nouveau* habillé en bourgeois et d'un garçon de classe qui portait un grand pupitre. Ceux qui dormaient se réveillèrent, et chacun se leva comme surpris dans son travail. (Flaubert 2001: 47; original emphasis)

This beginning already contains several features that start to mark off the style of the author: the use of italics for 'nouveau', where none are necessary, stresses it and creates a distance between the denotative meaning of the term – here 'a new boy' – and the meaning that it holds in the text. Flaubert often uses italics in this way in *Madame Bovary*. The new boy is dressed 'en bourgeois', which here means not in uniform, but which gives, in French, an indication through connotation of the class of the boy. The sleeping boys hint at the boredom that Emma faces later in the novel. The 'Nous' which begins the novel was not in Flaubert's early drafts or his definitive manuscript and was added on the fair copy (*version copiste*).[9]

Davis' translation reads:

> We were in Study Hall, when the Headmaster entered, followed by a *new boy* dressed in regular clothes and a school servant carrying a large desk. Those who were sleeping woke up, and everyone rose as though taken by surprise while at work. (Flaubert 2011a: 3)[10]

'Study Hall' is an Americanism, though it conveys the meaning of the French. The italics for new boy are kept, which has the same distancing effect as in the French: both focusing attention on the character and making unclear what meaning the narrator is giving the term. The hint of class relationship is lost with 'regular clothes', but this is the pragmatic meaning of the French phrase. Davis follows Flaubert's tenses, though boundaries between them are more blurred in English (it is not always clear from verb endings alone if they are imperfective or perfective). The comma in the second sentence, which pauses the action of the sentence and which is not strictly necessary in syntactic terms, is maintained. Davis also maintains the non-standard capitalisation of 'Étude' and 'Proviseur'.

While these two sentences are innocuous enough, it is worth comparing them to Adam Thorpe's translation from 2011:

> We were in Study-hour, when the Headmaster entered, followed by a *new boy* dressed in his everyday clothes and by a classroom servant carrying a big desk. Those who were asleep woke up, and each of us rose as if caught working. (Flaubert 2011b: 3)

There are a surprising number of differences here, given that the translations are almost exactly contemporary and given Thorpe's stated goal of following Flaubert's syntax (Thorpe 2011: xxiv), a goal which sounds similar to Davis' goal of reproducing Flaubert's style. Thorpe also states that he plans to use period language, in other words English from before 1857. The formulation 'Study-hour' is less American than Davis' 'Study Hall' and therefore less connotative of the American environment (Thorpe is British and this will have affected his choice here). The boy is dressed in 'everyday clothes', which is very slightly different to Davis' 'regular clothes'. Her 'school servant' becomes a 'classroom servant' – a very slight modification that does, nonetheless, give a slightly different connotation, as it implies that there are servants for each classroom. Thorpe alters Flaubert's use of a verb, 'dormaient' ('were sleeping'), to the adjectival 'were asleep'. Davis' continuous imperfect 'were sleeping' is closer to the French syntax here, though both have the same pragmatic meaning. Thorpe adds an extra first person pronoun in the final clause: 'each of us'. Flaubert's original reads 'chacun leva' ('each person rose') and Davis maintains this impersonal structure. Thorpe's 'as if caught working' seems odd, given that students are supposed to be working in study time – the verb 'caught' suggests something negative, while Davis' 'as though taken by surprise while at work' follows the meaning of the French more precisely.

In terms of narrative, the two texts are very similar and a reader encountering them separately would not really notice the differences between them, nor question whether or not they were acceptable translations. One might argue that Thorpe's translation is more readable, but this would be a subjective argument. When compared, however, they appear different on the level of style; the differences are indeed fine-grained and minimal here, but over the course of the novel, the impression is magnified. The slight differences in the use of verb tenses, and in the use of a personal pronoun where none can be found in the source text, show where Thorpe does not follow Flaubert's syntax but rather adapts it for an English language audience. These adaptations are very common (and unexceptional) in translation practice. Davis' aim of recreating Flaubert's style means that she follows Flaubert's syntax carefully.

The following passage contains an example of the elasticity of Flaubert's style, as it combines the high-register speech of Homais (in both direct speech and free indirect style) and a response from Emma:

> Homais demanda la permission de garder son bonnet grec, de peur des coryzas.
> Puis, se tournant vers sa voisine:
> — Madame, sans doute, est un peu lasse? on est si épouvantablement cahoté dans notre *Hirondelle*!
> — Il est vrai, répondit Emma ; mais le dérangement m'amuse toujours ; j'aime à changer de place. (Flaubert 2001: 136)

The extract comes from the first dinner that the Bovarys have in Yonville, at the *Lion d'Or*, with Homais and Léon, who is the other guest there. Flaubert says of *bonnets grecs* in his *Dictionnaire des idées reçus*:

'Indispensable à l'homme de cabinet – donne de la majesté au visage' ('Indispensable for bookworms, it makes the face majestic'; Flaubert 1979: 493). The intertext sheds light on Flaubert's use of the 'bonnet grec' and indicates the position that he takes towards Homais. The way the character speaks and is presented will confirm this: the reader's first impression of Homais includes a feeling of pompousness that will not diminish throughout the novel. His choice of the word 'coryzas' instead of the more common 'rhume' for cold shows that he wants to appear educated and intelligent. His actual speech in this example is formal, but not marked as unusually so.

Davis translates as follows:

> Homais asked permission to keep his fez on, for fear of contracting a coryza. Then he turned to his neighbour:
> "Madame is a little tired, no doubt? One is so dreadfully shaken about in our *Hirondelle.*"
> "That's quite true," answered Emma; "but I always find disruption interesting; I like a change of scene." (Flaubert 2011a: 70)

The first sentence offers one (minor) departure from a literal translation of Flaubert's French. Davis adds the verb 'contracting' before 'coryza'; this is not strictly necessary as the sentence 'for fear of a coryza' would be acceptable. However, the verb reinforces the medical register that Homais would use: 'contract' is a more formal way of saying 'catch'. 'Coryza' itself is a more technical term for a cold. Davis adds a note[11] to explain that a coryza is a cold and that Homais 'tends to favor a specialized scientific vocabulary' (Flaubert 2011a: 326). This is true and retaining the use of 'coryza' in the translations maintains this aspect of Homais' characterisation. The translation of 'bonnet grec' as 'fez' is a slight change: 'Fez', being a Turkish word, suggests a different history. From images of both types of hat, it is unclear just how different they are as they look very similar, but I find it hard to believe that a fez (or indeed a bonnet grec) would help stave off a cold. The description of Homais' movement in French is in the gerund, 'tournant' ('turning'), while Davis makes this a finite verb, 'he turned'. This moves away from the very exact following of Flaubert's syntax that could be seen in the earlier example. Davis also changes the position of the adverbial phrase 'no doubt' to the end of the sentence: positioned after 'Madame', it would be very marked. The use of 'One' is more marked in English than in French and sounds somewhat pretentious in speech, which suits Homais' character and it is possible to imagine him using an overly formal register to highlight his social position. Davis adds a 'quite' to Emma's response that makes the statement more idiomatic. The use of 'a change of scene' is an

Americanism, but it also interprets the text, as, in French, Emma says she likes changing place. It is an idiomatic translation, but worth noting as a deviation from the occasional simplicity of Flaubert's constructions; it could be read as making Emma more worldly than she appears in the French. Davis does maintain the semicolons here; the one directly after the speech-reporting verb is idiosyncratic in English and is an uncommon usage. It is also worth noting that this translation has anglicised the punctuation for speech, using speech marks: this is not the case for Davis' translation of *Du côté de chez Swann*, which uses the em-dash punctuation that is normally used in French. There are, then, a number of relatively minor adaptations that Davis makes that move this away from a word-for-word translation.

It is illuminating again to compare Davis' translation to Thorpe's:

> Homais asked permission to keep on his bonnet-grec, for fear of a head cold. Then, turning to his neighbour:
> 'Madame, no doubt, is a little weary? One is so terribly tossed about in that *Hirondelle* of ours!'
> 'That's true,' said Emma; 'but disturbance always diverts me; I like changing places.' (Flaubert 2011b: 76–7)

Thorpe here follows the syntax more closely than Davis does in some instances and alters it more in others. He retains 'bonnet grec', though with a hyphen, though he changes 'coryza' to 'head cold'. Homais' pretentious use of medical terminology is thus elided, though the use of a foreign term to describe his head gear does offer a suggestion of pretentiousness. Thorpe's 'I like changing places' feels more down-to-Earth than Davis' 'a change of scene' and mirrors more precisely the diction of the source text at this point. Thorpe also keeps the semicolons, even though the first (after Emma) is not necessary in English (it should be a comma here).

Davis' aim of reproducing Flaubert's style should not be understood as an attempt to be entirely literal (in the sense of word-for-word translation), but does give her some leeway to adapt the syntax as and when necessary. She argues that translation should be balanced: it will at times be worse than the original, and at times better (Davis 2011b: 78). The small changes noted in the above example are very minor liberties and it seems clear that Davis' preferred translation style here is one that follows the source text closely, but not slavishly. In relation to her translation of Michel Leiris, Davis commented on '[the temptation] to go too far in the direction of a similar deliberate awkwardness' (Davis 1997b: xi). In this translation, that temptation has been reined in.

Julian Barnes' review of Davis' *Madame Bovary* also concludes that

Davis does not always follow Flaubert's style precisely (Barnes 2010). He locates several examples where Davis' sentences are less flowing than the original or draw more attention to themselves. Any long work will offer examples of unidiomatic or poorly written sentences, so it is not a surprise that Barnes finds them. Barnes' review is, however, balanced and his conclusion provides a good summary of Davis' translation work:

> Davis's *Madame Bovary* is a linguistically careful version, in the modern style, rendered into an unobtrusively American English. At its best, it conveys the precision – which some think dryness – of Flaubert's prose in this novel, while its syntactical mirroring of the French sometimes brings us closer to Flaubert. At its worst, it takes us too far away from English, and makes us less aware of Flaubert's prose than of Davis being aware of Flaubert's prose. And such defects come from something very old-fashioned: a lack of love for the work being translated. (Barnes 2010)

The impression of precision is also one that can be attributed to Davis' own writing. The complaint that it takes us too far away from English overlooks that a writer's style will often take us away from the language and show it to us in different ways. Indeed, Flaubert's French is not entirely characteristic of other French writers from the mid-nineteenth century. The lack of love conclusion is interesting, insomuch as it assumes a relationship between translators and their translations that Lawrence Venuti has called 'simpatico' (1995: 273–306) – in other words, a sense that the translator will identify with the writer being translated and feel a similarity with them. Yet Davis has been fairly explicit that *Madame Bovary* holds no special place for her (see, for example, Boddy 2010). When first asked to do the translation, she turned it down (Anderson 2010). She has spoken about her preference for Flaubert's later, unfinished *Bouvard et Pécuchet* (ibid.). What Davis seems interested in, from her interviews and from her introduction to the novel, is Flaubert's craft. As a translator, this offers an interesting challenge, but this does not mean that it has to appeal to her as a writer.

Davis' translation style in this translation aims to keep the style of Flaubert's novel, which she positions as a new development from the previous translations. As I have shown, however, this does not mean a slavish word-for-word translation. Indeed, while Davis does follow the shape of Flaubert's sentences often, by, for example, following their parentheses and syntax, she also makes minor alterations. The result is a translation which closely follows the source text but which remains readable in the target language. Davis follows the heteroglossia of Flaubert's writing, with its multiple different characterisations (for example, Homais).

Davis' translation here, as in the other cases I have looked at, affects how we see Davis as a writer, though the temptation to read a translation as an extension of her writing is misleading. When Davis translates, she works as a translator, aiming to recreate the voice of the other writer in the translation. Davis' translations allow what Cecilia Alvstad (2014) calls the 'translation pact' to function: though they are signed by her, they are mainly read as a work by the original author. There are certainly shared tendencies between Davis' work as a writer and as a translator, such as attention to language, but Davis' translations are not versions. To an extent, they reflect her reading of the text, as all translations will. But her work on them does not mean that she will adapt them to her own style. There are works by Davis where she takes another writer's work and translates, adapts, edits or imitates it. These flout Alvstad's 'translation pact' and are the focus of my final two chapters, but also the final part of this chapter, which will look at Davis' 'Ten Stories from Flaubert'. It is in these stories where we find much more blurring of boundaries between translation and writing, between the two sides of Davis as a writer and as a translator, which her translations (in the more traditional sense) draw away from.

Translating Flaubert?

The focus in this section is on the 'Ten Stories from Flaubert' that Davis published in *The Paris Review* in 2010. As a response to Flaubert, they offer another facet of the relationship between Davis' writing and her translation, highlighting the porosity between them. They also, as I shall argue in this section, problematise the border between original and derivative work. They range from observations about servants to discussion of executions, while two deal with Pouchet's wife's funeral. Each story is an encapsulated narrative in itself, a short short story. There are no paratexts beyond the title of the collection, a title for each story and a credit for Davis as the author. It is impossible from the presentation in *The Paris Review* to tell if they actually are stories from Flaubert, or if they are not, where they have come from, or how Davis has confected them.

In the original publication, the reader was left to guess at where from Flaubert's voluminous work they had been taken. A reader of the *Paris Review* version of the stories would take it on trust that they were indeed stories from Flaubert as no evidence is given to support or deny this. As the stories were published in the Fall 2010 edition of the periodical, they came just before Davis' translation of *Madame Bovary* was published and can, therefore, be read as a form of advertising for the new translation. It was public knowledge at this time that Davis was working on the translation and an excerpt had been published in the August 2010 edition of *Playboy* (see Halford 2010). As such, an initial reader might speculate that the stories originated in *Madame Bovary* and had been extracted in some way from that work. As many of the stories are in the first person, this initial hypothesis could soon be discarded as it was therefore unlikely they came from *Madame Bovary*.

Davis included the stories from Flaubert in her 2014 collection *Can't and Won't*. Here they have grown from ten stories to fourteen, though one ('Industry') is characterised as a 'Rant from Flaubert' (Davis 2014: 215). In addition, the texts have also been revised in minor ways (for example, the addition of clarifying expressions – see discussion of 'The Cook's Lesson' below). Unlike the original publication, where the stories were concentrated as a group, in *Can't and Won't*, the stories are spread throughout the book. *Can't and Won't* contains two other sequences which are similarly distributed throughout the book. One is a sequence of complaint letters which echo 'Letter to a Funeral Parlor' from *Samuel Johnson is Indignant* (Davis 2001: 74–5). Another is a sequence of dreams that developed from 'Swimming in Egypt: Dreams while Awake and Asleep' in *Proust, Blanchot and a Woman in Red* (Davis 2007b). These are the first sequences to appear in Davis' work, which normally consists of independent stories (or sequences within stories). The three sequences, though each is non-linear and each is distributed slightly differently throughout the volume, give *Can't and Won't* a cohesion that is clearer than in Davis' earlier collections (where structure is at best implicit). Each of these sequences builds on previous work, either Davis' own in the case of the complaint letters, or a reading of Leiris or Flaubert.

In the acknowledgements to *Can't and Won't*, Davis explains the origins of the stories (and rant) from Flaubert. She states that they come from the letters he was writing to Louise Colet at the time that he was composing *Madame Bovary*, namely the years 1853–4. Davis says the material was 'excerpted, translated from French, and then slightly rewritten' (Davis 2014: 289). That final 'slightly rewritten' is somewhat vague and it is unclear to the reader what she might mean by this. She goes on to say that the rewriting was in order to create a 'balanced story' although she also allowed herself 'liberties', such as putting together two letters or adding information (ibid.). This information gives us a much more precise idea of the process that Davis undertook when creating the stories, but it leaves unclear exactly how much editing she undertook.

If we look at a couple of examples of the stories in relation to their sources in the letters, the sort of 'liberties' that Davis has undertaken come to light. The first example is from the first story in the cycle, 'The Cook's Lesson':

> Today I have learned a great lesson; our cook was my teacher. She is twenty-five years old and she's French. I discovered that she *does not know* that Louis-Philippe is no longer king of France and we now have a republic. And yet it is five years since he left the throne. (Davis 2010: 121; original emphasis)

The version which is found in *Can't and Won't* is almost identical, except for the addition 'when I asked her' in the third sentence, a shift into the past tense of the verb in italics and a further shift into the perfect tense of the final sentence:

> Today I have learned a great lesson; our cook was my teacher. She is twenty-five years old and she's French. I discovered, when I asked her, that she *did not know* that Louis-Philippe is no longer king of France and we now have a republic. And yet it has been five years since he left the throne. (Davis 2014: 9; original emphasis)

The differences between the two texts are minimal in terms of the meaning of the sentences. There is also almost no change in register. However, the slight changes highlight the instability of texts and the risks of assuming that a text, once published, is fixed in form (as Davis had highlighted in her essay on Flaubert, discussed above). In fact, the slight changes here suggest the kind of textual evolution that Davis has discussed in relation to her translations: she makes changes between editions. In the case of *Swann's Way*, she records having made over 1,500 changes between the British and American editions (Davis 2011b: 88). This continuity of practice suggests that the stories from Flaubert can be read as part of Davis' translational work.

A comparison with the source text shows, however, that there are a number of minor changes taking place that are uncommon in Davis' usual translation practice. The source text is found in a letter to Louise Colet, dated 30 April 1853 (Flaubert 1980: 318–21). After a rant about the literary establishment, especially Abel-François Villemain, Flaubert switches topic to tell a story:

> J'ai eu aujourd'hui un grand enseignement donné par ma cuisinière. Cette fille, qui a 25 ans et est Française, ne savait pas que Louis-Philippe n'était *plus roi de France*, qu'il y avait eu une république, etc. (Flaubert 1980: 321; original emphasis)

> I had a great lesson today, given by my cook. This girl, who's 25 years old and French, didn't know that Louis-Philippe was *no longer king of France*, that there had been a republic, etc. (my literal translation)

Davis' first line in her story alters the text in form to make it more idiomatic, but does not alter the meaning of the sentence. Her second sentence, again, alters the form of the text a little but keeps the meaning. It is interesting that in the earlier version of the story, Davis provides the information about Louis-Philippe in the present tense, while in the later version this has been changed to the past tense, which follows the French more closely. Yet in that later version, Davis adds an interpolation: 'when I asked her', which does not appear in Flaubert's letter. In both versions, Davis adds an explanation that five years have passed since the end of Louis-Philippe's reign – a detail that would have been obvious to Louise Colet, the intended audience of Flaubert's telling of this story, but not to Davis' audience. Davis' story includes no dates, so it would be impossible for that audience to know when the statement was made in relation to Louis-Philippe's reign; the detail is therefore necessary to make the context clear.

In the continuation of the story, Davis alters a direct quotation into indirect speech, makes explicit the comparison being made and changes Flaubert's 'triple imbecile' into 'imbecile'. She also removes his final remark, 'C'est comme cette femme qu'il faut être' ('We should be like this woman'; Flaubert 1980: 321), leaving it implicit.

Despite the minor changes that Davis has made here, the story is still very similar to its source and recognisable in relation to it. In some of the other stories, Davis makes more significant changes. In 'The Coachman and the Worm' (Davis 2010: 125–6; Davis 2014: 78–9), which deals with a former servant who has a tapeworm, the name of the servant is changed from Louis in the letters (Flaubert 1980: 294) to Tolet. As Davis uses Louis in this sequence to refer to Flaubert's friend Louis Bouilhet, the change in name highlights that this story is about a different person. The only other obvious change in this story relates to 'trente sols de brioche', which is translated as 'some white rolls' (Davis 2010: 126; Davis 2014: 78). Brioche may have been exotic once, but it is available in English-speaking countries (in, for example, almost any supermarket in England). The transformation of it into white rolls removes the cultural specificity of the term as well its historic resonances in French, but leaves in place the connotation of a specific taste for food. The effect is a loss of evoked meaning, but not one that derails the narrative of the story. Davis elides the more obviously culturally specific 'trente sols', for which there is no real equivalent, as 'shillings' has its own connotations in English and would seem considerably more than the thirty sols does.[12] Yet still, the translation 'some white rolls' can still be recognisably derived from 'trente sols de brioche', even if it represents a much less culturally specific form of it. The point of the translations in the stories from Flaubert is not to be accurate, however, but to provide the raw material for a story: in terms of the narrative, the fact that he wants brioche is less important than the fact of wanting a specific foodstuff.

In the story 'The Visit to the Dentist' (Davis 2010: 123; Davis 2014: 31), which is based on another part of the 30 April 1853 letter to Louise Colet (Flaubert 1980: 321), Davis adds some background to the tale and rearranges the material so that it has more of a narrative development. Flaubert begins by discussing the emotions of fear that people must have felt when entering the market square to be executed, a feeling mirrored by his own fear of a tooth extraction, before recounting seeing blood on the paving stones there as a six or seven year old. Davis, on the other hand, recounts this before having the speaker reflect on the shared nature of the fear. Davis' alterations to the order of information presentation mean that it appears to develop from an observation and the ensuing memory suggested by that observation, then to the empathic reflection: it feels more like a story.

In the end, there are a number of minor changes made to the texts in translation, but they still remain recognisable in relation to their sources. This is where the problem lies. They are still recognisably stories taken from Flaubert, but at the same time, they are stories presented by Lydia Davis. They have, therefore, a dual authorship and a dual status as a creative work and a work that is derivative of something else. The translation pact, as described by Alvstad (2014), whereby a translation is read with only the implied author in mind, as the translator is forgotten, does not come into play here: the translator is visible, present and lays claim to authorship. Davis' stories, after all, are presented as stories by Davis in both the magazine publication and in the book version, but in both they are also presented with the paratext 'stories from Flaubert'.

In this duality, the stories resemble found objects. The use of found objects in visual arts dates from Marcel Duchamp's 1913 *Bicycle Wheel*, which was a bicycle wheel on a chair. Duchamp later called these objects 'readymades' (cited in Gale 1997: 97), as they were indeed ready made. His later *Bottlerack* (1914) was, as the title suggests, a bottle rack. As Matthew Gale (1997: 100) points out, these readymades highlight the importance of context in the work of art: by placing them in a museum or gallery along with an artist's signature, they become works of art. Yet they also remain the objects that they always were.

Duchamp's readymades were everyday objects that almost anyone in his audience would recognise. The recognition is the source of the duality.[13] If the audience does not recognise the bottle rack as a utilitarian object, it becomes an abstract sculpture signed by Duchamp. Later viewers of replicas of the readymades may indeed view them as such, given that the objects are no longer in production, as is the case of the bottle rack, or due to the accretion of art historical discourse around them: one looks at Duchamp's *Fountain* (1917) not as a urinal but as a work of art by Duchamp.

The difficulty with Davis' stories from Flaubert is the likelihood of her audience knowing the source texts. Flaubert scholars may well be familiar with his letters, especially those dealing with the creation of *Madame Bovary*. Students reading *Madame Bovary* at university may have come across extracts from them, as they show just how much trouble writing the book was for Flaubert, or they contain sentences that clarify his conception of the work such as 'Vouloir donner à la prose la rythme du vers (en laissant prose et très prose) et écrire la vie ordinaire come on écrit l'histoire ou l'épopée (sans dénaturer le sujet) est peut-être une absurdité' ('Wanting to give prose the rhythm of poetry (while leaving it as prose and very much prose) and to write an ordinary life as you would write history or an epic (without denaturing the subject) might well be an absurdity'; Flaubert 1980: 287). But Davis did not translate Flaubert's passages dealing with artistic creation, rather the stories from the letters. They are seldom the main part of the letter, but rather observations or anecdotes that fill it out. As such, it is unlikely that a reader of Davis' stories would know the source texts without going looking for them.

As the stories are not likely to be recognised in relation to their source, they are read in relation to the paratextual note 'story from Flaubert', which is present in the title of the *Paris Review* publication of the stories and also in each story in *Can't and Won't*. The reader assumes they come from Flaubert's work. Their actual textual origin becomes irrelevant to the experience of reading them, because, due to that paratextual connection to Flaubert, they are never read entirely without Flaubert in mind. As Davis' stories, they maintain the dual authorship of both Davis and Flaubert, even if the reader is unsure of their exact connection to Flaubert.

There is a connection here with how I have been reading Davis' more conventional translations. In the case of a translator like Davis who is also a writer, then the dissipation of the translator, that Alvstad (2014) argues is part of the translation pact and the experience of reading a translation, is minimised as the name recognition of the translator leads to the text being viewed also as part of their work and connected to it in some way. Davis' stories from Flaubert highlight the difficulty of assigning authorship to a translation. They collapse boundaries between translation and writing, between writer and translator.

Further, reading *Madame Bovary* with Davis' 'Ten Stories from

Flaubert' in mind encourages the reader to notice anecdotes in the novel. The following, which is taken from Davis' translation, reads in a similar way to many of the 'Ten Stories':

> The caretaker, who is at the same time gravedigger and beadle in the church (thus deriving from the parish corpses a twofold profit), has taken advantage of the empty piece of ground to plant potatoes in it. Year by year, however, his little field shrinks, and when an epidemic occurs, he does not know whether he ought to rejoice at the deaths or lament at the graves. (Flaubert 2011a: 64)[14]

There are other stories that become foregrounded in a similar way, such as Félicité's story about the Guérin girl (Flaubert 2001: 170–1; Flaubert 2011a: 95). They offer small, encapsulated stories that are not necessary to the development of the main plot. The existence of Davis' stories thus suggests a different way of reading Flaubert: not as a writer of long novels, but as a collector of anecdotes that can be redeployed in longer narratives. The derivative work affects how we read the source and changes our perception of it.

The stories from Flaubert show how translation can be seen to be central to Davis' work as a writer and how the border between her persona as a translator and as a writer is porous. They are a more obvious form of response to translating a writer than the responses I analysed in the earlier chapters. They are also less combative: they are more like mini-homages to Flaubert than the sorts of deconstructions or rewritings of Proust, Blanchot and Leiris that I have been looking at. Yet they are also less appropriative than other translational works by Davis, which I turn to in the next two chapters.

Notes

1. Her rewriting of *Bob, Son of Battle* (Ollivant 2014) might also be considered an interlingual translation or a translation from English dialect. She has also been publishing translations of very short stories by the Dutch writer A. L. Snijders in periodicals (see Duijsens 2014).
2. This is available in the Library of Congress. Apter (2013: 267) reports that Sherwood was the pen name of John Stirling; this is confirmed by the Library of Congress which combines both Stirling and Sherwood in its catalogue. Barnes (2010) states that the first published translation was Eleanor Marx-Aveling's translation of 1886, but this is the first British publication.
3. In this way, it is similar to Jean Renoir's *La Régle du jeu* (1939) – Renoir's use of the title precedes Leiris' – which was first seen as a realist film but which came to be understood as having more modernist elements, especially in terms of sound design (Wollen 2002: 151–62.)

4. Davis (2011b: 73) attributes the first translation to Eleanor Marx-Aveling.
5. My understanding of style is therefore more historical and intertextual, if not Bakhtinian (see Bakhtin 1981), than the version of style as choice and effect described by Jean Boase-Beier (2015: 16–20).
6. This is how Borges conceptualises the differences in the identical texts by Cervantes and Pierre Menard in his story 'Pierre Menard, autor del Quijote' (Borges 1997: 41–55) – they are separated in time and as such their identical sentences have different meanings. For the phrase 'la verdad, cuya madre es la historia' ('truth, whose mother is history'), the narrator says that, in the case of Cervantes, this is just 'un mero elogio de la historia' ('mere praise of history'; Borges 1997: 53). When reading Menard, however, the idea is 'asombrosa' ('astonishing'): 'La verdad histórica, para él, no es lo que sucedió: es lo que juzgamos que sucedió' ('Historical truth, for him, isn't what happened; it's what we judge to have happened'; ibid.). The narrator is reading the texts through their contemporary intellectual climates, which affects how they are interpreted. A similar process takes place in Buchloch's (2003) reading of two similar, monochromatic triptychs by Rodchenko and Klein respectively: Buchloch argues that difference in meaning between them is based on their different historical moments and the different audience reactions to them.
7. As we saw in the earlier chapter on Davis and Proust, the 'retranslation hypothesis' (Williams and Chesterman 2002: 72) builds on a similar line of argument. Sharon Deane-Cox's (2014) recent work, which draws on British publications of *Madame Bovary* as one of its case studies, has questioned this hypothesis, as once there are multiple retranslations then the degree of formal similarity varies and there are many different approaches to the source text.
8. Deane-Cox (2011) gives quite detailed information about when Marx-Aveling's translation was republished.
9. Flaubert's drafts are available at <http://www.bovary.fr> (last accessed 2 April 2015).
10. I am using the British edition of the text for my close readings, which was published one year after the American edition, hence it is Flaubert 2011a rather than Flaubert 2010.
11. Davis' notes are not marked in the text itself by numbers. They are given at the end of the novel with page numbers and then the relevant term in bold. This means that a reader need not refer to them if they do not want to, but if there is a word or expression that needs further explanation, they can look in the notes to see if it is included. The notes and critical apparatus are not therefore intrusive, as they might be in a scholarly edition.
12. Sols is a synonym for sous, of which there were twenty in the old French *livre* currency.
13. Linda Hutcheon makes a similar argument about adaptations: 'we experience adaptations (*as adaptations*) as palimpsests through our memory of other works that resonate through repetition with variation' (Hutcheon 2006: 8; original emphasis). The variations in Davis' stories from Flaubert and Duchamp's readymades are much more minor than might be expected in most forms of adaptation.
14. The French reads: 'Le gardien, qui est en même temps fossoyeur et bedeau

à l'église (tirant ainsi des cadavres de la paroisse un double bénéfice), a profité du terrain vide pour y semer des pommes de terre. D'année en année, cependant, son petit champ se retrecit, et, lorsqu'il survient une épidémie, il ne sait pas s'il doit se réjouir des décès ou s'affliger des sépultures' (Flaubert 2001: 128).

Chapter 6

Marie Curie and Parody

Lydia Davis' story 'Marie Curie, So Honorable Woman' problematises the border between translation and other forms of intertextual writing, especially parody, and therefore also the border between author and translator in Davis' *œuvre*.[1] As we saw, this border was already questioned by Davis' use of extracts from her translation of Proust in one of her stories (Chapter 4) and by her use of translations from Flaubert's letters as her stories from Flaubert (Chapter 5). 'Marie Curie, So Honorable Woman' (Davis 2001: 99–119) goes one step further. Davis' story is constructed through translation but at the same time is not a translation. This chapter explores how it plays with and disrupts the boundaries between translation and other intertextual forms of writing, ultimately questioning the idea of representation inherent in these practices.

Intertextual writing and translation both produce a target text from a source text, taking material and manipulating it in order to create a new work. This similarity has been explored by several theorists in the past.[2] However, other forms of intertextual creation do not have such a strong 'relation norm' (Chesterman 1997: 69–70) as translations, which can be considered to provide 'full-scale representations' (Hermans 1998: 17) of their source texts. This has been seen in preceding chapters where Davis' translations are recognised as 'full-scale representations' of their source texts. These expectations of translation operate at the base of what Cecilia Alvstad (2014) calls the 'translation pact', where the implied author of the translation does not include the translator. There is more expectation that there will be alteration and manipulation in adaptation (Hutcheon 2006: 7) and indeed the adaptor will often be understood to have more of an authorial role.[3]

This chapter begins by analysing how 'Marie Curie, So Honorable Woman' is presented as a text, drawing on its publication history and the introduction provided with its original magazine publication (Davis

2000a, 2000b) which highlights its intertextual nature. The story is then compared with other stories by Davis that are based on quotation from another writer's work, such as 'Extracts from a Life' (Davis 1986: 57–61) and 'Lord Royston's Tour' (Davis 1997a: 84–114). These stories resemble translations in their relation to a source text. 'Marie Curie, So Honorable Woman' differs from the other stories as it is constructed from translated elements, which I analyse in the next section. Yet the text is not strictly a translation, as it abridges the text and purposely mistranslates terms. In the section 'Parody and Translation', I discuss how it might be better described as a parody, drawing on legal definitions and Linda Hutcheon's theory of parody.

The Presentation of 'Marie Curie, So Honorable Woman'

Lydia Davis' story 'Marie Curie, So Honorable Woman' does not declare itself to be either a translation or a derivative work in the general sense. There is no source text cited in its publication history in book form (in Davis 2001, 2002c and 2009) or in its original publication in *McSweeney's Quarterly Concern* [hereafter *McSweeney's*] (Davis 2000a). The original publication was accompanied by an exchange of letters between the editors of *McSweeney's* and Davis (Davis 2000b), where Davis alluded to a biography of Marie Curie that she once translated. Although Davis does not explicitly identify the text in the letters, she is referring to Giroud's *Une femme honorable* (1981), which Davis published a translation of, entitled *Marie Curie: A Life*, in 1986. If the work is derivative, in the legal sense of being an adaptation according to British law (Copyright, Designs and Patents Act 1988 (ch. 48), Section 21(3)(a)(i)) or a derivative work according to American law (17 USCode Section 101), then it would require some sort of acknowledgement.[4] Davis' lack of acknowledgement of a source text makes the status of the story ambiguous. In this section, I will demonstrate how paratextual material accompanying its first publication reduces that ambiguity and focuses readers on the intertextual elements of the story.

Reading the story, it is difficult to divine that there is an intertextual relationship with Giroud's biography. 'Marie Curie, So Honorable Woman' is made up of thirty-nine short sections, ranging from one line to around a page. There is a clear narrative, albeit a compressed one: the text tells the story of Marie Curie's life, from birth to death. The story is marked stylistically by a certain 'awkward English', as Davis (2000b: 27) describes it. There are, for example, unidiomatic constructions, such as 'In two months she will be twenty four years'. There is even the incorrect use of gendered pronouns, such as 'It is a daughter of the earth'. The English throughout the text is also marked by non-standard collocations, such as 'brief angers' (all these examples from Davis 2001: 100).

The editors of *McSweeney's* felt the English to be uncomfortably strange. In response to it, they initiated the letter exchange that functions as a preface to the magazine's publication of 'Marie Curie' with the following letter:

> Dear Ms. Davis,
>   We just read the first few sections of the Madame Curie piece and we think we should stop. We think we first need to read an introduction, of your devising, explaining the process by which you've created this. We are, because we are stupid, still unsure about the piece's provenance—who wrote, who translated, are you abridging, etc. (Davis 2000b: 27)

The awkwardness of the English in 'Marie Curie' is integral to the story, which Davis had to explain to the publishers of what was considered an avant-garde journal[5] in order for the story to be accepted. Davis provided the editors of *McSweeney's* with an explanation of the provenance of the text:

> I once had to translate a biography of Marie Curie (I've often had to accept jobs I didn't like) that was written in a rather 'cute' style that is not uncommon in some permutation in certain French writers/publications. As usual, though I was bored and irked by the job, I was also amused by the style and its possibilities, so after a while, I began copying out into awkward English the more absurd sequences or sentences. I always envisaged using bits like these to compose a shortened 'life' of Marie Curie in awkward translationese. (Davis 2000b: 27)

Here Davis provides a full explanation of the composition of the text, along with her reasons. She made an even clearer statement later in the exchange: 'this Marie Curie piece is my abbreviated and deliberately awkward and literal translation of excerpts of a real book by a real French author' (ibid.). Davis therefore suggests her story is a form of appropriation which was motivated by seeing the potential for text to be something other than it was.

Davis eventually agreed that some sort of introduction to the text might be necessary, but voiced concern: 'The trouble is, if there is an intro or even an afterword, the piece is radically changed: it is reduced to an exercise, something more mechanical than I want it to be' (2000b: 28). With a clear introduction explaining the mechanics of the piece, the story becomes reduced to nothing more than an example, appearing arbitrary and losing its narrative impact. The solution chosen by

McSweeney's and Davis was to create a more subtle form of introduction: the exchange of letters becomes the introduction to the piece, although separated from it by over 100 pages. It is quite possible that readers would not see the introduction, or if they did, they might choose not to read it. The story is left to stand alone, but there is an explanation available should one be necessary and should the reader take the initiative to find it. The exchange of letters is not reproduced in any of the book publications of the story, suggesting that Davis later felt an introduction unnecessary. With no introduction, readers are left with only the title as a clue to the source of the story, which obscures its status as an intertextual work.

The other concession Davis made to the editors of *McSweeney's* was to change the title of the piece to 'Translation Exercise #1: Marie Curie, Honorable Woman'. On the first page of the story (Davis 2000a: 139), the title appeared like this, although in a different font, and with the subtitle much bigger than the title:

TRANSLATION EXERCISE #1:

MARIE CURIE,
HONORABLE WOMAN

The normal title/subtitle hierarchy is reversed: the subtitle appears larger and thus more important than the actual title, which is now the significantly smaller 'Translation Exercise #1'. Although the text presents itself as some form of translation, there is no reason to assume that it is, bearing in mind that it is fiction and its title may not reflect its origins. Given its context, the text could be a pastiche of the 'awkward English' of 'translationese' (in other words, English which sounds as if it is translated word for word from another language without regard for English norms of style or expression).

The title 'Translation Exercise #1' encourages readers to approach the style of the text with suspicion: it becomes seen as a rhetorical embellishment, rather than central to the text. By reverting to the original, non-explanatory title in the book publications, Davis indicates that the style is central to her conception of the story. Indeed, in the correspondence with the editors of *McSweeney's* she notes that what 'interests [her] about this [piece] is the two forms of awkward English . . . combined with what is an interesting and moving life story' (Davis 2000b: 27). The style for Davis is therefore counterbalanced with the narrative; a reasonably clear and emotionally striking story is cloaked in an awkward narration. Davis is interested not only in formal experimentation but also in some sort of narrative or emotional charge. As I mentioned in Chapter 3, Marjorie Perloff has noted how Davis' fiction reconnects words and their referents (Perloff 1989: 21). Stories such as 'Letter to A Funeral Parlor' (Davis 2001: 74–5) and 'Grammar Questions' (Davis 2007a: 27–9) develop around language structures but tell stories of mourning. In the case of 'Marie Curie, So Honorable Woman', this emotional element appears in the real Marie Curie's story, which is a story of overcoming adversity and losing loved ones. By removing the introduction and the title 'Translation Exercise #1' in the book publications, Davis indicates that she wants readers to pay attention to the story rather than the process of its creation.

Davis' Abridged Biographies

More is at stake here than a simple use of Giroud's biography as a source for a story, especially considering how Davis states that it originated as translations of extracts of the biography. Davis has written more stories which are abridgements of other texts, including 'Extracts from a Life' (Davis 1986: 57–61), based on Shinichi Suzuki's autobiography *Nurtured by Love* (1969), 'Lord Royston's Tour' (Davis 1997a: 84–114), which draws on the Reverend Henry Pepys' memoirs of Lord Royston (Royston 1838), and 'Our Village' (Davis 2013), based on Sidney Brooks' *Our Village* (1995). All three of these stories acknowledge their sources in their respective volumes, despite that not being strictly necessary for 'Lord Royston's Tour', which was based on a work which was in the public domain and so legally required no attribution. The acknowledgement for 'Extracts from a Life' notes that the text is 'used by permission of Exposition Press' (Davis 1986, n.p.): the process of abridgement in this text was thus viewed as creating a derivative work. In this section, I want to consider how these abridgements are similar to translations in their creation of second order texts.

Both 'Extracts from a Life' and 'Lord Royston's Tour' have formal similarities with 'Marie Curie, So Honorable Woman' in addition to their status as abridgements of other texts. All three stories are built around multiple sections which have their own subheadings. In the case of 'Marie Curie, So Honorable Woman', these subheadings are Davis' own. The device of subheadings disappears in the later 'Our Village', which is also the only one to be written in verse. All four stories recount compressed biographies, in the first person for 'Extracts from a Life' and 'Our Village', and in the third person for 'Marie Curie, So Honorable Woman' and 'Lord Royston's Tour'. 'Lord Royston's Tour' is different from the other extract stories as it deals with only a short period of its subject's life, but it resembles them in other respects. The compressed narrative with section titles is a form that Davis uses in some other stories, e.g. 'Mrs. D. and Her Maids' (Davis 2007a: 87–111) or 'What You Learn About Baby' (Davis 2007a: 115–24). The form allows the texts to have narrative development and, at the same time, be discontinuous. The section subheadings have a distancing effect as they are comments on the narrative, but they also act like inter-titles in silent film, providing a summary and introducing the next scene.

Davis' extract stories develop from her sense of the potential in the source texts. Talking to Larry McCaffery about 'Extracts from a Life' and 'Lord Royston's Tour', Davis noted that 'both started with [her] reading something with pure delight and pleasure', and that she saw a potentiality in both: 'this other text [that] seemed to be there *in potential* – there was something a great deal more interesting in [them] than what [she] was reading, the same language with a different shape and intention' (McCaffery 1996: 74; original emphasis). The motivation for the two earlier excerpt texts is not so different from the motivation for 'Marie Curie, So Honorable Woman', which also stems from an interest in the 'style and its possibilities' (Davis 2000b: 27). The same features appear in 'Our Village' and are, in fact, highlighted by the use of verse. Each text, then, works through a recontextualisation of the narrative elements: each one uses its source text as raw material and Davis sculpts her story from the block of the other text. In 'Marie Curie, So Honorable Woman' there is a second process which is the translation of the source text into English, but the selection and editing is similar to that used for 'Extracts from a Life', 'Lord Royston's Tour' and 'Our Village'.

McCaffery suggested to Davis that the process of abridgement and selection in these stories 'shares a lot with translation'. While Davis agreed, she also saw a difference: 'it's obviously more of a transformation. But it must be related' (McCaffery 1996: 74). Both processes entail reworking a source text into a target text which is distinct from its source but bears traces of its origin. There is a recontextualisation of the material, leading to a change in meaning, although how this change is effected is different between translation and abridgement: translation recontextualises the whole text into a different cultural and linguistic context, while abridgement takes the material out of its original context and places it into a new, reduced context without changing the language. The products of both processes can thus be read doubly: (1) as independent texts, without reference to their source texts or (2) as a reworked form of their source texts. This doubleness was operative in Davis' 'Ten stories from Flaubert', discussed in Chapter 5. How the texts are read depends on readers' previous knowledge of the texts in question. In the case of 'Lord Royston's Tour' and 'Marie Curie, So Honorable Woman', only very erudite readers may know the original, as neither Pepys' memoir nor Davis' translation of *Une femme honorable* was reprinted.[6] In the case of 'Our Village', the source text was written by a relative and held as a manuscript by her father before finally being transcribed and published by the Historical Society in 1995, so it is very unlikely that readers will have encountered the source text. *Nurtured by love*, the source text for 'Extracts from a Life', was more popular, going through at least eighteen printings, but may still be unknown to Davis' readers. As such, these stories would be read in the context of Davis' work. Translations in general, on the other hand, are more likely be read in the context of the works by the writer of the source text: Davis' translation of *The Way by Swann's*, for example, is more likely to be read in the context of Proust's work than as a piece of writing by Davis.

Translation in 'Marie Curie, So Honorable Woman'

Despite the possibility of reading the text as autonomous, as Davis' lack of paratexts in the book publications suggests, 'Marie Curie, So Honorable Woman' can also be read in relation to a source text. In this section, I argue that it contains (mis)translations from Giroud's *Une femme honorable* (1981) which connect it to its source, but at the same time this deliberate strategy of mistranslation makes it something other than a translation.

If an extract from 'Marie Curie, So Honorable Woman' is read alongside the corresponding text from *Une femme honorable*, the similarity between the two texts becomes quite clear:

> Pierre Curie has come on stage in Marie's life at the precise moment at which it was suitable that he should appear.
> The year 1894 has begun. Marie is assured of obtaining her license in July. She is beginning to look beyond, she is more available, and the spring is beautiful. Pierre is already captive to this singular blonde person. (Davis 2001: 103)

> Pierre Curie est entré en scène dans l'existence de Marie au moment précis où il convenait qu'il apparût.
> L'année 1894 est entamée. Marie est assurée d'obtenir sa licence en juillet. Elle commence à regarder au-delà, elle est plus disponible, et le printemps est beau. (Giroud 1981: 64)
> Pierre Curie est déjà captif de cette singulière petite personne blonde. (Giroud 1981: 66)

Davis' text appears to be an almost word-for-word translation of the French. Davis does make minor adjustments, such as translating 'existence' as 'life' (rather than its cognate term) and moving adjectives before nouns. There are, however, elements in the English which are markedly unidiomatic or non-standard. Davis retains the perfect tense of the first sentence, although in standard English this would probably be rendered as a past simple, referring as it does to an event in the distant past. The French text uses the present perfect tense to imitate speech (as spoken French avoids the *passé simple*) in an attempt to make the register less formal. Conversely, the present perfect tense in English makes the text seem awkward and unidiomatic as it is incorrectly used. Davis also uses cognate words for French terms, which leads to phrases in the story being incomprehensible: Marie's licence, for instance, is not a licence but a bachelor's degree. The metaphor of Pierre being a captive seems less marked in French than in English, where the more common expression would be the phrase 'captivated by', which appears forty-nine times in the British National Corpus, rather than the phrase 'captive to', which only appears four times. The sense of these phrases is also different: 'captivated by' suggests being deeply interested in something, whereas 'captive to' suggests a relation that is much more negative.

Davis' story can also be seen to abridge the source text. In the above example, the sentence about Pierre Curie is found two pages later in the source text than the first part of the paragraph. Davis omitted much of the material, as the story is around twenty pages in length and the biography is around 360 pages. Lawrence Venuti (1998: 64) notes that if a translation omits or alters a significant amount of material from the source text, it might not be legally regarded as a translation but rather as an adaptation or some other derivative work. As Davis' story is a heavily abridged version of Giroud's biography, it cannot legally be considered a translation. It is therefore another form of derivative writing, which one would expect to be accompanied by an acknowledgement of its source.

Davis' full translation of *Une femme honorable* fulfils the expectations of a professional translation much more than the story does. It does not abridge material in the same way. A reading of the text which corresponds to the above example also shows that Davis followed the norms of standard English usage:

> Pierre Curie entered Marie's life at just the right time.
> The year 1894 was nearly half over. Marie was sure of receiving her degree in July. She was beginning to look ahead, she had more time on her hands, and the spring was beautiful.
> . . .

Pierre Curie was already captivated by the unusual little blonde woman. (Giroud 1986: 48–9)

Davis translates using more colloquial and idiomatic expressions than she uses in her story. Rather than translating 'licence' with its cognate 'licence', she uses the equivalent 'degree'. She avoids the marked expression 'is captive to' by using the more idiomatic 'captivated by'. It is clear, then, that Davis' translation in 'Marie Curie, So Honorable Woman' is doing something other than offering an appropriate English rendering of the text.

The prior existence of a full translation suggests a very different aim to the two texts. It could be argued that because 'Marie Curie, So Honorable Woman' does not repeat the exact wording of either *Une femme honorable* or *Marie Curie: A Life* it is a new piece of writing. In copyright law, only the way a text is expressed can be copyrighted, not the ideas in the text (Goldstein 2001: 184–5). Siva Vaidhyanathan (2001: 105–12) reports that a significant precedent for reading the difference between expression and ideas in copyright law is the case *Sheldon* v. *Metro-Goldwyn* (1934). Learned Hand, the judge in the Second Circuit Court of Appeals in New York, gave his opinion when the case was appealed in 1936 that, when judging the similarity of two works, one must pay attention to the 'very web of the author's expression' (cited in Vaidhyanathan 2001: 109). This 'web of expression' Hand clarified by suggesting different elements that combine to make up the work: 'plot, character, means of revelation, setting, themes' (ibid.). In relation to these categories, Davis' story is in many ways significantly similar to Giroud's biography: it contains the same characters, the same plot, the same setting and the same themes. The main difference is the way in which Davis' story presents the material: it is compressed into a considerably shorter frame and it is written in a style which is marked by the fact that it is not idiomatic and seems, in many ways, to be a pastiche of bad writing. It should be clear that Davis' story 'Marie Curie, So Honorable Woman' is not supposed to provide a full biography of Marie Curie in the same way as *Une femme honorable* and *Marie Curie: A Life* do; rather, it appears to be a parody or critique of certain forms of writing. This difference in aim, intent and market clearly separates the two works. It could still be argued that Davis' story is derivative of Giroud's book, forming an adaptation or appropriation of it.

Parody and Translation

'Marie Curie, So Honorable Woman' is different from Davis' other excerpt stories as it does not acknowledge a source text. Such an acknowledgement shows that the stories can legally be regarded as derivative. But why does this story not do so? If 'Marie Curie, So Honorable Woman' was regarded as a parody, then, according to Paul Goldstein (2001: 300), it would be exempt from the usual requirements for authorisation. In this section, I want to argue that the story may legally be a parody, but in literary terms its status is less clear. It is first necessary to review what is meant by parody in the law and in literary theory.

Parody is one of the extensions of the fair-use rule that allows people to copy copyrighted works for certain purposes, such as personal study, scholarship or some educational uses. As Goldstein notes, 'though nowhere expressly exonerated in the Berne text, [parody] is widely accepted across the Berne Union as a permitted use, presumably on the ground that it meets Article 9(2)'s standards' (2001: 300). Article 9(2) protects the idea of fair use:

> It shall be a matter for legislation in the countries of the [Berne] Union to permit the reproduction of such works in certain special cases, provided that such reproduction does not conflict with a normal exploitation of the work and does not unreasonably prejudice the legitimate interests of the author. (Berne Convention, Paris Text 1971, Article 9(2))

The convention is vague here: it does not specify what these 'certain special cases' might be and each individual country can interpret the phrase differently. In the UK, the Copyrights, Designs and Patents Act 1988 explicitly states what the law understands as permitted uses of copyrighted material (Sections 28–76). US law also makes clear what is to be understood by 'fair use' (17 US Code Section 107). Parody is not explicitly mentioned in either country's law.

Goldstein suggests that all parodies *must* identify their source text:

> In common law countries such as the United Kingdom and Canada, parody may be assimilated to the fair dealing exemption for the purpose of criticism so long as the parody meets the statutory requirement of sufficiently identifying the original work and its author. (Goldstein 2001: 301)

From a literary theoretical perspective, on the other hand, Linda Hutcheon argues that parodies *do not* normally announce their source text: 'Like parodies, adaptations have an overt and defining relationship to prior texts, usually revealingly called "sources." *Unlike parodies*, however, adaptations normally announce this relationship' (Hutcheon 2006: 3; my emphasis). Parodies may still overtly suggest to the audience that there is a source text, even an identifiable one. For example, the film *Shaun of the Dead* (dir. Wright, 2004) parodies the earlier *Dawn of the Dead* (dir. Romero, 1978), but does not announce its affiliation in any other way than by the rhyme in the title: there is no explicit recognition of the earlier text as a source. Many European nations, according to Goldstein (2001: 300), allow parodies so long as they do not present a direct conflict with the original work's sales or marketability, i.e. they '[do] not conflict with a normal exploitation of the work and [do] not unreasonably prejudice the legitimate interests of the author' in the words of the Berne Convention. As noted earlier, 'Marie Curie, So Honorable Woman' is a very different work to Giroud's *Une femme honorable*. It is therefore unlikely that the story would be confused with the biography and, consequently, would not affect its sales or reputation.

The law does not explicitly define parody as a concept, in a similar way to how it does not define translation. The landmark parody case in American law is *Campbell* v. *Acuff-Rose Music, Inc* (1994), where the US Supreme Court offered the following rule of thumb for deciding if a work is a parody: 'whether a parodic character may reasonably be perceived' (cited in Goldstein 2001: 301). In previous musical parody cases, according to Vaidhyanathan (2001: 146–7), courts decided whether or not a song was parodic by asking if it criticised or satirised the original song. Justice David Souter, the US Supreme Court judge in the case of *Campbell* v. *Acuff-Rose Music, Inc*, decided that Two Live Crew's song did criticise Roy Orbison's song (ibid. 146–8). Parody is therefore legally viewed as a form of criticism and can be accepted as a form of fair use according to US law.

One of the defining characteristics of parody, then, is a critical distance from the source text. Indeed, parody is generally viewed as having 'a humorous or satirical purpose' (Wales 2001: 286) which would demonstrate a critical distance from the text parodied. Hutcheon criticises the narrow range of intent normally accepted for parody in her *Theory of Parody*. Her definition offers a similar view to the legal reading of parody as a form of criticism: 'Parody is . . . repetition with critical distance, which marks difference rather than similarity' (Hutcheon 1985: 6). This critical distance is common to the theorist's and the jurors' definitions. Without it, the parody is no longer a parody, but some other form of specific intertextual relationship, for example plagiarism, adaptation or translation. Hutcheon elsewhere establishes a distinction between parody and adaptation by calling adaptation 'repetition without replication' (Hutcheon 2006: 7): 'critical distance' is not neces-sarily part of adaptation (as we saw in Davis' stories from Flaubert in Chapter 5, which were adaptations that did not criticise their source).

For Davis' 'Marie Curie, So Honorable Woman' to be a parody of *Une femme honorable* there should be some sort of criticism apparent of that text. In its magazine publication, a critical reading is facilitated by the introduction in the letters pages. In the book publications, however, the text appears as a narrative piece, without commentary or explication. Therefore there must be something within the text itself that encourages readers to interpret the text as a parody.

The translation in 'Marie Curie, So Honorable Woman' suggests the parodic intent of the story, as it is hyperbolic. As I discussed earlier, the text uses cognate words (so-called 'false friends') and non-standard syntax, emphasising the influence on its structures from the source text.[7] The title itself, 'Marie Curie, So Honorable Woman', already demonstrates that there is a tendency in the text to use non-standard English. If it is compared with the title of Giroud's biography, *Une femme honorable*, an element of distortion is already present: the *so* of 'So Honorable Woman'. This *so* is not present in the title of the version published in *McSweeney's*, 'Translation Exercise #1: Marie Curie, Honorable Woman' (Davis 2000a). The *so*, therefore, can be read as subtly announcing the parodic intent of the piece. As an intensifier, it pushes the text towards hyperbole, which is also what much of Davis' translation strategies do in the story.

'Marie Curie, So Honorable Woman' also becomes parody in its selec-tion of material. Rather than fairly representing Giroud's book, Davis selects only those bits which appear awkward or amusing to English lan-guage readers. Davis' introduction supports this reading, as she remarks that she copied out 'into awkward English the *more absurd* sequences or sentences' (Davis 2000b: 27; my emphasis).[8] The following example shows a moment of high pathos in the text, but the serious nature of the narrative events is undermined due to the way it mixes the trivial and the profound:

> The body is removed to a police station. An officer picks up his telephone. But Pierre Curie no longer has ears to be annoyed that he belongs, in death as in life, to the number of those for whom one disturbs the Minister of the Interior. (Davis 2001: 108)

The small details seem incongruous: why is it important that an officer picks up his telephone? Pierre's humility is described here, but the expression 'no longer has ears' is not common in English, as there is no record of it in the British National Corpus, which contains a sampling of over 100 million words. The strangeness it represents derails the reader's concentration. There are two records in the British National Corpus for 'in death as in life', but it appears uncommon and possibly too formal for the context. The French text that this extract is based on shows that 'in death as in life' is another example where Davis has translated in a hyperbolic manner:

> Et il [le commissaire] prend son téléphone. Mais Pierre Curie n'a plus d'oreilles pour s'agacer d'appartenir, même dans la mort, au nombre de ceux pour qui l'on dérange le ministre de l'Intérieur. (Giroud 1981: 181)

> And he [the commissioner] picks up his phone. But Pierre Curie can no longer hear and get annoyed that, even in death, he is someone for whom the Minister of the Interior can be disturbed. (my translation)

Here the expression is 'même dans la mort', which could be translated as 'even in death'. There is, therefore, an element of caricature in the story. In addition to this, Davis has added the detail of Pierre's being moved to the police station: in the French text he is still lying dead in the street. The removal of any other context and the cumulative effect of so much 'awkward English' forces readers to pay attention to the style, especially how it seems inappropriate, in English at least, to the narrative it is telling.

So it seems that 'Marie Curie, So Honorable Woman' could be considered a parody in the legal sense: it demonstrates a critical distance to the source text and at the same time represents no threat to a 'normal exploitation of the work and does not unreasonably prejudice the legitimate interests of the author' (Berne Convention, Paris Text 1971, Article 9(2)), as it in no way tries to compete with Giroud's text as an authoritative (if somewhat *sui generis*) biography of Marie Curie. This would account for the lack of acknowledgement in book form, as acknowledgement would not strictly be necessary. The text still uses translation as means of composition, but cannot strictly be considered a translation due to its abridged form and its tendency to exaggerate the interference from the source.

In artistic terms, the status of the text as a parody is less certain. Hutcheon stresses how parody relies on the reader's recognition of the parodic text as parodic, which entails their knowledge of the text being parodied:

> When we speak of parody, we do not just mean two texts that interrelate in a certain way. We also imply an intention to parody another work . . . and both a recognition of that intent and our ability to find and interpret the backgrounded text in its relation to the parody. (Hutcheon 1985: 22)

For Hutcheon, the reader should have access to the source text and be familiar with it to be capable of seeing how the parodic text is critically distanced from it. Davis' 'Marie Curie, So Honorable Woman' is a parody of a biography in a different language which is nowhere referred to by name. For the reader to recognise it as a parody, they must find the French text and compare it with Davis' story. Monolingual English readers would not be able to complete this exercise and so for them 'Marie Curie, So Honorable Woman' cannot be said to be a parody of Giroud's *Une femme honorable* in Hutcheon's sense.

The status of Davis' story is problematic. It could legally be considered a parody, but it does not make clear its relationship with its little-known source text. As such, it can be seen to produce a text that is double coded – both independent and referring to another text – but where the source side is barred. Readers only have access to the target text, unless they find out the provenance of the text and can read it in French.

A better description of Davis' story is an appropriation of Giroud's text. Appropriations, according to Julie Sanders (2006: 26), do not always explicitly acknowledge their sources. She argues that appropriations in literature often stem from a 'political or ethical commitment' (ibid.: 2) on the part of their creator. Sanders can be read as suggesting that appropriations should be judged on their capacity to fulfil that commitment. But what sort of ethical or political commitment is being played out in this appropriation?

As I have already argued, the presentation of Davis' story in its book publications as 'Marie Curie, So Honorable Woman' draws attention away from the intertextual origin of the story to focus on the subject of Marie Curie's life. However, readers cannot fail to notice the style of the text, which is marked as awkward and unidiomatic. Readers are therefore guided to question how style affects representation.

The story can be read as asking readers to reconsider the framework of what Andrew Chesterman has called, in relation to translation, an 'ethics of representation' (Chesterman 2001: 139–40). This approach suggests that translations should give a fair representation of their source texts. More widely, it suggests that texts should fairly represent their subjects, be they human or non-human. 'Marie Curie, So Honorable Woman' shows how style affects representation: the story it tells is inseparable from the style in which it is told. Both Giroud and Davis present different interpretations of Marie Curie's life story. 'Marie Curie, So Honorable Woman' highlights how their representations of that life story always show evidence of their interpretations. The text demonstrates, in its very construction, that any representation is always a form of interpretation. In a similar way, as Hermans (2007:

27–51) among others has shown, translations always contain traces of their translator's interpretive choices. The reference to translation in the story's title when it was published in *McSweeney's* highlights its criticism of the idea of translation as a fair representation. Davis' own appropriation of Giroud's text in 'Marie Curie, So Honorable Woman' questions further this 'ethics of representation'. The story does not fairly represent its source text, but it does not intend to do so either. As a parody, it intends to criticise the source text. It never hides that it is an interpretation and does not fulfil the criteria that are expected of translations, despite containing translations. The story does not follow an 'ethics of representation'. Instead, it brings into question those very ethics.

Davis' story is an appropriation of another text which criticises not only that text but wider cultural assumptions. Davis' story questions the reader's understanding and expectations in relation to (1) representation, (2) translation, (3) parody, (4) the use of intertextuality, (5) the correct use of the English language, among other things. The story unsettles readers rather than comforts them, presenting a challenge to accepted ideas. It proposes a hybrid form that mixes translation, parody and abridgement. Importantly, this hybrid form brings together Davis' work as a translator and her work as a writer in a yet more complex way than even her stories from Flaubert, which retained a paratextual reminder of their origin. Here the text stands alone. It is presented as a story by Lydia Davis, without any link to another text. Yet at the same time it does have a translational origin and a traceable source text. Translation, albeit in a non-standard form, becomes central to the process of writing. In the next chapter, I turn to other works by Davis which similarly break down the boundaries between original and derivative writing by using the work of other authors.

Notes

1. An earlier version of this chapter was published as 'At the Borders Between Translation and Parody: Lydia Davis's Story about Marie Curie' in *TTR*, 25:2 (2012), 167–91.
2. Gérard Genette's survey of intertextual writing, *Palimpsestes*, argues that translation is a form of transposition (Genette 1992: 293–300). Other theorists, including Georges Bastin (1998) and Linda Hutcheon (2006: 171), have discussed how translation can be placed in the wider field of adaptation. Richard Dyer (2007: 34) even includes translation in his study of pastiche, as he argues that it is a form of acknowledged imitation. As John Milton and Marie-Hélène C. Torres (2003: 14) point out, the border

between translation, adaptation and other forms of intertextual production is not fixed. Milton (2009) has also suggested ways in which adaptation studies and translation studies address similar concerns.

3. Thomas Leitch (2007: 236–57) points out how, in film adaptation, the director's role as author may be contested by the various claimants to authorship. While this refers to film, in literary adaptation there are still (at least) two authorial figures involved and their positions as authors of the adapted text are in competition.

4. While I refer to copyright law in my analysis of Davis' story, this chapter should by no means be read as actually questioning the legal status of the text.

5. Albeit one which was planning to 'rush headlong into the *World of Normaler* [*sic*] *Fiction*' (*McSweeney's* 2000: n.p.; original emphasis).

6. Both only have records for their first editions in COPAC, a catalogue of British academic libraries' holdings, which includes the holdings of the British Library, itself a copyright repository.

7. It shows, in other words, what Gideon Toury has termed '*negative transfer*' (Toury 1995: 275; original emphasis).

8. In conversation with Larry McCaffery, Davis also mentions writing down 'an absurdly accurate translation of a sentence that was already sentimental and stupid' (McCaffery 1996: 75).

Chapter 7

Translation as Composition

As Davis' responses to her translated texts have shown, there is a porous border between authorship and translation in her work, with connections appearing between her translations and her writing. Davis goes further in some of her stories: her 'Stories from Flaubert' and 'Marie Curie, So Honorable Woman' use translation as a form of composition. This chapter focuses on other instances in Davis' stories where she has used a discernible source text as a basis for her own work. 'The Walk' (Davis 2007a: 72–82), for example, cites different translations from Proust's *Du côté de chez Swann* to demonstrate different characters' perceptions of an event, while 'Kafka Cooks Dinner' (Davis 2007a: 9–18) is a pastiche of Kafka's style. 'Southward Bound, Reading *Worstward Ho*' (Davis 2007a: 68–71) combines citation and pastiche in a way that allows it to comment on Beckett's *Worstward Ho* (1999) while at the same time recounting its own narrative. The citational nature of all of these stories means that they recontextualise material from elsewhere, creating moments in the text which are doubly coded, pointing the reader to another text while also forming part of Davis' story. This process is similar to what happens with translations, where the target text is both a new text and a representation of the source text.

This sort of double coding is often associated with postmodern art, which Linda Hutcheon (1988: 4) characterises by its rewriting and revising of past art forms. Certainly, in postmodern American fiction – the literary context for Davis' work – there is much rewriting of other texts. Christian Moraru dedicates his book *Rewriting* (2001) to the rewritings in prose authors such as E. L. Doctorow, Robert Coover, Paul Auster, Kathy Acker and others. In poetry, too, there is no shortage of writers using elements of others' work in their own work, as Marjorie Perloff has explored in her *Unoriginal Genius* (2010). But the use of others' texts is not limited to postmodernism, or contemporary literature: Gérard Genette's *Palimpsestes* (1992) covers examples from the ancient

Greeks onward. Davis is not alone or unique in her use of other writers' material as the basis for her own.

Davis' use of intertexuality resembles translation and can, I argue in this chapter, be read as a non-conventional form of translation. The stories that I analyse in the first half of this chapter resemble translation in their use of other texts as sources and references. They differ, crucially, in their status as Davis' stories: they are attributed to Davis, and while they refer to, cite and mimic other writers, they are part of Davis' *œuvre* of stories. They are first read as works by Davis, secondly as intertexts. This is the reverse of translation, which is often read first in the context of the source author, and then, if at all, in the context of the translator (although, as I have been demonstrating throughout the book, there is value in reading translations in this way).

There is a significant parallel between Davis' intertextual stories and her translations. They are two sides of the same coin, offering Davis the chance to write in another's words. The first half of this chapter investigates her use of other writers' texts in her own stories. The result is a similar space to translation, but one that has been internalised into Davis' work. The concepts of collage and montage, with the recontextualisation inherent in these practices, provide a framework for understanding Davis' intertextual stories. The distinction between her translations and her own stories is problematised here. The second half of the chapter changes tack, questioning the use of translation as a figure that appears in Davis' stories, most importantly 'The Letter' (Davis 1986: 49–56). The stories do not translate another text in the sense of creating an equivalent text in another language, but they present characters translating within the diegetic frame of the story itself. Translation, in these stories, becomes central to Davis' storytelling.

Collage, Quotation and Pastiche

Collage and montage are two practices that use quotation as part of the creative act. Perloff notes in *The Futurist Moment* that collage, as it is currently understood, is very much a product of the early twentieth century, although the idea of sticking different materials together, as the French word *collage* literally means, has been around a lot longer (Perloff 1986: 45–7). Modernist collage is a more specific practice, according to Perloff, which 'always involves the movement of materials from one context to another, even as the original context cannot be erased' (ibid.: 47).

Collage is a familiar feature of modernist and later poetry, which will often quote and incorporate earlier texts. Perloff writes about the collages created by protomodernist and modernist poets such as Apollinaire, William Carlos Williams and T.S. Eliot (ibid.: 72). A more postmodernist work like Ted Berrigan's *Sonnets* (2000), for example, is also created from a collage of his own earlier work, citations, conversations and other textual materials.[1] Collage can be subtler, for example where an artist may use material from somewhere else as an element in their own work, rather than basing the entire work around cutting-and-pasting. Davis uses this more subtle form of collage in her use of quotations in stories such as 'The Walk' and 'Once a Very Stupid Man'.

Davis' use of quotation sometimes borders on montage. Whereas collage produces abstract images, montage generally uses already existent images in combination to create a new figurative image. One of the more famous visual examples is Richard Hamilton's 'Just What Is It that Makes Today's Homes So Modern, So Appealing?' (1956).[2] In this montage, the viewer is presented with an image of a sitting room, with sofas and easy chairs, posters on the walls and a tape player in the bottom centre. The two inhabitants of the room are both pictured in black and white, while the rest of the work is in colour, highlighting the different provenance of the images. The man appears to be a weight-lifter, and is carrying a giant lollipop, while the woman sits on the sofa. Both appear to be naked. The ceiling of the room is a picture of the moon. On the back wall there is a poster, which on further inspection turns out to be the cover of a magazine, *Young Romance*. Hamilton's picture is made from quotations from other works. Hamilton's sources are magazine and advertising images, rather than any prestigious or canonical source. The individual parts of the picture are therefore doubly recontextualised: first into the picture itself, and the representational meaning that it has, and secondly they are placed into a context of 'fine art' rather than popular culture.

A literary montage would have to create a cohesive whole, linked together by narrative or argument. Modern poetry allows for a discontinuity that narrative does not; poetry's lines need not connect to each other in a logical fashion, nor need there be an overall meaning to the poem. There are, however, narrative works that use aspects of other works in a different situation, for example the rewritings of earlier texts analysed by Moraru (2001), or more concretely, a novel like Terry Pratchett's *Lords and Ladies* (1992), where the characters from his Discworld series are involved in the plot of Shakespeare's *A Midsummer Night's Dream*. William Burroughs (1993: 19–21) describes a related practice in his essay 'Les voleurs', where he suggests stealing parts of others' works, from the descriptive passages of Conrad to the 1930s backdrops of Hopper's paintings.[3] In all cases there is less quoted material than in a picture like Hamilton's. Literary montage would tend more to a parodic, adaptive use of its sources rather than the more literal quotation of visual montage.

Davis' 'Marie Curie, So Honorable Woman' (Davis 2001: 99–119; see Chapter 6) could also be considered a montage. It takes material from Giroud's *Une femme honorable* (1981) and recombines it into a new narrative frame. It would be an unusual montage, using only one source and keeping it in roughly the same order, but the principle of recombination of already existent elements is the same. Yet the fact that the material in 'Marie Curie, So Honorable Woman' is translated would alter the profile of that material. The distancing from the source text caused by the process of translation would mean that if 'Marie Curie, So Honorable Woman' was re-imagined as a pictorial montage then instead of using photographs pasted together to create a new image, it would use paintings of photographs, and the paintings would then be pasted together. The quotational origin of the material is obscured. It is also arguable that the actual origin of the material is rendered almost irrelevant by its placing in a figurative image in Hamilton's case or in a narrative text in Davis'.

Yet it is also possible to read the texts in relation to their source texts, as transformational works, as the previous chapter did with 'Marie Curie, So Honorable Woman'. Neither reading, either as original works or as derivative works, can really exclude the other, whose possibility remains as a trace; its absence makes it present. Texts that are built from quotations hinder or make impossible a comprehensive, holistic reading. This type of reading would expect some sort of unity in the text, in the fashion of Cleanth Brooks' 'well wrought urn' (see Brooks 1947). Even poststructuralist writers such as Gilles Deleuze and Félix Guattari (1991: 155) search for a unity to the text, which they say must 'tenir debout tout seul' ('stand up on its own').

A parallel again appears with translation, which produces a text which is intended to be read without access to its source. However, any reading of the translated text is complicated by the absent presence of the source text. The reader can ignore that source text, but as soon as the illusion of wholeness breaks down – the faults and 'discontinuities' of translation that Lawrence Venuti's (1995: 29) symptomatic reading searched for – then the source's spectral presence is felt. Where the collage of 'Marie Curie, So Honorable Woman' differs is its incorporation of that discontinuity into the form of the text itself, by offering a narrative that is interrupted by section titles that also serve to provide a framework which gives the appearance of continuity. Translations and collage forms cannot be reduced to being either original or derivative, as they produce texts that use other texts. Judith Halberstam notes that '[visual collage] references the spaces in between and refuses to respect the boundaries that usually delineate self and other, art object from museum, and the copy from the original' (Halberstam 2011: 136): translation also blurs these boundaries.

The recontextualisation of material need not be as transformative as it is in the case of translation and montage. Citation, while working on a smaller scale, takes elements of one work and places them in another. The cited material, just as in collage, points to another text, but at the same time forms an intrinsic part of the new text where it has been placed. Two stories by Davis use what appear to be long quotations from other texts: 'Once a Very Stupid Man' (Davis 1986: 137–41) quotes from a story from the English translation[4] of Martin Buber's *The Way of Man* (2002, translation first published 1950); the other story is 'The Walk' (Davis 2007a: 72–82), mentioned in Chapter 4, which quotes a passage from Proust's *Du côté de chez Swann* in both Davis' and Scott Montcrieff/Kilmartin's translations. The two stories are similar in their narrative and their use of quoted material; both redeploy the words of others to help show the state of mind of a character in the story.

In 'Once a Very Stupid Man' an unnamed woman is shown to be having difficulty dressing, which reminds her of a story she read on the subway, which she then reads to her male companion before thinking a little further about it. In 'The Walk' an unnamed female translator and an unnamed male critic wander round Oxford, ending up, magically, back at the place where they began, which reminds the woman of the passage in *Swann's Way* where the narrator's father would bring the family back from a long walk, suddenly stopping at a gate, only to demonstrate to the narrator and his mother that it was their house (Proust 1954: I, 114–15). Davis quotes this passage, in the Scott Moncrieff/Kilmartin translation, which she states was the version the critic preferred (Davis 2007a: 77). A second anecdote, this time about a librarian seeming to magically make a building appear also reminds her of the passage, which is then quoted in Davis' version of *The Way by Swann's*.

The announcements on the copyright pages of the books in which the two stories appear are worded differently, reflecting differing relationships with their source texts. In *Varieties of Disturbance* (Davis 2007a), where 'The Walk' first appeared in book form, the excerpts from the translations of Proust are named as 'quotations'. In *Break It Down* (Davis 1986), on the other hand, it states that 'The tale in "Once A Very Stupid Man" is adapted from a traditional Hasidic story recounted in Martin Buber's *The Way of Man*'. This designation suggests a greater distance from the source text than is the case in 'The Walk'. Indeed, there are several layers of disassociation here: the tale is 'adapted' rather than quoted, and the source itself is a retelling of a traditional story. The possibility of quoting a traditional story is questionable: traditional stories exist in no fixed form. The story itself would be in the public domain while Buber's retelling of it is not. Davis' adaptation is really of Buber's retelling, rather than the traditional story.

Adaptation seems too strong a word for the treatment the story receives in 'Once A Very Stupid Man'. It is quoted almost verbatim, and the two texts look like parallel translations. Nothing changes until the third sentence:

> There was once a man who was very stupid. When he got up in the morning it was so hard for him to find his clothes that at night he almost hesitated to go to bed for thinking of the trouble he would have on waking. One evening **he finally made a great effort, took paper and pencil** and as he undressed noted down exactly where he put everything he had on. The next morning, **very** well pleased with himself, he took the slip of paper in his hand and read: 'cap' – there it was, he set it on his head; 'pants' – there they lay, he got into them; and so it went until he was fully dressed. 'That's all very well, but now where am I myself?' he asked **in great consternation**. 'Where in the world **am I**?' He looked and looked, but it was a vain search; he could not find himself. 'And that is how it is with us,' said the rabbi. (Buber 2002: 22–3; **bold** text denotes material not in Davis' version)

> There was once a man who was very stupid. When he got up in the morning it was so hard for him to find his clothes that at night he almost hesitated to go to bed for thinking of the trouble he would have on waking. One evening he **took paper and pencil and with great effort,** as he undressed, noted down exactly where he put everything he had on. The next morning, well pleased with himself, he took the slip of paper in his hand and read: 'cap' – there it was, he set it on his head; 'pants' – there they lay, he got into them; and so it went until he was fully dressed. **But now he was overcome by consternation,** and he said to himself: 'This is all very well, **I have found my clothes and I am dressed,** but where am I myself? Where **am *I*? And** he looked and looked, but it was a vain search; he could not find himself. And this is how it is with us, said the rabbi. (Davis 1986: 138–9; **bold** text denotes material not in Buber's version)

Davis' change of word order in the third sentence (beginning 'One evening . . .') changes the meaning slightly, focusing the great effort on how he noted down the places where his clothes were. Buber's text locates the great effort in the act of noting down where things were, and possibly the process of thinking of this action. The fourth sentence is identical, but the fifth sentence is very different. Davis here stresses the man's consternation and trouble, making him 'overcome' by it. Her interjection in the man's utterance to himself, 'I have found my clothes and I am dressed' makes explicit an implicit process of thought in Buber's text. The man has succeeded in overcoming a practical problem, but has lost track of himself – it is ambiguous whether or not it should be read metaphorically, that is, losing himself in space as well as losing his identity. The stress Davis adds to 'Where am *I*?' highlights his losing a grip on himself, seemingly beginning to panic.

Davis' version of the story, while appearing very similar to the source text, does alter it, focusing on how the man was now, after having solved the material problem of his clothes, upset by the more metaphysical problem of his own position. The man in the story is made to mirror the woman in Davis' story, who is also having difficulty with her identity, as well as not being able to find her clothes. In the context of Buber's work, though, it becomes clear that the story itself is a parable. Before the tale is recounted it is explained, suggesting how the reader should interpret it: 'he must find his own self, not the trivial ego of the egotistic individual, but the deeper self of the person living in a relationship to the world' (Buber 2002: 22). The lost clothes are the outward appearances of the self, but in paying attention to those the very stupid man loses track of his relationship with the world.

Davis' character in 'Once A Very Stupid Man', and to a lesser extent in 'The Walk', is appropriating the quotation as an expression of her own thought. The changes in the Hasidic tale show evidence of the character's preoccupations and her own waning feeling of selfhood – on the next page she calls herself a 'bearded man' (Davis 1986: 140). In a move typical of Davis, the character then wonders about the causality involved: she is unsure if she was reminded of the tale, or if, rather, reading the tale made it possible for her to lose her clothes. In the same way, later in the same paragraph and at the very end of the story, she cannot decide if there is a great noise outside coming in, or if 'something in [her] had gone out into the street to make such a great noise' (Davis 1986: 141). Her sense of self is no longer limited by her body, but she seems different to the man of Buber's story; she is not focusing on her 'trivial ego', but is excessively open to outside influence, to the point that she can no longer distinguish between herself and other. Perloff suggests that the woman and the character in the parable are quite different, as the man sees that identity is spiritual, whereas the woman's 'quite contrary perception [is] that we cannot . . . tell where the "clothes" end and the inner person begins' (Perloff 1989: 212). Both characters can be seen to suffer a breakdown of identity, but the man in the parable loses himself, whereas the female character loses the sense of her own boundaries (just as the quotation problematises the boundaries of the text). While there is a difference here, the two perceptions are still related as perceptions of identity loss.

Other stories by Davis use quotation in a way analogous to how these characters do; the text is appropriated and used for a purpose that fits its new environment. In 'Kafka Cooks Dinner' (Davis 2007a: 9–18), a first person narrator, assumed to be Kafka, describes the anxiety caused by preparing dinner for a certain Milena, who, if the characters are related to their real counterparts, was Kafka's Czech translator. The anxiety is exaggerated by the memory of a dinner prepared for a previous fiancée, Felice.[5] The story feels absurd because Kafka's style, which it pastiches, appears overwrought for the everyday activities it describes: 'What a man! He must have moved mountains! – whereas I did almost nothing but mix the kasha as instructed by Ottla' (Davis 2007a: 16). There is an acknowledgement in *Varieties of Disturbance* that '[s]ome of the material in [the story] was taken from *Letters to Milena* by Franz Kafka' (Davis 2007a: viii), although there is no notification of permission being granted for citation on the copyright page. It is difficult to know from this acknowledgement what that material might be; nor are any quotations clearly marked in the text. There is something unusual in this, as Theo Hermans notes that quotations 'tend to be signalled and bracketed to separate them from the surrounding discourse' (Hermans 2007: 69); this is the case with the citations in 'The Walk' and 'Once A Very Stupid Man'. However, in artistic montage, the signalling tends to be less explicit in form, for example the different colour schemes of pieces in Hamilton's 'Just What Is It that Makes Today's Homes So Modern, So Appealing?' In literary montage there may even be no acknowledgement of sources, as in 'Marie Curie, So Honorable Woman'. Reading Kafka's letters (Kafka 1990) reveals that there are passages which Davis has adapted, often attributing them to another speaker or otherwise disguising them. For example, the image of Kafka floating under a bridge in a boat, of which in the story a friend says 'it was as if Judgment Day had arrived and my coffin had been opened' (Davis 2007a: 13), is a reworking of the story in the letters (Kafka 1990: 16–17) where the comparison is made by an employee in slightly different words. Davis does not quote the anecdote verbatim, but rephrases and recontextualises it, meaning that, for legal purposes, it is not a quotation.

There are statements in the story which are hyperbolic when related to cooking: 'As I plan this meal, I feel like Napoleon would have felt while designing the Russian campaign, if he had known exactly what the outcome would be' (Davis 2007a: 12). In the letters, a similar remark is made about Kafka's travel plans: 'I feel like Napoleon must have felt if, while at the same time he was designing the Russian campaign, he had known exactly what the outcome would be' (Kafka 1990: 24). Similarly, the quote above about moving mountains comes from the reaction to something in Milena's letter (Kafka 1990: 9), and not from Felice's description of Kafka's food, as the story has it (Davis 2007a: 16). The doom-laden tone of such statements fits the popular image of Kafka, influenced by the atmosphere in his novels *The Trial* and *The Castle*, where the characters appear unable to escape their fate.[6] Davis' text plays on the image of Kafka's despair and morbidity, extending it into absurdity by juxtaposing it not with existential problems but with everyday worries. The story begins 'I am filled with despair as the day approaches when my dear Milena will come' (Davis 2007a: 9), a statement that appears overly dramatic – especially when the source of such despair would appear to be the normally pleasant visit of a loved one. The trouble is caused by the choice of what to offer her: the narrator wants to avoid potato salad as it is 'no surprise to her anymore'. The description of his struggle to find a suitable menu is elaborate: 'Now and then I summon all my energy and work at the menu as if I were being forced to hammer a nail into a stone, as if I were the one hammering and also the nail' (ibid.).

The reader is constantly teased throughout this piece by passages that sound like Kafka, but may only be pastiches. Pastiche is deformative: 'it selects, accentuates, exaggerates, concentrates' (Dyer 2007: 56). It plays not with the thing itself, but rather with the stereotyped image of that thing. While 'Kafka Cooks Dinner' does contain reworked quotations from *Letters to Milena*, one of the effects of the pastiche of Kafka's writing style is that the whole text appears as if it could be citation. The text is received as if it were a montage, and the reader cannot, without recourse to the source text, decide what is original to the story and what is taken from the source. Here 'Kafka Cooks Dinner' is different from 'Once A Very Stupid Man' and 'The Walk', which explicitly mark their quotations as quotations, but similar to 'Marie Curie, So Honorable Woman' and the excerpt stories, especially in the way that citations are altered in 'Marie Curie' by translation into English. 'Kafka Cooks Dinner' is received by the reader as if it were made from quotations, although it also contains elements written by Davis.

In the visual arts, there are some works that operate on a similar principle: they appear, on first viewing, to be found objects, but after some study turn out to be fabricated by the artist. An example would be Jeff Koons' *Popeye Series* (2002–ongoing),[7] where what appear to be inflatable swimming pool toys, for example a giant lobster, turn out to be made from aluminium and painted to resemble rubber toys. The 'toys' are placed in positions that would be impossible for rubber shapes to maintain, such as a boat filled with heavy objects and maintaining a rigid shape, or as load-bearing parts of a chain. The viewer's acceptance of the authenticity of the objects is thus challenged by the works, which seem physically impossible. The *Popeye Series* plays with the expectations of the viewer, who has come to accept the use of found objects and other heterogeneous materials in modern art, and so accepts the 'rubber toys' at face value, at least initially.

The reader of 'Kafka Cooks Dinner' also expects a citational work, as the acknowledgements page suggests it might be, and accepts passages that appear Kafka-esque as being citations from Kafka, whether or not they are. Davis, like Koons, is playing with the reader's literary competence and knowledge of the tradition of quotational works – collage, montage, found object – that other of her stories play a part in. 'Kafka Cooks Dinner' appears as an ironic addition, taking part in and at the same time refuting the tradition.

Davis' use of pastiche can be considered, like translation, to set up a correspondence between her work and the work of the author who is the object of the pastiche. It encourages the reader to associate that author with Davis' author-function (Foucault 1994) and to draw comparisons. Davis' *œuvre* is therefore made more porous by her use of pastiche and translation. It is not just made up of her own writing, but of the voices of multiple authors.

This can be seen in her story 'Southward Bound, Reads *Worstward Ho*' (Davis 2007a: 68–71), which also plays with citation and pastiche, combining the two in a text that provides explicit and implicit commentary on its source, Samuel Beckett's *Worstward Ho* (1999, first published 1983). In the story's publication in *Mark Joseph: New and Used* (Joseph and Krukowski 2006: 25–7, 29), the two parts were published separately, although the function of one part as a commentary on the other is still implied by their proximity in position and content.[8] In its book publication, which will be the focus here, the text is split in two by the placement of one part in the position of a series of footnotes to the other, recalling conventions of academic commentary.

Although there are more words in the footnotes, the part of the text that is not in footnotes is typographically identified as the main part. It narrates the tale of a woman reading Beckett's *Worstward Ho* on a bus. It is written in a pastiche of the extremely terse style of Beckett's text:

> In van, heading south, sits on right or west side, sun in through windows from east. Highway crosses and recrosses meandering stream passing now northwest and now northeast under. Reads *Worstward Ho*: On. Say on. Be said on. Somehow on. Till nohow on. Said nohow on. (Davis 2007a: 68)

Davis quotes from Beckett's text throughout both parts of her story, and while the citations are not marked off by quotation marks in the main text, they are clearly identified as citations by being prefaced by the verb 'reads', as in the example above. Passages from Beckett's text are thus incorporated into the pastiche, allowing the reader to see how it differs. Davis' main part is not as severely minimalist as *Worstward Ho*, which tends to more staccato rhythms and shorter sentence structures, for example 'The eyes. Time to try worsen. Somehow try worsen. Unclench' (Beckett 1999: 27). There is the flavour of Beckett's style in the repetitions in the second sentence above, 'crosses'/'recrosses' and 'now northeast and now northwest under'. The syntax is surprisingly straightforward, however, with only the parenthesis 'passing now northeast and now northwest' breaking a strictly logical sequence in this sentence. The initial sentence, constructed of several fragments, is closer to the style of *Worstward Ho*. Davis' sentences contain more information, using commas where Beckett uses full stops. Davis has commented on her early fascination with Beckett's syntax (McCaffery 1996: 66) and this text plays out some sort of homage, with Davis mimicking Beckett's late style, although producing a more fluent version of it.

The other part of the story is told in footnotes which appear to be comments on the main text. They do not comment, however, in the discursive sense of commentary, but offer a retelling of the same passage in a more conventional narrative form. For example, the first paragraph of the main body reads: 'Sun in eyes, faces east, waits for van bound for south meeting plane from west. Carries book, *Worstward Ho*' (Davis 2007a: 68). The sentence structure is elliptical, with no clear sense of who the subject may be. There are references to directions which structure the sentence in such a way that there appears to be a clockwise movement around the compass dial. The two forms of transport also offer structuring elements to the sentence. There is then a paratactic connection with the second sentence. The first footnote, in contrast, reads as follows:

> She waits near the highway before the entrance of HoJo's for the van going south. She is going south to meet a plane from the west. Waiting with her is a thin, dark-haired young woman who does not stop walking back and forth restlessly near her luggage. They are both early and wait for some time. In her purse she has two books, *Worstward Ho* and *West with the Night*. If it is quiet and she reads *Worstward Ho* on the way south, when she is fresh, she can read *West with the Night* on the way back north, when it will be later and she will be tired. (Davis 2007a: 68)

Here the footnote provides information that the main body of the text does not give, including other characters and an explanation of why she has *Worstward Ho*. The footnote text connects to the main body through words which appear in both versions (south, west, plane, book,

Worstward Ho). The footnotes are paraphrases of the main text – translations into the same language according to Roman Jakobson's notion of 'intralingual translation' (Jakobson 1959: 233). Yet at the same time they provide more information than a paraphrase would normally allow for: the sparse narrative of the main text, which is filled with the movement of the van and the character's reading, is fleshed out to include other travellers and several stops of the bus in the other footnotes.

The story, as a whole, produces a commentary on *Worstward Ho*. It narrates the character's reading of that text, first in a form that mimics the source text, and then, in the footnoted section, in a more narrative form. The narrative itself focuses on the reading, and finishes with its end. The character has had mixed reactions to the book, liking some sections and not others, notably the beginning and the end. The connecting thread that drives the action, such as it is, then, is the reading of Beckett's text, and the character's reactions to it. This does not yet account for the pastiche of the main part, which reproduces the style of the text being read by the character in the tale. The pastiche acts in tandem with the narrative in the footnotes, and can be seen as providing a commentary in a different manner. The imitation of Beckett's style is the product of a reading, which is not explained, as it is in the footnotes, but rather performed in the construction of the text itself. It can be viewed as homage, although the criticisms in the other part suggest that this homage is not unequivocal. However, the levels of the commentary are different: the intradiegetic comments belong to the character, whereas the implicit comment performed by the pastiche belongs to the implied author of the story. Translation and reading in 'Southward bound, Reads *Worstward Ho*' appear as both the form and the content of the story. The content is the narrative of the reading of *Worstward Ho*. The form involves translation/reading doubly: first as the paraphrase of one part of the story by the other; secondly in the reading of Beckett that the text itself performs.

Like the other texts in this section, the story complicates any attempt to read it in a unified way: the citations of Beckett's work push the reader towards that work, just as the pastiche mimics and questions his style. Davis incorporates the work of others into her own work in these stories in a way, just as her translations of Leiris, Proust and Flaubert do, which places her in a dialogic relationship with those other writers. However, that relationship is never simple and her use of pastiche as well as quotation provides a critical distance. Sometimes the readings of the works are delegated to characters in the stories, as in the case of 'The Walk', 'Once an Honest Man' and 'Southward Bound, Reads *Worstward Ho*', which disrupts any identification of their opinion with Davis' own. Some of the characters appropriate the texts as expressions of their own thoughts, creating a double coding that allows the original significance of the quoted material to be obscured. The meaning of these works remains unstable as the original significance is never fully erased – if the reader knows about it then it can affect their acceptance of the character's reading. The citations are never fully recontextualised in Davis' stories. Like translations, they become part of her work while still remaining the work of others. The stories in this section, then, highlight how similar translation is to other intertextual practices, and how they are brought together in Davis' work, which produces translational writing.

Translation in Davis' Stories

There are other stories by Davis that take translation as a starting point, but not in the form of another text that is translated. Davis sometimes uses translation as a theme, writing about translation within the diegetic frame of her stories. In other stories, characters are seen translating, and their translation drives the story along. Here translation becomes a narrative device. Some of the characters in Davis' stories are translators. The narrator and her husband in 'The Bone' (Davis 1986: 88–90) were living in Paris, 'translating art books' (ibid.: 88) at the time of the story, which does not go on to mention translation but rather narrate how her husband was saved from choking. Similarly, in 'Thyroid Diary' (Davis 2001: 76–91), the narrator is a translator, but the story focuses much more on the problems of having an underactive thyroid gland. The significance of the central character's professional status as a translator is much more prominent in 'The Walk' (Davis 2007a: 72–82), which was analysed in the previous section: she appropriates a passage from her translation of Proust to help express her own state of mind, which comes about as the result of a walk around Oxford, which forms the main narrative of the story. In *The End of the Story* (1995) and 'The Letter' (Davis 1986: 49–56), the fact that the central character is a translator is much more significant: in 'The Letter' the character's reading of a poem in French forms the second half of the story, and provides insights into her personality while also allowing a narrative development through her reactions to the letter itself. In addition she, like the narrator of *The End of the Story*, translates in a time of personal crisis. Since *The End of the Story* begins by mentioning a story very similar to 'The Letter', leading Christopher Knight to note that it 'echoes' it (Knight 2008: 205), translation in both texts will be analysed together.

Rather than focusing on the representation of the translator, as has been a recent trend in translation studies,[9] this section focuses on how translation is used within the story as a device to shape the narrative. Importantly Davis' story and novel do not belong to the group of texts that Waïl S. Hassan (2006: 754a) has called 'translational literature': their narratives do not take place between cultures, but rather within a highly educated part of American culture, where the characters have knowledge of a foreign language and use it in their professional activities, but do not draw a hybrid identity from that knowledge. The narrator of *The End of the Story* recounts how if she is 'at a party and [says] to a man that [she is] a translator, he often loses interest immediately' (Davis 1995: 85) and walks away. There is nothing here of the romanticised traitors (Anderson 2005: 174–9), cross-cultural lovers (Wilson 2007: 386–7) or devious textual manipulators, as in Italo Calvino's *If on a Winter's Night a Traveller* (1981: 126–7). Davis' texts do not bring 'attention to the "invisible" agency of translators and to the "fluency" and "transparency" of their translations' (Hassan 2006: 754b), but rather the characters translate as a professional activity: only the reading of the letter, which is the centre of the story 'The Letter' but is also mentioned in *The End of the Story* (1995: 96–7), brings a contact between their professional and personal lives.

Before reading 'The Letter', there is another story by Davis that, while it does not place translation at its centre, builds around reading a book in French. 'Foucault and Pencil' (Davis 1997a: 10–12) shows a character reading and reflecting about a book by Foucault at the same time as they are thinking about an argument they are having with someone else.[10] The way in which the character in 'Foucault and Pencil' uses reading as a means of avoiding approaching a conflict they are having with another person who is absent is a more important connection with 'The Letter'. Here too reading and translation are used as a way of intellectualising a delicate interpersonal situation in order to deal with it. The fact that the character in 'Foucault and Pencil' is reading in a foreign language implies a possibility of translation, and through reporting in English parts of the text being read Davis' story actually performs an act of translation, for example in the phrase 'harder to understand when subject of sentence was noun like thought, absence, law' (ibid.: 12). The nouns would not be these words in a French text, but rather their French equivalents. The story does not focus on translating the text, despite containing translations within it. There is also a metaphorical translation between Foucault's book and the argument, where the difficulties of comprehension are carried over from one domain to another.

'Foucault and Pencil' is quite elusive on details of the argument that the character is involved in, or even their identity. All the sentences are written in a subjectless notational form, which avoids the normal deictic markers of identity, that is, his, her, my; for example, 'Sat down to read Foucault with pencil in hand' (ibid.: 9). The subject of the main verb is left unclear. Habit would suggest that such a notational form would refer back to the speaker, as it mimics note-taking which presumes the identity of the subject of the sentence is already known.

The story develops along two axes. The first is the understanding of Foucault's book, and the second is the understanding of the situation of conflict that the central character finds themself in. The character alternates between thinking about the argument and trying to read Foucault, and the growing understanding of both is presented in parallel, although in neither understanding does anything become clear other than the problem itself. As the last sentence states:

> Put down Foucault and pencil, took out notebook and made note of what was now at least understood about lack of understanding reading Foucault, looked up at other passengers, made note of same question about argument as before though with stress on different word. (Davis 1997a: 12)

The solution is not that the narrator now understands the problem in either case, but rather that they understand the conditions of the problem.

Reading is just one of the processes of understanding, but the exploration of that process, or moreover its failure, forms the centre of this story. Rather than solely describing a character reading, the story develops through the process of reading: it is the fits and starts that are of interest. Davis uses the process of understanding a text as a metaphor for understanding a situation, through the juxtaposition of the two narratives. The character thinks first of how to understand the argument, before attempting again to read Foucault and noticing the difficulty. Then they think again of the argument, using a different metaphor than previously. They go back to reading Foucault, realising that there are some points that are easier to understand and some harder. Their problem with Foucault is not solved, but framed in a way that makes a solution possible. Their rethinking of the argument is positioned in this space of possibility. The understanding of the book and the argument appear to build upon each other: it is as if they are one and the same. The character seems to be experiencing greater clarity of mind as the story goes on, allowing them to understand both the situation they are in and the book they are reading.

Reading substitutes for thinking about the argument, as if an abstract idea allows the central character to comprehend something more emotional and less yielding to analysis. Josh Cohen remarks that 'self-consciousness serves . . . as a passage to incomprehension' (Cohen 2010: 502) in Davis' work. The move into abstraction would sidestep the negative results associated with self-consciousness: by analysing a proxy situation, which has little or no relation to the emotional disturbance, the character can achieve an understanding that would have eluded them if they had approached the problem head on. Other characters in stories by Davis, notably 'Grammar Questions' (Davis 2007a: 27–9), analysed in Chapter 3, or 'Break it Down' (Davis 1986: 20–30), utilise abstract problems to work through emotional difficulties; where they try to work out the problems directly, as in 'Story' (Davis 1986: 3–7), they reach an impasse.

Translation in a linguistic sense becomes central in the story 'The Letter' (Davis 1986: 49–56). Here, too, the character uses translation as a form of intellectual proxy for an emotional problem. The central character in this story is a translator who is suffering the after-effects of a love affair. The first half of the story recounts her difficulties with the end of the relationship, which are quite similar to the narrator's in Davis' novel, *The End of the Story*. The relationship ended 'stormily' (Davis 1986: 49), and the translator still thinks of her ex-lover, with different friends providing information regarding his whereabouts and situation. The story is set about a year after the break-up, when she receives a letter from him. In the meantime she has been translating 'because it was the only thing she could do' (ibid.: 51): translation serves as a way of taking her attention away from the pain of the break-up.

If this were the sole use of translation in the story, it would present an interesting slant on the representation of the translator, but 'The Letter' also makes translation a central device in its narrative progression. The second half of the story shows the translator character's attempts to read the letter that her ex-lover has sent. She collects it from the post office, half recognising the handwriting; when she realises whose handwriting it is she 'swears aloud over and over' (ibid.: 52). Hoping that it will contain a cheque for some or all of the money he owes her, she opens the letter, which turns out not to be a letter but rather a poem in French, copied out in his handwriting, and signed by him as if it were a letter. The poem is never identified, although a reference to '*pure things*' (Davis 1995: 97) when speaking of a letter/poem from a lover in *The End of the Story* suggests that the poems may be the same poem in both texts. The novel's narrator cannot find the poem in an anthology where she was looking for it. However, she does give a translation of the first line: '*We have thought pure thoughts*' (ibid.). The poem appears to be Paul Valéry's 'Le bois amicale' (Valéry 1929: 13) although it is misquoted: Davis' '*nous nous retrouvions*' (Davis 1986: 55) appears in the poem as 'nous nous sommes trouvés' (Valéry 1929: 13, line 13). The text is otherwise obscured by the handwriting, which the character finds difficult to read, and which is not presented in the story. The reader of 'The Letter' is therefore unlikely to identify the poem, although Davis provides enough information for the reader to understand its significance in the story.

The rest of the story narrates the central character's attempt to understand the letter. She postpones the moment of confrontation that reading the letter represents, first going to a meeting that she is already late for, then by continuing work on a translation. When she speaks to her current lover, she does not mention the letter, although she does talk about the translation. Finally she takes the letter to bed with her to read it. Her secrecy and the act of reading the letter in bed suggests that, at some level, she views the letter as a substitute for her ex-lover; she shields her current lover from a potential source of jealousy.

She begins her interpretation of the letter not with the words, but with the material features: envelope, postmarks, handwriting, before moving on to the paper of the letter. Johnny Payne (1993: 170) notes that the central character has 'formidable powers of observation', and she is rigorous in her reading of the external features of the letter, even down to the traces of decisions not made: 'He might have hesitated writing her last name, because there is a small ink blot in the curve of one letter' (Davis 1986: 53). She is here unable to know whether or not he hesitated, or indeed what that hesitation might mean, despite there being marks that could be interpreted as pointing towards that conclusion. Karen Alexander (2008) sees this type of analysis as a central feature in Davis' work, and there is a consistency between the character's reading of the outward features of the letter in this story and the narrator's obsessive dissection of the costs of a romantic trip in 'Break it Down' (Davis 1986: 20–30), or the narrator's obsessive rehashing of her lover's story in 'Story' (Davis 1986: 3–7). Perloff also notes how, despite the character's speculation about the conditions in which the letter was sent, there is only one fact: the place of the postmark (Perloff 1989: 209). Yet there is also a return address, which Perloff chooses not to view as a fact, possibly as it is not as 'objective' as a postmark, which is imposed by a system outside of the control of either the letter's writer or its reader. The woman in the story chooses to overlook the address, or rather to ignore its function as locating her former lover. This is a wilful avoidance of the possibility of contact, just as the poem avoids the personal contact that a real letter would involve. The central character is ambivalent towards this possible reopening of communication with her ex-lover, an attitude also present in her mix of happiness and anger at receiving a message from him.

After examining the materials of the letter, she moves on to its content. She notes first the date, May 10, and her name at the top. The form the letter takes is: 'The date, her name, comma, then the poem, then his name, period' (Davis 1986: 54). The poem, as the character notes, is the letter. She reads it several times, unable to decipher a specific word. She guesses that it should be '*obscures*' as that rhymes with '*pures*' (ibid.). In the story the French words are written in French in italics, and given a gloss in English, meaning that a reader with no knowledge of French should be able to follow the narrative. At the same time, giving the words in French forces the reader into an analogous position to the central character: the reader must try to interpret the words. The presence of the original French words, which were absent in 'Foucault and Pencil', means that there are blocks to comprehension: they must be read and pronounced, separate from the meanings assigned to them by the gloss, which comes to exhibit only the semantic meaning of the words.

The poem itself is never quoted in full, only as short phrases. It is about two people, one described as a '*compagnon de silence*, companion of silence' (ibid.: 55), who die and find each other again. Her interpretation lingers over this finding each other again, double checking that is the meaning. She sees this as the message of the poem/letter: that her ex-lover still thinks there is a possibility, in the future, of them meeting up again. But then she doubts this, questioning her interpretation. Finally, she gives up reading it, only to sniff it, hoping to smell him, yet all she 'is probably smelling is the ink' (ibid.: 56). As Johnny Payne notes, the central character inhabits a 'misery-ridden space of lovelorn interpretation, heartsick hermeneusis' (Payne 1993: 171); she interprets to try to find the trace of her ex-lover, yet this interpretation brings her no closer to him. Although, if her attitude towards him is ambivalent, her incomplete interpretation is a symptom of that ambivalence: she cannot read the poem because she does not want an unequivocal answer. Her questioning of her own reading is a movement away from any knowledge of her ex-lover. Her self-conscious questioning leads to a willed lack of comprehension.

'The Letter' presents another case where reading and interpreting are central to the narrative development of one of Davis' stories. The character's reading of the letter is what drives the story forward. If it be the case that this analytic narrative is characteristic of Davis, then what makes this story and 'Foucault and Pencil' stand out from the rest of Davis' stories is the use of an explicit act of reading or translation. Rather than solely performing the action of interpreting or analysing, as a story like 'Break it Down' (Davis 1986: 20–30) does, these stories dramatise the act of reading.

The stories make translation into a central trope. The interaction between the characters takes place as an act of translation – metaphorically in 'Foucault and Pencil', and literally in 'The Letter'. Payne also links the narrator's interpretation in the latter story to translation. He argues that 'The Letter' enacts the secondariness of translation, and, in association, femininity (Payne 1993: 178–9). The act of interpretation is seen as a secondary act, and female secondary to the male – the two concepts have been commonly linked throughout Western history (Chamberlain 2004: 306). As Payne points out, however, '[t]he letter never appears integrally . . . but rather as a function of the woman's process of interpretation' (Payne 1993: 178). The whole story is presented from the viewpoint of the female recipient of the letter; she cannot be viewed as secondary in her relationship to the man. Indeed, Payne goes on to note how the story shows that 'the original masculine idiom depends at all points on her "necessary" and active cognition' (ibid.: 181). As such the female reading is necessary for the masculine writing, reversing the traditional gendered view of translation. Payne (ibid.: 179–80) explicitly compares this to Jacques Derrida's notion of the indebtedness of the original to the translation (Derrida 1985: 152), where the original needs the translation to survive: the reading of the letter is essential for the survival of the letter, meaning that the reader becomes more primary than the text.

Davis' story does not accept translation or interpretation as a secondary activity. Both are activities that are important to the character's possibility of understanding her situation, and so are primary activities to her, and by extension, to the narrative. As Payne (1993: 181) succinctly notes, the reader 'is forced back onto the woman's process of reading, rather than onto the letter'. Yet this reading could not happen without the letter. The process of reading is reliant on something to read, but at the same time need not be secondary to it: the text interpreted need not be more important than the interpretation.

Payne deems that the central character's activity as a translator only substitutes 'one object of interpretation for another' (ibid.: 179). The character in 'The Letter' does use the act of translation as a way of making herself busy to avoid thinking about her ex-lover – first when they are splitting up (Davis 1986: 51), and secondly as she postpones reading the letter (ibid.: 53). The narrator in *The End of the Story* also translates to avoid thinking about her former lover (Davis 1995: 158–9), explaining more fully that translation work and thinking about words stop 'his image [swimming up] between me and the work and causing a fresh pain' (ibid.: 159). The intellectual activity of translation is used, as reading is in 'Foucault and Pencil', as a way of not facing a direct emotional challenge.

I would argue that there is, however, a difference between the receipt of a letter and reading a literary text: letters are addressed to a recipient, and there is an assumed communication between the sender and the receiver. Letters imply a transferable meaning. Literary texts, on the other hand, have no clear addressee. The process of interpretation involved in reading a letter is different from translating a literary text: the first results in the deciphering of a message, whereas translation results in the creation of an equivalent text in another language. Translation as working practice places the translator in a writer's position, unable to read the work as a message, but reading a letter places the reader in the position of a receiver. The narrator's translation activity can be seen as an attempt to maintain control, which reading the letter would make her relinquish.

Translation serves as a narrative device in 'The Letter' as reading does in 'Foucault and Pencil': it pushes forward the narrative, although there is no real conclusion in either of the stories. Both stories use interpretation of texts as a way of dealing with emotional situations, although in 'The Letter' the text itself is the cause of the problem. Translation is, importantly, possible where reading is not – the character in 'The Letter' can translate various parts of the poem into English, and work on commissioned translations, yet she cannot read the letter: she cannot interpret its meaning with regard to her relationship with its sender. When she tries to find its message, she enters into the same space of doubt and continual questioning as Davis' other characters do when they try to face an emotional problem directly. While she can find other ways of producing signifying patterns, she cannot reach a single understanding of what those patterns might mean: she can only arrive at a range of possibilities.

Both of the stories in this final section produce a commentary on an absent text, Foucault's book in 'Foucault and Pencil' and the unnamed poem in 'The Letter'. They show the character struggling with a text that is not revealed to the reader, and so participate, like the other texts in this chapter, in the production of a barred double code: they refer to and point the reader towards another text, but remove access to that text at the same time. On the other hand, it is not important to know what the text referred to is to read and understand the stories: a knowledge of Foucault will not help understand the argument that the character is having in the first story, and access to Valéry's 'Le bois amicale' will not clarify the intent or the meaning of the letter in the second story. Something in each story remains incomprehensible beyond the story's intertexts.

Translation is both a thematic and formal component of these stories: the boundaries between Davis' activity as a writer and as a translator implode as the two come together in 'The Letter'. There is an important interaction between the translation and storytelling in this story. Translation becomes a means of moving the narrative forward. Yet all the stories analysed in this chapter, as well as 'Marie Curie, So Honorable Woman' and 'Ten Stories from Flaubert', go some way to blurring the boundaries between translating and writing stories: either by making translation into composition, as is the case in 'Marie Curie, So Honorable Woman', or by demonstrating how translation is one of a range of intertextual tools, rather than a singularly different process, or, finally, by making translation into a narrative device. Translation becomes central to the writing process.

The intertextual stories in this chapter rely on a manipulation of material into a new form; in 'The Letter' and 'Foucault and Pencil' this manipulation is obscured by its incorporation into a narrative, but there still remain strong intertextual impulses which disrupt a fully unified reading of the stories. Translation as a conventional activity, that is, the production of texts that are recognised and acknowledged as translations for a public that does not know the source language, still remains distinct, however, from the use of translation as part of a creative strategy, due in part to the problems of copyright, but also because this form of translation has a very different goal. In stories that use translation or other forms of intertextuality, the source material is presented in a new context, with new material to interact with. In a translation, the context does change, but the text is presented as a whole; the structures tying it together remain, even if altered.

Davis' incorporation of translation into her stories, either thematically or practically, brings her translation work into the heart of her own writing. Translation becomes part of her own stories. The use of intertextual elements has a similar effect, presenting multiple grafts of other writers' work onto Davis' *oeuvre*. The boundary between her work and other writers' becomes ever more porous. Davis' work is effectively decentred by this grafting; the perception of her as an author cannot be focused solely on her stories, but must also take into account her translations and how they resonate throughout her work. As we have seen throughout this book, Davis' translations, especially of Blanchot, Leiris, Proust and Flaubert, enter into a dialogue with her own stories, which in turn dramatise and explore translation. Davis' work is haunted by translation, either in its conventional, recognised form, or in a less restricted sense.

Davis' writing challenges the possibility of the work as a closed system; it always opens out through its inclusion of other writers' work within it. Davis's work is therefore filled with voices and texts other than her own. Translation is just one among many ways in which her work can be seen to fracture, breaking down its own boundaries. This mirrors the constant movement towards the other in Davis's stories and the porosity of subjectivity that leads characters to use other people's words to express themselves (for example, 'A Very Stupid Man', discussed in this chapter) or rely on external supports for their memories (for example, *The End of the Story*, see Chapter 4).

It seems important to note, in closing, that most of the writers she has been in dialogue with are white, male, canonical writers.[11] Davis' translations, responses and intertextual stories are a form of negotiating with the canon, which is traditionally masculine (Brooke-Rose 1989: 55). As Sandra Gilbert and Susan Gubar (2000: 76) argue, nineteenth-century female writers often rewrote and revised stories and images from men's writing. This questioning of the canon can also be found in more recent women writers (Sage 1992). Yet Davis' use of translation seems a more collaborative action than the sorts of aggressive rewriting to be seen in the work of writers such as Kathy Acker (see Moraru 2001: 143–55) or the parody of Giroud in Davis' own 'Marie Curie, So Honorable Woman'. Certainly, there are responses to Blanchot, Leiris, Proust and Flaubert in her own stories, but the act of translating them is a form of accommodation. Translating a writer gives them new life in the target language and can make their work available to new audiences (as was the case of the first translations of Blanchot and Leiris), or lead to a new way of reading that author in that language (which is one of the functions of the retranslations of Proust and Flaubert). There is a form of careful reading and creative rewriting in Davis' translations which is inherent in their recognition as acceptable, reliable versions of the original works – Davis is not appropriating their work, but rather doing it a service. At the same time, the translations also align her with key canonical authors, as their translator, which affects how Davis' own work is read. The use of translation as a form of speaking in another's voice is beneficial for both Davis and the original writer. Davis' responses to these authors deepen the dialogue that is present in the translations, sometimes bringing in more critical overtones. Through this continuing interaction with other writers in her translations and her stories, Davis shows that literature is created by many voices in interaction, not just that of the identified author of the piece. Davis demonstrates how translation, rewriting and intertextuality all question conventional ideas of authorship and national literatures; they offer us, as readers, a way of enlarging our own understanding of how literature works.

Notes

1. Judith Halberstam sees in collage a 'feminist and queer' practice and traces its practice in visual arts from Hannah Hoch to Kara Walker (Halberstam 2011: 136).
2. The image can easily be found on the internet by searching for its title. I found it at http://upload.wikimedia.org/wikipedia/en/f/ff/Hamilton-appealing2.jpg (last accessed 24 April 2015).
3. This latter would be difficult in a written work, although the mood of Hopper's paintings has arguably been borrowed by innumerable works.
4. There is nothing in the 2002 edition to state this is a translation, other than a different copyright date (1948) from the date of the original British publication (1965), but there is a book published by Buber in 1948 called *Der Weg des Menschen, nach den chassidischem Lehre* ('The Way of Man, after the Hasidic teachings') which would appear to be the source text.
5. Davis' story 'Meat, My Husband' (Davis 1997a: 5–7) also centres on the anxiety caused by having to prepare dinner for a loved one.
6. James Hawes (2008) has tried to dispel this image of Kafka.
7. Exhibited at the Serpentine Gallery, London, from 2 July to 13 September 2009.
8. The two parts of the text were, according to the copyright page of *New and Used*, originally published separately: one in 1989 and one in 1993. The *Varieties of Disturbance* version highlights the links between them.
9. See, for example, Anderson 2005, Curran 2005, Mihalache 2005, Maier 2006, Wilson 2007, Cronin 2009, Kaindl and Spitzl 2014.
10. The gender of the character is unknown, and rather than using the neologistic pronoun 's/he' or even 'he/she', it seems preferable to use a gender neutral plural 'they'. It should also be noted in passing that Davis translated an interview with Foucault which was published as part of an anthology of his work on ethics in English (Foucault 1997), though this knowledge is not significant for an understanding of the story.
11. I've generally avoided a gendered approach throughout the book in order to avoid characterising Davis as a 'woman writer', following Christine Brooke-Rose's (1989: 67) discussion of the problematics of this phrase and the way in which it inhibits the recognition of the innovative nature of experimental writing by people who just happen to be identified as women. I have also tried to avoid the sexist linking of translation and feminity (Chamberlain 2004).

Bibliography

Alexander, Karen (2008), 'Breaking It Down: Analysis in the Stories of Lydia Davis', in Ellen Burton Harrington (ed.), *Scribbling Women & the Short Story Form: Approaches by American & British Women Writers*, New York: Peter Lang, pp. 165–77.

Allen, Brooke (2010), '"Bovary" & le mot juste', *New Criterion*, 29, 10–14.

Alvstad, Cecilia (2014), 'The translation pact', *Language and Literature*, 23:3, 270–84.

Anderson, Jean (2005), 'The double agent: aspects of literary translator affect as revealed in the fictional work by translators', *Linguistica Antverpiensa*, New Series 4, 171–82.

Anderson, Linda (2011), *Autobiography*, 2nd edn, London: Routledge.

Anderson, Sam (2010), 'Knee-Deep in Bovary', *New York* <http://nymag.com/arts/books/features/68712/> (last accessed 6 April 2015).

Antonioli, Manola (1999), *L'écriture de Maurice Blanchot: Fiction et théorie*, Paris: Éditions Kimé.

Apter, Emily (2013), *Against World Literature: On the Politics of Untranslatability*, London: Verso.

Auster, Paul (1974), *Unearth*, Western, CT: Living Hand.

Auster, Paul (1998), *The Art of Hunger: Essays, Prefaces, Interviews & The Red Notebook*, London: Faber. First published 1997.

Badinter, Elizabeth (1995), *XY: On Masculine Identity*, trans. Lydia Davis, New York: Columbia University Press.

Bakhtin, Mikhail Mikhailovich (1981), *The Dialogic Imagination: Four Essays*, ed. Michael Holquist, trans. Caryl Emerson and Michael Holquist, Austin: University of Texas Press.

Barnes, Julian (2010), 'Writer's Writer and Writer's Writer's Writer', *London Review of Books*, 32:22, 7–11 <http://www.lrb.co.uk/v32/n22/julian-barnes/writers-writer-and-writers-writers-writer> (last accessed 27 March 2015).

Bassnett, Susan (2006), 'Writing and Translating', in Susan Bassnett and Peter Bush (eds), *The Translator as Writer*, London: Continuum, pp. 173–83.

Bassnett, Susan and Alejandra Pizarnik (2002), *Exchanging Lives: Poems and Translations*, London: Peepal Tree.

Bastin, Georges L. (1998), 'Adaptation', trans. Mark Gregson, in Mona Baker (ed.), *Routledge Encyclopedia of Translation Studies*, London: Routledge, pp. 5–8.

Beckett, Samuel (1999), *Worstward Ho*, London: John Calder. First published 1983.

Benjamin, Walter (1977), 'Zum Bilde Prousts', *Gesammelte Schriften*, ed. Rolf Tiedmann and Herman Schweppenhäuser, 7 vols, Frankfurt: Suhrkamp, II, 310–24.

Benjamin, Walter (1999), *Illuminations*, trans. Harry Zohn, London: Pimlico. First published 1968.

Berlant, Laurent and Lee Edelman (2014), *Sex, or the Unbearable*, Durham, NC and London: Duke University Press.

Berman, Antoine (1984), *L'épreuve de l'étranger*, Paris: Gallimard.

Berman, Antoine (1995), *Pour une critique des traductions: John Donne*, Paris: Gallimard.

Berman, Antoine (1999), *La Traduction et la lettre ou l'auberge du lointain*, Paris: Seuil.

Bernofsky, Susan (2005), *Foreign Words: Translator-Authors in the Age of Goethe*, Detroit: Wayne State University Press.

Berrigan, Ted (2000), *The Sonnets*, ed. Alice Notley, New York: Penguin. First published 1964.

Blanchot, Maurice (1943), *Faux pas*, Paris: Gallimard.

Blanchot, Maurice (1949), *La Part du feu*, Paris: Gallimard.

Blanchot, Maurice (1951), *Au moment voulu*, Paris: Gallimard.

Blanchot, Maurice (1953), *Celui qui m'accompagnait pas*, Paris: Gallimard.

Blanchot, Maurice (1955), *L'Espace littéraire*, Paris: Gallimard.

Blanchot, Maurice (1957), *Le Dernier homme*, Paris: Gallimard.

Blanchot, Maurice (1959), *Le Livre à venir*, Paris: Gallimard.

Blanchot, Maurice (1969), *L'Entretien infini*, Paris: Gallimard.

Blanchot, Maurice (1975), 'Death-Halt', trans. Lydia Davis, *Living Hand*, 4 (Winter 1975), 3–28.

Blanchot, Maurice (1976), 'Death Sentence', trans. Lydia Davis, *Georgia Review*, 30:2, 379–403.

Blanchot, Maurice (1977a), *L'Arrêt de mort*, Paris: Gallimard, Collection L'Imaginaire. First published 1948.

Blanchot, Maurice (1977b), 'The Madness of the Day', trans. Lydia Davis, *Tri-Quarterly*, 40, 168–77.

Blanchot, Maurice (1978), *Death Sentence*, trans. Lydia Davis, Barrytown, NY: Station Hill Press.

Blanchot, Maurice (1981a), *The Madness of the Day*, trans. Lydia Davis, Barrytown, NY: Station Hill Press.

Blanchot, Maurice (1981b), *The Gaze of Orpheus, and other literary essays*, ed. P. Adams Sitney, trans. Lydia Davis, Barrytown, NY: Station Hill Press.

Blanchot, Maurice (1982a), *The Siren's Song*, ed. Gabriel Josipovici, trans. Sacha Rabinovitch, Brighton: Harvester.

Blanchot, Maurice (1982b), *The Space of Literature*, trans. Ann Smock, Lincoln: University of Nebraska Press.

Blanchot, Maurice (1985), *When the Time Comes*, trans. Lydia Davis, Barrytown, NY: Station Hill Press.

Blanchot, Maurice (1987), *The Last Man*, trans. Lydia Davis, New York: Columbia University Press.

Blanchot, Maurice (1993), *The One Who Was Standing Apart From Me*, trans. Lydia Davis, Barrytown, NY: Station Hill Press.

Blanchot, Maurice (1999), *The Station Hill Blanchot Reader*, ed. George Quasha, trans. Lydia Davis, Paul Auster and Robert Lamberton, Barrytown, NY: Station Hill Press.

Blanchot, Maurice (2002), *La Folie du jour*, Paris: Gallimard. First published 1973.

Block, Haskell M. (1981), 'The Writer as Translator: Nerval, Baudelaire, Gide', in Marilyn Gaddis Rose (ed.), *Translation Spectrum*, Albany: State University of New York Press, pp. 116–26.

Boase-Beier, Jean (2015), *Translating the Poetry of the Holocaust: Translation, Style and the Reader*, London: Bloomsbury.

Boddy, Kasia (2010), 'Lydia Davis', *The Telegraph* <http://www.telegraph.co.uk/culture/books/8113668/Lydia-Davis.html> (last accessed 6 April 2015).

Borges, Jorge Luis (1997), *Ficciones*, Barcelona: Libro del bolsillo.

Bowie, Malcom (1998), *Proust Among the Stars*, London: Fontana.

Brooke-Rose, Christine (1989), 'Illiterations', in Ellen G. Friedman and Miriam Fuchs (eds), *Breaking the Sequence: Women's Experimental Fiction*, Princeton: Princeton University Press, pp. 55–71.

Brooks, Cleanth (1947), *The Well Wrought Urn: Essays in the Structure of Poetry*, New York: Harcourt Brace World.

Brooks, Sidney (1995), *Our Village*, Harwich, MA: Harwich Historical Society.

Buber, Martin (1948), *Der Weg des Menschen, nach des chassidischen Lehre*, The Hague: Boucher.

Buber, Martin (2002), *The Way of Man*, trans. unknown, London: Routledge.

Buchloch, Benjamin (2003), 'The Primary Colours for the Second Time: A Paradigm Repetition of the Neo-Avant-Garde', in Jason Gaiger and Paul Wood (eds), *Art of the Twentieth Century: A Reader*, New Haven, CT: Yale University Press, pp. 98–106.

Burroughs, William S. (1993), *The Adding Machine: Selected Essays*, New York: Arcade. First published 1986.

Butor, Michel (1986), *The Spirit of Mediterranean Places*, trans. Lydia Davis, Malboro, VT: Marlboro Press.

Callus, Ivan (2014), 'Exhausted Replenishment: Experimental Fiction and the Decomposition of Literature', *Word and Text*, 4:1, 116–35.

Calvino, Italo (1981), *If On A Winter's Night A Traveller*, trans. William Weaver, London: Secker & Warburg.

Chamberlain, Lori (2004), 'Gender and the Metaphorics of Translation', in Lawrence Venuti (ed.), *The Translation Studies Reader*, 2nd edn, London: Routledge, pp. 306–21.

Chesneaux, Jean (1979), *China, the People's Republic 1949–1976*, trans. Paul Auster and Lydia Davis, Hassocks: Harvester.

Chesneaux, Jean, Francoise Le Barbier and Marie-Claire Bergère (1977), *China from 1911: Revolution to Liberation*, trans. Paul Auster and Lydia Davis, Hassocks: Harvester.

Chesterman, Andrew (1997), *Memes of Translation*, Amsterdam and Philadelphia: Benjamins.

Chesterman, Andrew (2001), 'Proposal for a Hieronymic Oath', *The Translator*, 7:2, 139–54.

Cicero, Marcus Tullius (1997), 'Translating Greek Orations into Latin', trans. E. W. Sutton and H. Rackham, in Douglas Robinson (ed.), *Western Translation Theory from Herodotus to Nietzsche*, Manchester: St Jerome, p. 7.

Cockerill, Hiroko (2006), *Style and Narrative in Translations: The Contribution of Futabatei Shimei*, Manchester: St Jerome.

Cohen, Josh (2005), 'Aesthetic Theory, Psychoanalysis and the Ironic End of Art', *Parallax*, 11:4, 71–80.

Cohen, Josh (2010), 'Reflexive incomprehension: on Lydia Davis', *Textual Practice*, 24:3, 501–16.

Copeland, Rita (1991), *Rhetoric, Hermeneutics, and Translation in the Middle Ages: Academic Traditions and Vernacular Texts*, Cambridge: Cambridge University Press.

Cronin, Michael (2009), *Translation goes to the Movies*, Abingdon: Routledge.

Culler, Jonathan (1982), *On Deconstruction: Theory and Criticism after Structuralism*, Ithaca, NY: Cornell University Press.

Culler, Jonathan (2002), *Structuralist Poetics: Structuralism, linguistics and the study of literature*, London: Routledge. First published 1975.

Curran, Beverley (2005), 'The fictional translator in Anglophone literatures', *Linguistica Antverpiensa*, New Series 4, 183–99.

Davis, Lydia (1976), *The Thirteenth Woman and other stories*, New York: Living Hand.

Davis, Lydia (1981), 'A Note on the Translation', in Maurice Blanchot, *The Gaze of Orpheus and other literary essays*, ed. P. Adam Sitney, Barrytown, NY: Station Hill Press, pp. xiii–xv.

Davis, Lydia (1983), *Story and other stories*, Great Barrington, MA: The Figures.

Davis, Lydia (1986), *Break It Down*, New York: Knopf.

Davis, Lydia (1995), *The End of the Story*, New York: Farrar Straus Giroux.

Davis, Lydia (1997a), *Almost No Memory*, New York: Farrar Straus Giroux.

Davis, Lydia (1997b), 'Translator's Note', in Michel Leiris, *Scratches*, trans. Lydia Davis, Baltimore and London: Johns Hopkins University Press, pp. ix–xi.

Davis, Lydia (1999), '"Remembering the Van Wagenens"', in Charles Baxter (ed.), *The Business of Memory: The Art of Remembering in an Age of Forgetting*, Saint Paul: Graywolf Press, pp. 87–105.

Davis, Lydia (2000a), 'Translation Exercise #1: Marie Curie, Honorable Woman', *McSweeney's*, 5, 139–51.

Davis, Lydia (2000b), [Letters to the Editor], *McSweeney's*, 5, 27–9.

Davis, Lydia (2001), *Samuel Johnson is Indignant*, Brooklyn, NY: McSweeney's.

Davis, Lydia (2002a), 'Translator's Introduction', in Marcel Proust, *The Way by Swann's*, trans. Lydia Davis, London: Allen Lane, pp. xxii–xxxvii.

Davis, Lydia (2002b), 'A Problem Sentence in Proust's *The Way by Swann's*', *The Literary Review*, 45:3, 473–8, in *Proquest* <http://0-literature.proquest. com.fama.us.es/searchFulltext.do?id=R01616215&divLevel=0&area=abell &forward=critref_ft> (last accessed 6 March 2016).

Davis, Lydia (2002c), *Samuel Johnson is Indignant*, New York: Picador.

Davis, Lydia (2004), 'Loaf or Hot Water Bottle: Closely Translating Proust', *Yale Review*, 92:2, 51–70.

Davis, Lydia (2007a), *Varieties of Disturbance*, New York: Farrar Straus Giroux.

Davis, Lydia (2007b), *Proust, Blanchot and a Woman in Red*, Paris: Centre for Writers & Translators, AUP; Lewes: Sylph Editions.

Davis, Lydia (2009), *Collected Stories*, New York: Farrar Straus Giroux.

Davis, Lydia (2010), 'Ten Stories from Flaubert', *The Paris Review*, 194, 121–7.

Davis, Lydia (2011a), 'Introduction', in Gustave Flaubert, *Madame Bovary*, London: Penguin, pp. ix–xxvi.

Davis, Lydia (2011b), 'Some Notes on Translation and on *Madame Bovary*', *The Paris Review*, 198, 65–96.

Davis, Lydia (2013), 'Our Village', in Lydia Davis and Eliot Weinberger, *Two American Scenes*, New York: New Directions, pp. 5–36.

Davis, Lydia (2014), *Can't and Won't*, London: Hamish Hamilton.

Dawn of the Dead, film, directed by Georges A. Romero. USA: Laurel Group, 1978.

Deane-Cox, Sharon (2011), 'Flaubert and the retranslation of *Madame Bovary*', *Flaubert*, 6 <http://flaubert.revues.org/1538> (last accessed 15 March 2015).

Deane-Cox, Sharon (2014), *Retranslation: translation, literature and reinterpretation*, London: Bloomsbury.

Deleuze, Gilles (1970), *Proust et les signes*, 2nd revd edn, Paris: Presses Universitaires de France.

Deleuze, Gilles and Félix Guattari (1991), *Qu'est-ce que la philosophie?*, Paris: Minuit.

Derrida, Jacques (1979), 'Living On', trans. James Hulbert, in Harold Bloom, et al., *Deconstruction and Criticism*, London: Continuum, pp. 62–142.

Derrida, Jacques (1985), *The Ear of the Other: Otobiography, Transference, Translation*, trans. Peggy Kamuf, Lincoln: University of Nebraska Press.

Derrida, Jacques (1986), *Parages*, Paris: Galilée.

Detrez, Conrad (1984), *A Weed for Burning*, trans. Lydia Davis, New York: Harcourt Brace Jovanovich.

Detrez, Conrad (1986), *Zone of Fire*, trans. Lydia Davis, New York: Harcourt Brace Jovanovich.

Dimock, Wai Chee (2006), *Through Other Continents: American Literature Across Deep Time*, Princeton: Princeton University Press.

Du Bouchet, André (1976), *The Uninhabited: selected poems of André Du Bouchet*, trans. Paul Auster, New York: Living Hand.

Duffy, Nikolai (2005), 'Inter Alia: Steve Ericskon, Rosmarie Waldrop, Lydia Davis and the Lightening of Meaning', unpublished PhD thesis, London, University of London.

Duijsens, Florian (2014), 'Notes from the Netherlands: On Lydia Davis' Translations of A.L. Snijders', *The Quarterly Conversation*, 35 <http://quarterlyconversation.com/notes-from-the-netherlands-on-lydia-davis-translations-of-a-l-snijders> (last accessed 17 April 2015).

Dupin, Jaques (1974), *Fits and Starts: Selected poems of Jacques Dupin*, trans. Paul Auster, Salisbury: Compton Press.

Dyer, Richard (2007), *Pastiche*, Abingdon: Routledge.

Eakin, Paul John (1999), *How our Lives Become Stories: Making selves*, Ithaca, NY: Cornell University Press.

Edson, Russell (1994), *The Tunnel: Selected poems*, Oberlin: Oberlin College Press.

Evans, Jonathan (2011), 'Translation in Lydia Davis's Work', unpublished PhD thesis, Portsmouth, University of Portsmouth.

Felstiner, John (1998), 'Translating as Transference: Paul Celan's Versions of Shakespeare, Dickinson, Mandehlstam, Apollinaire', in Kurt Mueller-Vollmer and Michael Irmscher (eds), *Translating Literature Translating Cultures*, Stanford: Stanford University Press, pp. 165–75.

Fish, Stanley (1980), *Is there a Text in this Class?*, Cambridge, MA: Harvard University Press.

Fitch, Brian T. (1992), *Lire les récits de Maurice Blanchot*, Amsterdam and Atlanta: Rodolpi.

Flaubert, Gustave (1881), *Madame Bovary: A Tale of Provincial Life*, trans. Mary Neal Sherwood, Philadelphia: T. B. Peterson and Brothers.

Flaubert, Gustave (1886), *Madame Bovary: Provincial Manners*, trans. Eleanor Marx-Aveling, London: Vizetelly and Co.

Flaubert, Gustave (1979), *Bouvard et Pécuchet*, ed. Claudine Gothot-Mersch, Paris: Gallimard. First published 1881.

Flaubert, Gustave (1980), *Correspondence*, Vol. 2, Paris: Bibliothèque de la Pléiade.

Flaubert, Gustave (2001), *Madame Bovary*, ed. Thierry Laget, Paris: Gallimard. First published 1856.

Flaubert, Gustave (2010), *Madame Bovary: Provincial Ways*, trans. Lydia Davis, New York: Viking Penguin.

Flaubert, Gustave (2011a), *Madame Bovary: Provincial Ways*, trans. Lydia Davis, London: Penguin.

Flaubert, Gustave (2011b), *Madame Bovary: Provincial Morals*, trans. Adam Thorpe, London: Vintage.

Foucault, Michel (1994), 'Qu'est-ce qu'un auteur?', in Daniel Defert and François Ewald (eds), *Dits et écrits*, 4 vols, Paris: Gallimard, I: 789–821.

Foucault, Michel (1997), 'Polemics, Politics and Problematizations: An Interview with Michel Foucault', trans. Lydia Davis, in Paul Rabinov (ed.), *Ethics: Essential Works of Michel Foucault 1954–1984 vol. 1*, New York: The New Press, pp. 111–19.

Freud, Sigmund (2006), 'Beyond the Pleasure Principle', trans. John Reddick, in Adam Philips (ed.), *The Penguin Freud Reader*, London: Penguin, pp. 132–95.

Friedländer, Saul and Mahmoud Hussein (1975), *Arabs and Israelis: A dialogue*, trans. Paul Auster and Lydia Davis, London: Holmes & Meier.

Friedman, Ellen G. and Miriam Fuchs (eds) (1989), *Breaking the Sequence: Women's Experimental Fiction*, Princeton: Princeton University Press.

Gaddis Rose, Marilyn (2000), 'Twentieth-Century Thinkers', in Peter France (ed.), *The Oxford Guide to Literature in English Translation*, Oxford: Oxford University Press, pp. 296–300.

Gale, Matthew (1997), *Dada and Surrealism*, London: Phaidon.

Genette, Gérard (1972), *Figures III*, Paris: Seuil.

Genette, Gérard (1992), *Palimpsestes*, Paris: Seuil. First published 1982.

Gentzler, Edwin (1996), 'Translation, Counter-Culture and *The Fifties* in the USA', in Román Álvarez and M. Carmen-África Vidal (eds), *Translation Power Subversion*, Clevedon: Multilingual Matters, pp. 116–37.

Gilbert, Sandra M. and Susan Gubar (2000), *The Madwoman in the Attic: The Woman Writer and the Nineteenth Century Literary Imagination*, 2nd edn, New Haven, CT: Yale University Press.

Gill, Carolyn Bailey (ed.) (1996), *Maurice Blanchot: The Demand of Writing*, London: Routledge.

Gillespie, Stuart (2011), *English Translation and Classical Reception: Towards a New Literary History*, Chichester: Wiley-Blackwell.

Giroud, Françoise (1981), *Une femme honorable: Marie Curie, une vie*, Paris: Fayard.

Giroud, Françoise (1986), *Marie Curie: A Life*, trans. Lydia Davis, London: Holmes & Meier.

Goethe, Johann Wolfgang von (1962), 'Übersetzungen', *Werke*, ed. Erich Trunz, 14 vols, Hamburg: Wegner, II, 255–8.

Goethe, Johann Wolfgang von (2012), 'Translations', trans. Sharon Sloane, in Lawrence Venuti (ed.), *The Translation Studies Reader*, 3rd edn, Abingdon: Routledge, pp. 64–6.

Goldstein, Paul (2001), *International Copyright Law: Principles, Law and Practice*, New York: Oxford University Press.

Gray, Margaret E. (1992), *Postmodern Proust*, Philadelphia: University of Pennsylvania Press.

Grieve, James (2005), 'Working with the Demented', *Meanjin*, 64:4, 99–103.

Haase, Ullrich and William Large (2001), *Maurice Blanchot*, London: Routledge.

Halberstam, Judith (2011), *The Queer Art of Failure*, Durham, NC: Duke University Press.

Halford, Macy (2010), 'I buy it for the Bovary', *New Yorker* <http://www.newyorker.com/books/page-turner/i-buy-it-for-the-bovary> (last accessed 16 April 2015).

Hand, Seán (2002), *Michel Leiris: Writing the Self*, Cambridge: Cambridge University Press.

Hart, Kevin (2004), 'The Gospel of *L'Arrêt de Mort*', *Journal of Philosophy and Scripture*, 1:2 <http://www.philosophyandscripture.org/Issue1-2/Kevin_Hart/kevin_hart.html> (last accessed 18 March 2008).

Hass, Robert and David Lehman (eds) (2001), *The Best American Poetry 2001*, New York: Scribner Poetry.

Hassan, Waïl S. (2006), 'Agency and Translational Literature: Ahdaf Soueif's *The Map of Love*', *PMLA*, 121:3, 753–68.

Haviland, Beverly (1989), 'Missed Connections', *Partisan Review*, 56:1, 151–7.

Hawes, James (2008), *Excavating Kafka*, London: Quercus.

Heep, Hartmut (1996), *A Different Poem: Rainer Maria Rilke's American Translators Randall Jarrell, Robert Lowell, and Robert Bly*, New York: Peter Lang.

Hennard Dutheil de la Rochère, Martine (2013), *Reading, Translating, Rewriting: Angela Carter's Translational Poetics*, Detroit: Wayne State University Press.

Hermans, Theo (1998), 'Translation's Representations', Συγρισŋ/*Comparaison*, 9, 14–30.

Hermans, Theo (2007), *The Conference of The Tongues*, Manchester: St Jerome.

Hess, Deborah M. (1999), *Complexity in Maurice Blanchot's Fiction: Relations Between Science and Literature*, New York: Peter Lang.

Hill, Leslie (1997), *Blanchot: Extreme contemporary*, London: Routledge.

Hutcheon, Linda (1985), *A Theory of Parody: The Teachings of Twentieth Century Art Forms*, New York and London: Methuen.

Hutcheon, Linda (1988), *A Poetics of Postmodernism: History, Theory, Fiction*, London: Routledge.

Hutcheon, Linda (2006), *A Theory of Adaptation*, Abingdon: Routledge.

Jakobson, Roman (1959), 'On Linguistic Aspects of Translation', in Reuben A. Brower (ed.), *On Translation*, New York: Oxford University Press, pp. 232–9.

Jakobson, Roman (1960), 'Closing Statement: Linguistics and Poetics', in Thomas B. Seboek (ed.), *Style in Language*, Cambridge, MA: MIT Press, pp. 350–77.

James, Henry (1946), *The Turn of The Screw*, Harmondsworth: Penguin. First published 1898.

Jardin, André (1988), *Tocqueville: A Biography*, trans. Lydia Davis and Robert Hemenway, London: Peter Halban.

Jarolim, Edie (1985), 'Ideas of Order', *Poetics Journal*, 5, 143–5.

Joseph, Marc and Damon Krukowski (eds) (2006), *Marc Joseph: New and Used*, Göttingen: Steidl.

Jouve, Pierre Jean (1926), *Le Monde désert*, Paris: Mercure de France.

Jouve, Pierre Jean (1995), *Hélène*, trans. Lydia Davis, Evanston: Marlboro Press/Northwestern University Press.

Jouve, Pierre Jean (1996), *The Desert World*, trans. Lydia Davis, Evanston: Marlboro Press/Northwestern University Press.

Jouve, Pierre Jean (1997a), *Hecate*, trans. Lydia Davis, Evanston: Marlboro Press/Northwestern University Press.

Jouve, Pierre Jean (1997b), *Vagadu*, trans. Lydia Davis, Evanston: Marlboro Press/Northwestern University Press.

Kafka, Franz (1990), *Letters to Milena*, trans. Philip Boehm, New York: Shocken.

Kaindl, Klaus and Karlheinz Spitzl (eds) (2014), *Transfiction: Research into the Realities of Translation Fiction*, Amsterdam: Benjamins.

Kaplan, Steven (1989), *Robert Bly and Randall Jarrell as Translators of Rainer Maria Rilke: A Study of the Translations and their Impact on Bly's and Jarrell's Own Poetry*, Frankfurt am Main: Peter Lang.

Katz, Daniel (2007), *American Modernism's Expatriate Scene: The Labour of Translation*, Edinburgh: Edinburgh University Press.

Knight, Christopher J. (1999), 'An Interview with Lydia Davis', *Contemporary Literature*, 40:4, 525–51.

Knight, Christopher J. (2008), 'Lydia Davis's Own Philosophical Investigation: *The End of the Story*', *Journal of Narrative Theory*, 38:2, 198–228.

Kristal, Efraín (2002), *Invisible Work: Borges and Translation*, Nashville: Vanderbilt University Press.

Kristeva, Julia (1974), *La révolution du langage poétique*, Paris: Seuil.

Lacan, Jacques (1966), *Écrits*, Paris: Seuil.

Lacan, Jacques (1973) *Le Séminaire Livre XI: Les quatre concepts fondamentaux de la psychanalyse*, ed. Jacques-Alain Miller, Paris: Seuil.

Lefevere, André (1992), *Translation, Rewriting, and The Manipulation of Literary Fame*, London: Routledge.

Lefevere, André (2012), 'Mother Courage's Cucumbers: Text, System and Refraction in a Theory of Literature', in Lawrence Venuti (ed.), *The Translation Studies Reader*, 3rd edn, London: Routledge, pp. 203–19.

Lehman, David (ed.) (2003), *Great American Prose Poems: From Poe to present*, New York: Scribner.

Leigh, James (1978), 'The Figure of Autobiography', *Modern Language Notes*, 93:4, 733–49.

Leiris, Michel (1961), *Nuits sans nuit et quelques jours sans jour*, Paris: Gallimard.

Leiris, Michel (1987), *Nights as Days, Days as Nights*, trans. Richard Seiburth, Hygiene, CO: Eridanos Press.

Leiris, Michel (1989), *Brisées: Broken Branches*, trans. Lydia Davis, San Francisco: North Point Press.

Leiris, Michel (1997a), *Scratches*, trans. Lydia Davis, Baltimore and London: Johns Hopkins University Press. First published 1991.

Leiris, Michel (1997b), *Scraps*, trans. Lydia Davis, Baltimore and London: Johns Hopkins University Press.

Leiris, Michel (2003), *La Règle du jeu*, Paris: Gallimard, Bibliothèque de la Pléiade.

Leitch, Thomas (2007), *Film Adaptation and its Discontents: From Gone with the Wind to The Passion of the Christ*, Baltimore: Johns Hopkins University Press.

Lejeune, Philippe (1975), *Lire Leiris: Autobiographie et langage*, Paris: Klinkseick.

Lewis, Philip E. (2004), 'The Measure of Translation Effects', in Lawrence Venuti (ed.), *The Translation Studies Reader*, 2nd edn, London: Routledge, pp. 256–75.

Louth, Charlie (1998), *Hölderlin and the Dynamics of Translation*, Oxford: Legenda.

Lyotard, Jean-François (1979), *La Condition postmoderne*, Paris: Minuit.

McCaffery, Larry (1996), 'Deliberately, Terribly Neutral: An Interview with Lydia Davis', in Larry McCaffery (ed.), *Some Other Frequency: Interviews with Innovative American Authors*, Philadelphia: University of Pennsylvania Press, pp. 59–79.

McSweeney's (2000), [Front Matter], *McSweeney's*, 5, n.p.

Madeleine, Jacques (1972), [En somme, qu-est ce?], in Jacques Bersani (ed.), *Les Critiques de notre temps et Proust*, Paris: Garnier, pp. 13–20.

Maier, Carol (2006), 'The Translator as *Theôros*: Thoughts on Cogitation, Figuration and Current Creative Writing', in Theo Hermans (ed.), *Translating Others*, vol. 1, Manchester: St Jerome, pp. 163–80.

Manguso, Sarah (2008), 'Interview with Lydia Davis', *The Believer*, <http://www.believermag.com/issues/200801/?read=interview_davis> (last accessed 7 April 2010).

Marcus, Ben (2007), 'Analyze This' <http://www.bookforum.com/inprint/014_01/172> (last accessed 8 July 2009).

Marcus, Laura (1994), *Auto/biographical discourses: Theory Criticism Practice*, Manchester: Manchester University Press.

Mihalache, Iulia (2005), 'Le jeu de scène: traductions et traducteurs à travers les cultures et les genres littéraires', *Linguistica Antverpiensa*, New Series 4, 139–54.

Milton, John (2009), 'Between the Cat and the Devil: Adaptation Studies and Translation Studies', *Journal of Adaptation in Film and Performance*, 2:1, 47–64.

Milton, John and Marie-Hélène C. Torres (2003), 'Apresentacão', *Cadernos de Tradução*, 1:11, 9–17.

Moraru, Christian (2001), *Rewriting: Postmodern Narrative and Cultural Critique in the Age of Cloning*, Albany: SUNY Press.

Nicol, Bran (2006), '"The memoir as self-destruction" *A Heartbreaking Work of Staggering Genius*', in Jo Gill (ed.), *Modern Confessional Writing: New Critical Essays*, London: Routledge, pp. 100–14.

Nida, Eugene (2004), 'Principles of Correspondence', in Lawrence Venuti (ed.), *The Translation Studies Reader*, 2nd edn, London: Routledge, pp. 153–67.

Novalis (1997), 'Translating Out of Poetic Morality', trans. Douglas Robinson, in Douglas Robinson (ed.), *Western Translation Theory from Herodotus to Nietzsche*, Manchester: St Jerome, pp. 212–13.

Ollivant, Alfred (2014), *Bob, Son of Battle: The Last Gray Dog of Kenmuir*, A New Version by Lydia Davis, New York: New York Review Books.

Payne, Johnny (1993), *Conquest of the New Word: Experimental Fiction and Translation in the Americas*, Austin: University of Texas Press.

Pérez-González, Luis and Şebnem Susam-Saraeva (2012), 'Non-professionals Translating and Interpreting. Participatory and Engaged Perspectives', *The Translator*, 18:2, 149–65.

Perloff, Marjorie (1986), *The Futurist Moment: Avant-Garde, Avant Guerre, and the Language of Rupture*, Chicago: Chicago University Press.

Perloff, Marjorie (1989), 'Fiction as Language Game: The Hermeneutic Parables of Lydia Davis and Maxine Chernoff', in Ellen G. Friedman and Miriam Fuchs (eds), *Breaking the Sequence: Women's Experimental Fiction*, Princeton: Princeton University Press, pp. 199–214.

Perloff, Marjorie (2010), *Unoriginal Genius: Poetry by Other Means in the New Century*, Chicago: Chicago University Press.

Pound, Ezra (1954), *Literary Essays*, ed. T. S. Eliot, London: Faber and Faber.

Pratchett, Terry (1992), *Lords and Ladies*, London: Gollancz.

Prendergast, Christopher (2002), 'General Editor's Preface', in Marcel Proust, *The Way by Swann's*, London: Allen Lane, pp. vii–xxi.

Prose, Francine (1997), 'Lydia Davis', *Bomb Magazine*, 60, <http://www.bomb site.com/issues/60/articles/2086> (last accessed 20 March 2009).

Proust, Marcel (1954), *À la recherche du temps perdu*, ed. Pierre Clarac and André Ferré, 3 vols, Paris: Gallimard, Bibliothèque de la Pléiade.

Proust, Marcel (1960), *Swann's Way*, trans. C. K. Scott Montcrieff, London: Chatto & Windus. First published 1922.

Proust, Marcel (1981), *Rememberance of Things Past*, trans. C. K. Scott Montcrieff and Terence Kilmartin, 3 vols, London: Chatto & Windus.

Proust, Marcel (1982), *A Search for Lost Time: Swann's Way*, trans. James Grieve, Canberra: Australian National University.

Proust, Marcel (2002), *The Way by Swann's*, trans. Lydia Davis, London: Allen Lane.

Pym, Anthony (1998), *Method in Translation History*, Manchester: St Jerome.

Quasha, Georges and Charles Stein (1999), 'Afterword: Publishing Blanchot in America: A Metapoetic View', in Georges Quasha (ed.), *The Station Hill Blanchot Reader*, Barrytown, NY: Station Hill Press, pp. 511–27.

Reynolds, Matthew (2011), *The Poetry of Translation*, Oxford: Oxford University Press.

Royston, Philip Yorke (1838), *The remains of the late Lord Viscount Royston: with a memoir of his life* by Rev. Henry Pepys, London: J. Murray.

Sage, Lorna (1992), *Women in the House of Fiction: Post-War Women Novelists*, Basingstoke: MacMillan.

Sanders, Julie (2006), *Adaptation and Appropriation*, Abingdon: Routledge.

Sartre, Jean-Paul (1977), *Life/Situations: Essays Written and Spoken*, trans. Paul Auster and Lydia Davis, New York: Pantheon.

Sartre, Jean-Paul (1978), *Sartre in the Seventies: Interviews and Essays*, trans. Paul Auster and Lydia Davis, London: André Deutsch. [English edition of Sartre 1977; identical apart from the title and absence of note on the author.]

Sauret, Patrick (1995), *Inventions de lecture chez Michel Leiris*, Paris: L'Harmattan.

Shapard, Robert (1986), 'Introduction', in Robert Shapard and James Thomas (eds), *Sudden Fiction: American Short Short Stories*, Salt Lake City: Peregrine Smith, pp. xiii–xvi.

Shaun of the Dead, film, directed by Edgar Wright. Hollywood: Universal, 2004.

Silliman, Ron (2001), 'Foreword', in Rae Armantrout, *Veil: New and Selected Poetry*, Middletown, CT: Wesleyan University Press, pp. ix–xvi.

Simenon, Georges (1979), *African Trio*, trans. Stuart Gilbert, Paul Auster and Lydia Davis, London: Hamish Hamilton.

Sorrentino, Gilberto (1986), 'Language – Lying and Treacherous', *The New York Times*, Sunday 25 May 1986 <http://query.nytimes.com/gst/fullpage.html?res=9A0DE1D6103CF936A15756C0A960948260&pagewanted=1> (last accessed 18 March 2008).

Stark, Susanne (1997), 'Marian Evans, the Translator', in Susan Bassnett (ed.), *Translating Literature*, Cambridge: D. S. Brewer, pp. 119–40.

Steiner, George (1998), *After Babel*, 3rd edn, Oxford: Oxford University Press.

Stewart Atwell, Mary and Alison Espach (2009), 'Little Plots of Real Life: A Conversation with Lydia Davis [interview]', *Fiction Writer's Review* <http://fictionwritersreview.com/interviews/little-plots-of-real-life-a-conversation-with-lydia-davis-interview> (last accessed 11 May 2010).

Suzuki, Shinichi (1969), *Nurtured by Love: A new approach to education*, trans. Waltraud Suzuki, New York: Exposition Press.

Thomas, Jean-Jacques (1975), 'A One-Dimensional Poetics: Michel Leiris', *SubStance*, 4:11/12, 3–43.

Thorpe, Adam (2011), 'Introduction' in Gustave Flaubert, *Madame Bovary: Provincial Morals*, London: Vintage, pp. xiii–xxiv.

Toury, Gideon (1995), *Descriptive Translation Studies and Beyond*, Amsterdam and Philadelphia, PA: Benjamins.

Updike, John (1982), 'No Dearth of Death', *New Yorker*, 11 January 1982, pp. 92–4.

Vaidhyanathan, Siva (2001), *Copyrights and Copywrongs: The Rise of Intellectual Property and How It Threatens Creativity*, New York: New York University Press.

Valéry, Paul (1929), *Poésies*, Paris: Gallimard.

Varney, Jennifer (2010), 'The "Wobbling" Translation: H.D. and the Transmission of the Classics', *The Translator*, 16:1, 1–18.

Venuti, Lawrence (1986), 'The Translator's Invisibility', *Criticism*, 28:2 (Spring 1986), 179–212.

Venuti, Lawrence (1995), *The Translator's Invisibility: A History of Translation*, London: Routledge.

Venuti, Lawrence (1998), *The Scandals of Translation: Towards an Ethics of Difference*, London: Routledge.

Wales, Katie (2001), *A Dictionary of Stylistics*, 2nd edn, London: Longman.

Walkowitz, Rebecca (2015), *Born Translated: The Contemporary Novel in an Age of World Literature*, New York: Columbia University Press.

Webb, Timothy (1976), *The Violet in the Crucible: Shelley and Translation*, Oxford: Oxford University Press.

West, Russell (1996), *Conrad and Gide: Translation, Transference and Intertextuality*, Amsterdam and Atlanta: Rodolpi.

Williams, Jenny and Andrew Chesterman (2002), *The Map: A Beginner's Guide to Doing Research in Translation Studies*, Manchester: St Jerome.

Wilson, Rita (2007), 'The Fiction of the Translator', *Journal of Intercultural Studies*, 28:4, 381–95.

Wollen, Peter (2002), *Paris Hollywood: Writings on Film*, London: Verso.

Wood, James (2005), *The Irresponsible Self: On Laughter and the Novel*, London: Pimlico. First published 2004.

Wood, James (2009), 'Songs of Myself: Lydia Davis's very, very short stories', *New Yorker*, 19 October 2009, pp. 88–91.

Yao, Steven G. (2002), *Translation and the Languages of Modernism: Gender, Politics, Language*, New York: Palgrave Macmillan.

Ziolkowski, Thad (1993), 'Lydia Davis', in *Dictionary of Literary Biography*, vol. 130, in *Literature Resource Center* database <http://go.galegroup.com/ps/i.do?&id=GALE%7CH1200000128&v=2.1&u=uniportsmouth&it=r&p=LitRC&sw=w> (last accessed 4 March 2010).

Ziolkowski, Thad (1997), [Interview with Lydia Davis], *Index Magazine* <http://www.indexmagazine.com/interviews/lydia_davis.shtml> (last accessed 20 March 2009).

Žižek, Slavoj (2006), *How to Read Lacan*, London: Granta.

Index